Praise for Debra Monroe

"Fine and funky, marbled with warmth and romantic
confusion, but not a hint of sentimentality."
—*Boston Globe*

"Rangy, thoughtful, ambitious, and
widely, wildly knowledgeable."
—*Washington Post*

"Her characters, like her prose, have hard edges.
They also have big hearts, dark humor, and purely
unique ways of opening themselves up for our
inspection. This book makes you want to take the
author out for a drink and tell her your troubles."
—ANTONYA NELSON

"If this book were a country song,
Lucinda Williams would sing it."
—*Atlanta Journal-Constitution*

"Prose that shimmers like a jazz solo."
—JONIS AGEE

"Her intelligence tilts the world and offers her every
encounter an almost hysterical spin. In a [book]
laden with trenchant notes on our new world, Debra
Monroe offers us a lively quest—a woman caught
between the romantic and the semantic evaluates
all the fangled possibilities for human connection."
—RON CARLSON

"Intelligent . . . deliciously wacky."
—*Publishers Weekly*

On the Outskirts of Normal

On the Outskirts of Normal

FORGING A FAMILY AGAINST THE GRAIN

Debra Monroe

THE UNIVERSITY OF GEORGIA PRESS
Athens & London

Published in 2015 by
The University of Georgia Press
Athens, Georgia 30602
www.ugapress.org
© 2010 by Debra Monroe
All rights reserved
Designed by Kaelin Chappell Broaddus
Set in 10/13 Kepler Std by Kaelin Chappell Broaddus
Printed and bound by Thomson-Shore, Inc.
The paper in this book meets the guidelines for
permanence and durability of the Committee on
Production Guidelines for Book Longevity of the
Council on Library Resources.

Most University of Georgia Press titles are
available from popular e-book vendors.

Printed in the United States of America
15 16 17 18 19 P 5 4 3 2 1

Library of Congress Control Number: 2015945790

ISBN: 978-0-8203-4911-4 (pbk : alk. paper)
ISBN: 978-0-8203-4910-7 (e-book)

British Library Cataloging-in-Publication Data available

This book was first published in 2010 by
Southern Methodist University Press.

for Marie
(the moon, the stars, and the sun to me)

To the homemaker, no matter what gender,
age or marital status, we need help.
—from *Help! From Heloise*

Emotions really exist at the bottom
of the personality or at the top.
In the middle they are acted.
—IRIS MURDOCH

Can we agree that we're all haunted?
—JOHN LAHR

Contents

To the Reader

This story is true according to my memory—which is imperfect, not omniscient, not neutral. But I tried my best. The names of family members and cities have not been changed. For the sake of other people's privacy, I changed names and physical traits of some places and some people.

On the
Outskirts
of Normal

Mother Lore

I stood in the mail room at work, talking to my friend Tess. My daughter, Marie, age six, stood near me in a polka-dot tutu because we'd come straight from her dance class. Tess said, "Are those new bandages?" I glanced at my arms. "I had new blood tests," I said. Then I noticed a woman I didn't know—a temporary instructor? a new secretary from the dean's office?—across the room, staring. My daughter is black. I'm white. The woman was making goo-goo eyes at Marie, meanwhile telegraphing glances at me that said: how interesting, lovely. In fact, Marie is lovely. But no stranger would point this out if we weren't conspicuous; I forget we're conspicuous. I don't think about the fact our skin doesn't match until someone else does. The woman smiled, waiting to initiate a chat, to give me a compliment, I guess, then ask for the story of how we came to be.

Tess said, "Do you have the test results back? Do you need to eat? Let's go to my office, and you can eat your eggs there. I can always tell you've been there, scattered bits of eggshell on the floor." I was on a high-protein diet, doctor's orders, and hard-boiled eggs seemed like the most portable form. I carried them in my briefcase. I kept sausage in my purse. I had a thermal-lined bag for when I had to be away from home for hours.

I told Tess, "I accidentally put raw eggs in my briefcase yesterday—so gross. Thank God they're sticky. They scooped right out with a paper towel, and then I damp-sponged the lining." I apologized to Tess for my stray eggshell bits. I always tried to peel eggs carefully, over a wastebasket. I thought how easy it would be to tidy up Tess's office with just the right vacuum. I had one at home that was compact and portable with a shoulder strap—it was good for small messes, also upholstery, baseboards. I love vacuum cleaners, and I collected them the way a middle-aged man might collect vintage cars. When I added onto my house, I designed a special closet for storing my vacuum cleaners.

Then I stopped thinking about eggs and best possible cleaning methods because Marie had edged closer to the woman across the room, who was holding out her silver bracelet for Marie to inspect. I started to call Marie back, but suddenly I felt too tired. I was on the last edge of being able to summon the tact required for these exchanges that always seemed, at first, like small talk. Curiosity about Marie—her relation to me—is natural. It's usually kind. But it was constant then. This would be the second time in one day.

I said to Tess, "Man cannot live by food alone. Or woman."

Being sick made my mind wander, I realized.

I wanted a glimpse of the big picture. I wondered how I'd arrived at this juncture. Marie had health problems. I did. I was taking care of Marie, taking care of myself, meantime keeping up the light-hearted banter meant to persuade myself and anyone listening that I was fine, that Marie was, that this apparently experimental motherhood was fine too. To outsiders, I probably seemed like a scout on the way forward. I'd adopted Marie just after the Multiethnic Placement Act had been amended to say a child could never be denied a parent nor a parent denied a child on account of race, and so, as families go, we were rare, the minority's minority. We lived in a small Texas town—with its staid norms, its unflinching gaze—twenty miles outside of San Marcos, the sleepy college town where I taught. So the sense that we weren't mainstream seemed magnified.

Lately I obsessed about my mother. Had I become her?

Long before I realized I didn't have clout, I'd been angry about my mother's lack. Married to my dad, she'd felt isolated—his drinking, his dark side. When he'd asked for a divorce, I'd felt certain her life would improve. She had her productive hobbies, her cooking, gardening, sewing. "You can do all that and not subject yourself to his bad moods," I'd tell her by phone. "You'll feel fulfilled and self-sufficient now." What did I know? I was young. "You're a catch," I said the next time she called. "You have pretty eyes. Some man will come along, marry you, and think he went to heaven." She doubted it. She lived in Spooner, Wisconsin. How many eligible men could there be? One day she called and said: "You couldn't have been more wrong. Life alone is just lonely."

Next thing I knew she was married. Life with this new husband, a drunk with a worse temper than my dad's—but he didn't cheat—was less lonely, she reported. His bad temper felt familiar. "I don't want to spend my leisure time with someone who expects me to act normal," she added. This logic seemed twisted, so I said: "Fine, but don't expect sympathy. Don't call me to come to the rescue." I thought I was being a feminist. Or practicing tough love, a phrase that got tossed around a lot then. "I'm not enabling this bad marriage," I said. But my sister told her: "Night or day, at home or in a bar, one mile or a thousand, I'll come and get you." My sister did sometimes rescue my mother.

Once my new stepfather stubbed out a lit cigarette on my brother-in-law's neck as my brother-in-law bent to lift my mother's suitcase—to get her out for a few days, a week. But she always went back. My sister couldn't ignore my mother. My sister isn't the ultimatum type. And for the first years of my mother's second marriage, before her husband took her thousands of miles away, my sister lived the next county over. My brother was four hours away. I was in another state—in Kansas then—a nomadic student following scholarships, writing my master's thesis, which involved analytic thinking including (though not primarily) a meticulous assessment of how much drug intake sparked my creativity while leaving short-term memory intact. Age twenty-three and divorced for the first time, I also had my social life. If I got too secluded, I thought, I'd fall for anyone. So I'd put on an angora sweater and go to clubs. I liked the way my lipstick stained the butts of harsh cigarettes. I wanted to be soft yet tough. I wanted to be left alone, but at times I relapsed, found someone, latched on. And if I sometimes wondered how my mother had sunk so low, I never noticed my own sinking, the same fall.

One of my classmates put cover-stick over her blackened eye. Another wandered night streets with purpose—stalking—keeping up with her lover who wandered night streets with a different purpose. And I worked at being detached but ended up partly-attached, which hurt the same way a loose tooth does: low-grade, constant, one tricky boyfriend after another. One of them said once, taking my clothes off, "Your patience is endless."

Staying keeps the men you don't want away, I'd reasoned. A bad-tempered man you know is better than a worse-tempered man in the offing. So you ride out his moods and inattention, unfinished business with his last boss or cruel father. You've heard about love since you first heard stories. A kiss will wake you, your parents standing vigil. (Snow White: seven eunuchs standing guard.) A kiss does wake you. Then an old force moves like wind, like weight, below, beneath. Sex is good. You feel good getting it. You can't admit it because you're young. Sex you don't want is everywhere. You go for a walk alone, and a construction crew whistles—you're Red Riding Hood bypassing a pack.

My mother gave me a birds and bees talk once, too late. "I never understood the hoopla," she'd said. I glanced up, the data collector in me, the research side of my brain dominant, and said: "Did you have an orgasm?" She looked puzzled. "Did you come?" I asked.

She said, "I felt enjoyment."

I said, "It's not like a man's orgasm, but you'd know if you had one."

It was years ago when I said this. She hadn't met my mean stepfather yet. She was forty.

I'd thought at the time: she's past needing all that now.

Now I was forty, lonely, anxious, sick, wanting sex, and, yes, I was a mother. I wondered if my mom had needed that bad husband so she'd be consumed by a pressing, immediate problem that blocked out all other problems, the harm he caused—bruises, broken dishes—keeping her mind off trouble that didn't rise and fall by the day or hour but stayed unsolved. Marie was seeing three different doctors. I was seeing two. Not a week passed when I didn't drive one of us to a specialist. I was having a spate of bad luck.

I wanted my experiences to turn into a set of directions—the right way forward. But my escalating to-do list, the synchronized performance of unexpected crucial tasks, my jumbled-up simultaneity, made it impossible for me to see my experiences as a sequence, a pattern: consequence. I tried to pay attention, to capture and contain this passage of time, to transform haphazard events into meaning. So I lived my life while analyzing it too because my earliest sense of order—a pastor back-lit by sunlight passing through stained glass, the quiet heave of organ music as he pieced together stray facts to tell a story that always made a point—persists. I have faith: the conversion of life into stories. If hard luck won't beget meaning, then hard luck is only hard, I think. If I can't find the wisdom right away, I know it's because I don't have all the details yet, or enough insight to sort them out. If more time passed, I told myself, if I kept reshuffling and reconsidering, I'd discover my daily events and their upshot were governed not by chaos but purpose. I never stopped believing I'd find an orderly plot in my disorderly tangle of memory.

But right now I was picking up late papers from my university mailbox. I had to drive Marie home, cook dinner for us, get her ready for bed. Then housework and papers to grade.

"Debra, what about your new blood tests," Tess asked again, "the results?"

"I'm still undiagnosed. Underdiagnosed." The doctor had used that word.

Tess shook her head. "You're thin, and tired."

The woman who'd beckoned to Marie was crossing the room. Marie followed, carrying the silver bangle. The woman said, "I know you. I saw a photo of you and your little girl in the pediatrician's office, on that bulletin board where people hang up pictures. She was still a baby. But I commented on it to the doctor—you two are very striking."

Together, I thought. Apart, not so much.

She said, "Do you know what the pediatrician said? She said she'd never in her life met a mother so ready to love a baby as you when you brought her for the four-day check-up."

I smiled. "Thank you." The feelings I'd had that day came rushing back. I'd stared at Marie, six pounds, no ounces, her perfect body, eyes focused and merry. She already knew me—I belonged to Marie. It had actually been a six-day check-up because I didn't meet Marie until she was two days old. The receptionist called her name, and I didn't stand right away because it wasn't my name. Then I realized it was my daughter's name—it was *us*—and I carried her to the examination room. I set her on the baby scale, and I felt tremulous and awe-struck at the wrenching elation of loving a child—letting my heart exist outside my body, and, as she'd grow, letting my heart roam around the risky world.

I looked at Marie now, her hand on my leg. She grinned and shook her tutu. At dance class, I'd sat with my friend, Jana—in the room with the one-way window so mothers can see their daughters but daughters can't see their mothers. Jana's daughter had popped her head through the door and said, "Marie is good at the mambo." Jana and I sat apart from the other mothers who'd known each other since high school days. Jana has a full-sleeve tattoo; her son sometimes acts strange in public. Jana doesn't wear a wedding ring. The mothers had long ago scanned both our hands for wedding rings. One mother said to me, "That week you all didn't come to class, the rest of us got to talking and wondering. Is Marie is your biological daughter?" The question—just its timing—surprised me. The mother said, "Because you look alike." I said: "We do?" The mother said, "Well, you both have good posture." I nodded. "Thank you. She's adopted, though." Jana pinched me. Then the mother said, "So, do either of you two moms have a favorite song you'd like to choose for the girls to dance to for the Christmas recital?" I said, "I'm open. Nothing special." Jana—less likely to take guff than I am—said, "I'm thinking anything by Sid Vicious. Or Nick Cave and the Bad Seeds." The mothers looked nervous. "She's kidding," I said. Then class was over, girls mamboing out the door.

I said to the woman in the mail room, "It's nice you told me that. I like that pediatrician." But I hadn't seen her since she'd referred Marie to the specialists. Then I told Marie to give the bracelet back, and I turned my back on the woman—on the role I'd signed on for when I adopted: race ambassador—and I stepped close to Tess and whispered, "I fainted on Sunday. It freaked Marie out, as you can imagine. I hit my head." I showed Tess the bump. "And," I told Tess this next part quickly, "I've been jilted. At my age." I paused. It was so unsuitable. An ingénue's predicament—a few sobs on the pillow, sensible advice from an elder, then a fresh start. But I was a matron. Or not. What? "I'm the mother of a little child," I told Tess, "her role model." Did loneliness matter? No one dies of it, I thought. I stared at my arms, taped from the five-hour blood test. Tess looked at me. She was sixty then. She's a lesbian. This had forced her, even more than me, to search for love beyond the pale. She said, "You're right on schedule, I think. I had my biggest heartache at your age. I had more courage about needing love. You earn courage. But who you run across in your hour of need? That's luck."

That night, still searching for clues, I called my aunt. She got married at the same age as my mother, but she'd been mostly happy fifty years. I asked her what she knew my mother didn't. She said, "Not one thing. But as I got older, Debra, I understood that the meaning of life is not romance. The meaning of life is children and old people. And death."

How I Got Here

God was eternal, I'd heard. Still, he varied place to place, era by era—
John Milton's God wasn't exactly Nathaniel Hawthorne's, I realized, or
anything like my old Sunday School teacher's. By the time I was thirty
I found myself married again, this time to a short, tense man who
believed in nothing. I'd liked him in part because my first husband
had been tall and, as everyone said, so laid-back. My first husband
played guitar, also solitaire in his bathrobe while smoking pot. So I'd
mistaken my second husband's impatience for drive. It turned out to
be anger. His mother had been divorced and flat-broke in Houston in
the 1960s—when single mothers were perhaps encouraged to give up
their kids to foster care as they held down jobs and hoped to remarry.
He and his brothers spent years with an old woman named Mammo
who'd locked them in a pen with geese, who attacked. He'd grabbed
one goose by the neck and swung at the others to fend them off,
breaking the goose's neck, saving his brothers, heroic. I didn't know
this when I met him, but I learned quickly he had contempt for anything unseen: feelings, ethics.

So I kept my beliefs to myself. Yet I couldn't quell the sense I'd had
since I was a child that cues or hints are everywhere, blatant. That
said, my husband's hair-trigger anger was random—any moment

might turn harsh, irregular. I'd let him move in too fast. Back when he wasn't my husband, just someone knocking and not yet admitted, I couldn't spot trouble. My weirdometer never went off. I screened everyone and came to wrong conclusions anyway. By the third date he'd put his toiletries in a drawer where I kept a hammer, pliers, string. He'd be spending the night, he said. His family was close-knit, he said. His family now included a dictatorial stepfather and four bewildered stepsiblings, who lived on a smallish family homestead in east Texas. We flew there for Christmas. Amid insults, practical jokes, scuffles—the family's way of showing affection, my future mother-in-law explained—I got engaged. Everyone watched as I unwrapped a box filled with coal and, at the bottom, in a dusty little box, a little diamond ring.

My second husband turned out to be a wife-beater. And sometimes he kicked things I cared about across the room, for instance my great-grandmother's china, piece by piece. It was slapstick comedy gone awry: the ever imminent blow-ups, our on-the-spot maneuvers meant to keep the skirmishes secret, muted. Once, in a grocery store, he grabbed my hair to direct me to another aisle because he didn't like me wandering away from him in big stores, and I glanced around to make sure no one was watching and swung a loaf of soft bread at him, then steered on, checking items off my list, soap, lettuce, onions, tea. Another day he got angry while making chili con queso, and I gave up reasoning with him and walked out the door and got in my car. He stood in the driveway in a navy blue bathrobe and threw an unwrapped brick of Velveeta onto my hatchback. The cheese lodged there. Thirty miles later, I stopped at a gas station to find the ice scraper—it was summer—and scraped off the cheese as a truck driver watched, curious.

Each time my husband hit me, I got hurt. But, for him, it relieved stress. He felt tender afterward, taping my fingers, icing a bruise. When he was sorry, he looked like a little boy I ought to protect. Of course, he wasn't born violent. He'd been beaten first, long ago. I was a trigger too. If, for instance, he said I was the crazy offspring of crazy people and I'd never amount to anything, I'd get upset. He spouted these phrases ready-made, his childhood replaying itself. It was my childhood replaying too—parts of it—and I'd start crying, running, slamming doors. Sometimes I got in his face and yelled that he was mean. We were two sets of bad behavior: co-angry. I never hit him back, though. I knew if I did, I'd get hurt worse. I believed that hitting, slapping, kicking were bad habits, or sins, but that most husbands would lash out if they had a short fuse, a tough childhood, and someone preternaturally long-suffering standing by. In brief, people I came from tried not to hit or get hit, but we did, and we didn't talk about it—it was too private.

I married him in Utah. I'd moved there from Kansas to work on my PhD in English, specializing in the history and theory of the novel. I was living a modest, well-budgeted life on stipends. I was teaching classes, taking classes. I'd go to the BYOB potlucks with other students. But once I met my husband, he liked nicer things and, even though he usually had a job, he couldn't pay his bills. So I waitressed too. I'd waitressed on and off for fifteen years. Each time I quit a waitress job, stuffing my apron into the trash, I'd hope it was forever. So far, it wasn't. My husband had chronic trouble with jobs—he'd piss someone off and get fired. He lost his temper and jobs, he told me, because he pined for home, for Texas, where the rivers were wider, the sky so blue, the food tastier. Even traffic laws made more sense in Texas, he said once, tearing up a ticket.

A few days before I married him—my bankrupt, hot-tempered husband—I had a miscarriage. We'd been engaged almost two years and though I didn't exactly want to marry him, I'd wanted the baby. This was my third pregnancy. The first two—the first with my first husband, the second with a ne'er-do-well I'd dated on the rebound after my first husband left me, taking only a change of clothes and his guitar—had ended in miscarriage too. So once I knew I was pregnant, and I was engaged besides, I planned a wedding. I mailed invitations, found cake recipes, a dress. At three months, I started bleeding.

The baby was dead, a doctor said. He gave me pills to induce contractions.

My not-yet-husband got depressed about the looming miscarriage and lost another job.

I didn't feel I could call off the wedding.

I phoned my sister to tell her I was losing the baby. My contractions started. I called the English department to cancel the classes I was teaching, to leave messages for professors teaching the classes I was taking. I called in sick to the restaurant too. I went to bed. And the contractions stopped. I went back to work. As I strode through the restaurant, a tray hoisted above my head, the contractions started again. I went home. The contractions stopped. The next day I went to campus to teach, then to a class I was taking.

I took more pills.

That afternoon, in the bridal department at JCPenney, I stood in an octagon-shaped room lined with mirrors, being fitted for a dress I'd bought on the cheap ("Spring into Spring Sale"). A woman with pins in her mouth snipped a thread. I looked at my reflection, eight angles. My stomach rose and fell, a slight but unmistakable undulation. A day later, at home, thirty-six hours before my wedding, I stared out the window as the cityscape turned from dark to dawn—a milk-colored sky, black outlines of trees, halos of street lamps—and I finished the miscarriage. I'd stayed up all night doing a crossword, waiting.

My sister and dad and stepmother were arriving from Wisconsin that day.

My husband's mother and stepfather were flying in from Texas too.

A judge we'd found in the Yellow Pages performed the ceremony. Winter light shone through the windows of our rent house, a half-light caused by low cloud cover—an inversion that traps pollutants, cold air. Afterward, friends from school stopped by with bottles of wine. I'd made appetizers, also a poppy seed cake with white chocolate frosting.

I milled among my classmates and friends, friends of friends, including Shen, ex-Mormon, grad student, single mother of four. She'd had a miscarriage too, she confided. My dad was making conversation with my new in-laws: "She was too much to handle. When she was eleven, I told her if God wanted her to have pierced ears, she'd have been born with holes in her ears. Do you know what she said?" He started crying. He set his glass of whiskey down. My stepmother slid it away. My in-laws looked uneasy. "She told me if God wanted me to smoke, he'd have given me a chimney. Can you imagine a girl speaking like that to her father?" I didn't know if he was crying like the father in *Fiddler on the Roof* because I'd been his precocious little girl and now I was married, or if his feelings were still hurt. My sister said, "They went round and round. I felt like I was going to get an ulcer." I wondered if she was going tell my in-laws about the time he'd swung at me and I ducked and his hand went through sheetrock, because this is legendary in the family annals. She didn't. She spoke carefully to these strangers, new in-laws.

When I'd picked up my sister, stepmother, and father at the airport, I told them I'd had the miscarriage that morning. My dad said, "I don't understand. Is the wedding on?" Other than that, we didn't discuss it. People in my family feel that if talking about a miscarriage would make you cry then you don't talk—i.e., so you won't cry about it at a wedding, which would be unseemly. Meanwhile, at the wedding, I made sure everyone had food. Then I walked outside, carrying trash. My neighbors, devout Mormons, were outside too. Their five-year-old, Becky, shrieked. "Debra! Why are you getting married twice?"

I turned, in my ivory dress and matching lace-covered pumps. Of course, I had gotten married twice, but that's not what Becky meant. In conversations over the fence, Becky's mother had always referred to my fiancé, my roommate, as my "husband." I'd never corrected her. They let Becky come to my house to visit me, and I wanted them to think I was good enough. Becky would sit in my lap, prattle and laugh. And I'd wished she belonged to me. That afternoon, wearing my wedding dress, trash bag in hand, I stood on the sidewalk and couldn't think how to answer her. I got rid of the trash, went inside.

A few months later, my first book got accepted. This stunned me. I'd mailed out my work, and it always came back, a hundred rejection slips, but I hadn't known what to do except keep revising, keep carrying my manuscript to the post office. When I got the phone call saying my book would be published and had won a prize besides, I was giddy as a teenager. If people asked how I felt—and they did, including a reporter for the local paper—I gushed like a beauty pageant winner, *so lucky, just can't believe, a big thank you to those who made this possible.* Teachers, I meant: kind, generous ones here and there.

I graduated that year with my PhD and applied for jobs.

The job I got was in North Carolina. We moved. My husband went from being a sporadically employed husband of a student and waitress to the unemployed husband of a professor and author. The change unnerved him. He sat in front of a VCR. Car wheels screeched.

Guns exploded. "Freeze!" He'd always watched action movies, just not so many.

In North Carolina, we rented a run-down house in a good neighborhood. Kids up and down the street would come sit on the porch and visit after school. My husband liked kids too and, since he didn't have a job, he'd join the skateboarders in the street. The director of graduate studies lived across from us, and the dean of Arts and Sciences three doors down. The woman next door was like me—in an intolerable marriage. Our dining room windows faced each other, and once she saw my husband swinging a dining room chair at me. She called. I answered the phone in the kitchen. She couldn't see me as long as I stayed on the line. My husband raged, waiting for me to hang up, waiting to pounce. He wouldn't as long as she was on the phone because he was smart about keeping his outbursts secret— he aimed mostly for my gut, the back of my head, places bruises wouldn't show. Still, I felt tense, talking on the phone, pretending to be well-adjusted.

"Are you all right?" my neighbor asked.

As far as I knew, her husband yelled, called her stupid, but didn't hit her.

"I'm fine," I said.

So why didn't I leave?

I wanted my brass bed, my lamps, tables, chairs, vases. I'd been collecting these homey artifacts, set dressing for my piecemeal version of family life, since I was a girl. I thought that anger erupting like bad weather, like fire or earthquakes, was unavoidable. Boyfriends had hit me when I broke up with them. My dad hit me, when he was mad. My mother sometimes hit me too, but never hard. Mostly, she buffered me—hid my errors and mishaps from my dad. And once, when I was teenager, my mother hit my dad when they were out one night. He came home with his glasses broken. I never found out why, what he'd done, or didn't do. When I was little, he was in a bar one night and wouldn't take her phone call, so she couldn't tell him to come with the car. My brother, age two, had fallen downstairs and broken both arms. She called an ambulance, and she, my sister, and I rode with my brother to the hospital. I've always wondered why she hit my dad that one night—if she'd found out about his girlfriend at last, or if it was just another night in a gloomy series, unremarkable except that her patience had finally snapped.

If I left my husband, I thought, it would be my second divorce: twice-divorced and not yet thirty-two.

All the same, I asked my husband to move out, and he said no. One night I told him he had to get a job, and he kicked me. If you hold still, you get hurt less. It ends. If you fight back, you get beaten longer. I lay on the floor, still, and he stopping kicking. I jumped for the phone and called 911. When he understood I wasn't pretending to call 911—which I'd done before, pretended—he grew quiet, careful. I hung up, waited for the cops to come, and I started to cry. He worked on his demeanor: hen-pecked, dog-tired. He hoped I'd keep crying, speak incoherently, and the cops would write me off as deranged.

When the squad car pulled up, I opened the door, looked up and down the street—lights out, everyone asleep. The cops came in. One shone his flashlight in my mouth, which was bleeding. He looked at my hand, fingers swollen, not broken. I didn't tell him my right breast hurt because my husband had kicked it with his boots on. The officer said to my husband, "Do you have somewhere to go?" My husband said no. "Do you have friends, a job?" Not friends or a job either. The cop asked me if I had a job. I said I did, and he asked where. I told him. I saw us through his eyes. Man without a job, wife a professor: disparity. Of course these two fought. And would I press charges? I wouldn't.

Lucky for me, I thought, my neighbors hadn't yet noticed the squad car in front of my house. I wasn't ready to come out as a battered woman. I wanted people to think of more than that—more than my pathetic life, or how my husband seemed polite and kept to himself, standard ax murderer M.O.—when they waved hello. Or, because my colleagues lived up and down the street, when they read my annual review, made my teaching schedule, decided if I'd get tenure. How could I work with people who pictured me as a low-rent, fisticuffs wife? Someone who'd somehow caused the beating? Or didn't know enough to avoid it? Since I wouldn't press charges, which would disrupt my career, my sense of progress, I felt, calling the cops that night didn't change a thing. One cop said to my husband, "Go for a long walk, and don't come home until she's left for work." The second said, "You get mad at your wife, sure. But certain behaviors aren't civilized."

A few weeks later, I sat in the dining room, grading papers. I heard gunfire start up. An avenger with a thick accent said, "I'll be back." The movie soundtrack swelled and slowed, suspense: Will X murder Y? Or vice versa? According to Aristotle, vicarious danger is useful. Rage strikes the protagonist, not the audience, like lightning striking a pole: safe discharge, catharsis. Yet somehow catharsis always circumvented my husband. If Arnold Schwarzenegger got mad, so did my husband. I stood up and paced—step, step, a skittering-over-hot-coals lack of tempo. I went outside for a walk, that night, every night, an hour, another hour, until he was down for the count, a sleeping bully, imperturbable for six hours. Under the glow of street lamps, sprinklers hissing, tree frogs chirping, my footfalls turned rhythmic, metrical. I hatched a plan. I applied for jobs in Texas because he was from there, and I thought his family could get him his own job.

A year after we'd arrived in North Carolina, we packed again. My neighbors got together and hosted a going-away party—the woman next door; the director of graduate studies; the dean of Arts and Sciences; a couple across the street, Merck Pharmaceutical executives. The Merck executives gave us a bottle of wine. The academics gave us ceramic mugs made by local artists. The woman whose marriage was like mine (or better, since she hid just a bruised ego) gave me a mini-crockpot for potpourri. She said, "I'll miss you." I thought: you will? I'd lived in Wisconsin, Kansas, Utah, North Carolina; I was moving to Texas. In each place, I'd developed friendships that didn't survive the next migration. Sometimes I'd think of a person with whom I'd whiled away pleasant hours and could hardly remember what state I'd been in. Friends I did know well had moved on too. This failure to attach was partly a result of my itinerancy, have-books-will-travel: my apprenticeship, then my search for a job. But I also knew my calculated rootlessness, my knack for shedding friends as I shifted environments, wasn't normal.

My feelings for my husband weren't normal either. I felt like an orphan, though my parents hadn't died. I watched my neighbors commemorating my departure with high seriousness. If this were a novel,

I thought, these characters would show up in the next chapter, the next. But it wasn't a novel. It was my life. I stared into my next-door neighbor's brown eyes welling with tears. She said, "It won't be the same here without you." I said, "Thank you." She looked confused. Wrong answer. "Without you either," I amended.

My husband's mother and stepfather borrowed a trailer and helped us move to Texas.

I was broke—student loans, signature loans he'd talked me into for get-rich schemes (he'd wrecked his credit before I met him), and a big MasterCard bill because every month we'd needed more than I earned. In San Marcos, where I'd start teaching in the fall, I looked at apartment buildings designed for undergraduates. From parking lots, I heard competing bass lines—rap, country-western, alt-rock, heavy-metal. I left my husband at the motel and spent the day driving complex to complex with a property management agent who said he'd let me have an empty Taco Bell cheap. My mind raced—perhaps it could be furnished in a modern, dashing way, like a studio? But I had antiques, collectibles. "It has two bathrooms," he added. "Neither with a tub or shower," I said. He was bored. He wanted a real client. He kept his eye on the ball, profit. I persisted. A little house. Empty farmhouse. I could afford $400 a month. He shook his head.

That night, in a Motel 6, my husband flicked through reruns of *Kung Fu* and *COPS*.

I found a newspaper ad for a house in a village twenty miles away.

Fixer-upper in idyllic small town. I hadn't heard of the town, but my husband had. It was famous in Texas for being an airbrushed glimpse of the past. People were moving to it in droves from conservative enclaves in Dallas and Houston, escaping urban blight.

My husband rode along with me to see the cottage for rent.

The girlish realtor/property management agent who drove us around town—she didn't keep her eye on the ball, I came to understand years later when I read about her suicide in the local paper—chattered. "It's so cool you're a professor," she said. I thought so too. I still pictured myself as a student. Or someone with a private life so messy that if people found out they'd take back my job. After my family turned unreliable, school became my substitute structure: teachers like surrogate parents with interchangeable faces, alternately friendly or aloof. The harder I worked at school, the more I got praise. The harder I worked at family—the one I came from, the ones I tried to make myself—the more I felt crazy. So I concentrated on school. And I'd been surprised my work was above average. Growing up in Spooner, Wisconsin, I'd been sporadically smart but continually wild, smoking and drinking by the time I was twelve. It was a small town. Everyone knew my problems, my family's. But one high school English teacher had pulled me aside and told me if I used my brain for good, for good causes, I'd turn into someone besides the juvenile delinquent other people might think I was.

So teaching turned out to be the right job for me, every semester a chance to reciprocate, to try to turn a troubled student to the light. I thought the stories we studied, and ideal versions of the stories students tried to write, were shapely depictions of life in which, unlike life, every detail flickered with augury and hope. I was struck by the gap between what I read (mystical, consoling form) and how I lived (by accident, in disarray). But the sprawling mess of life is why we need stories, I'd tell students, a fleeting sense of order, so we return to life with the unproven but irresistible conviction our mistakes and emergencies matter, so life might make sense too. And, according to people who'd read my teaching evaluations—I hadn't, too nervous, but when supervisors mentioned my evaluations I pretended I had—students said I was good. In North Carolina, my fusty, tweed-wearing department chair told me: "I've never before seen evaluations in which students report so consistently that this was their best class, that it changed the way they think."

The realtor/property management agent who later committed suicide asked my husband, "And what do you do for a living?" I tuned him out. His answer would be complicated: a rhetorical contortion that turned various aborted jobs into a career. "As soon as I get my wife settled," he added, "I'm heading back east for a job I bid on. That's why we're just renting." He coughed. He did this when he amplified facts. The job he had lined up was house-sitting. I said, "We don't have anything close to a down payment." My husband glared. The agent said, "Gosh, I don't mind helping out. You have to live somewhere." I thought: She must have an underdog complex. Or she's kind.

Is there a difference?

In the back of her jeep, I whispered to my husband: "This house we're looking at will be too small for two of us when you get back." He shrugged. "We'll get a new place. We'll move again." I panicked. I sighed. I resisted. A mixture of serendipity and sheer will had brought me to this arid yet fertile sliver of the Southwest. I wanted to dig in. I wanted to graft myself onto others and issue forth: branches and off-shoots. But how?

The property management agent spoke up. "It's hard to rent here. It's so inbred. You have no idea. Everybody knows everyone. You're either on the ins with them, or on the outs, depending. Everybody's going to love you or not, depending. There's three groups."

"Groups?" I said.

"Cliques for grown-ups."

"Demographic factions," I suggested.

She said, "Right. Old-timers, real country shit-kickers. Then hippies came next, to make communes. Some stayed, but not the cream of the crop. And then there's new people who think they're relocating into a Norman Rockwell painting." She glanced in the rearview at me. "You'll excuse me for being blunt. It's just that, you know, you seem like none of the above. I'm telling you that being a realtor here is hard. For one thing, everyone buys. Hardly anyone rents. Places that do get rented, people hear about them word of mouth, and they're already promised to a family friend by the time the old tenant's out, and someone I work with, I am so pissed, was trying to hide this property from me. She had the file folder under her desk. That is wrong. Illegal. Oh my God, that's her behind us in her freaking Lincoln Towncar—trying to show the house ahead of me."

We'd pulled up in a driveway. "I'll take it," I said. I stared at a yellow rectangle, seven-hundred-and-fifty square feet. I wanted to see the inside, but I wanted to get rid of rival tenants first. "I'll wander over and tell her," our agent said, triumphant, slamming her door. I made my way through waist-high weeds to the porch. Sunlight spilled on the land like bleach. The sun itself—hazy, quivering—was like an image in a movie about end-time.

We went to the realtor's office, and I signed a lease. Before we drove back to the motel to phone my in-laws in east Texas, we stopped at the house for another look. I thought: Should I trim the weeds? Other houses had neat, green lawns. I supposed people watered. Could I afford to? My house was a short walk to the river and a dingy, 1950s-style resort—"modern plumbing! air-conditioned comfy cabins"—just like dingy resorts in the back-of-beyond Wisconsin county where I grew up. Except the county where I grew up has mysteriously deep lakes fed by melted snow. A high murder rate. Endemic alcoholism. Did I want to live in another small town? Country people are my subject matter, I told myself; I came from them. The commune-types didn't bother me. I'd fallen for that faux-pastoral idea myself. In Wisconsin, I'd loved visiting my friends who'd moved to an old farm and bought chickens and two pigs they'd named Ron and Nancy.

In Texas that day, I rolled down my window to hear shallow water rushing over white rocks. "Are you nuts?" my husband said. "No one rolls down windows in the summer here." I rolled it up. The road to town—my commute, I realized—curved. We were passing through a green tunnel. Above me, live oaks held branches together in an arc.

The next day my in-laws arrived with the loaded-up truck, pulling a stock trailer with cardboard fastened over the holes where you usually see cow's faces—to keep wind and dirt off my furniture. I stood on the porch. The day before, the realtor had unlocked the door for me. The doorknob is too close to the jamb. I used my right hand to twist the key to the left, my left to twist the knob to the right. I heard birdsong and cicada, and my stepfather-in-law yelling: "Don't drop your end of the table, you lame-brained jackass." My husband said, "Senile piece of shit, you old corpse." My husband's brother yelling at the two of them: "Screaming like a pair of nellies. I'll give you both a knuckle sandwich." I glanced at my mother-in-law who gave me a smile. We women, it said, would never be so hateful. I'd had high hopes for this family—too little contact with my own.

But that day as I was cranking the doorknob one way, the key the other, I found a tempo, turning, cranking, talking, a rant, a prayer: I don't believe in an interventionist God, God, and if You did intervene, You'd save it for the people who believe in intervention, but all religions say we should help the afflicted, and I hope I'm not exaggerating that I feel afflicted here, and I do help myself make a move to make the next move, but my point is: what next? The doorknob gave. "Ouch," I said. I smashed my hand.

My wedding ring was flattened out, no kidding, the tiny diamond shoved to the side.

The door opened.

God is unsubtle, I thought.

Still, I didn't leave my husband that night. He went back to North Carolina, to his house-sitting job. I slept on the floor of my new yellow house, thinking about scorpions. Daylight, I washed walls, blacked the woodstove. I scrubbed cupboards, placed every picture and knick-knack. Even the porch looked well-decorated because my furniture overflowed. When my husband came back six weeks later, his jacket hanging on a chair looked untidy in this house where everything had to be stowed shipshape. He didn't fit. Nothing fit here, besides me. I looked at him. I'd moved to Texas to save my marriage. So he'd be happy and get a job. Now my marriage felt unbearably cramped. How had I stood it?

I told my husband we had to split up. "You must have wanted a divorce too," I said.

He looked at the floor, hands in his pocket. Sometimes he used to stand like that and whistle. Those were moments I'd liked him best. This time he looked guarded. "I guess."

"You didn't seem like you were enjoying being married either."

If he hit me now, I thought: so what? I'd been hit before. I could call the cops for help getting him to leave. No audience—I didn't know anyone here yet. But he just nodded and went outside. He got back into his truck, idled, then asked if I'd ever loved him.

Yes, I told him, but bad love has a shelf life. I wanted constancy now. I wanted to be alone, no husband, no wild card. From inside my house, I could hear wind rustling through the trees. At night, stars glimmered. On worrisome days, I sat in the river and water pounded my shoulders like jets in a spa. I said, "You were right about Texas. It is better."

Slamming the gear-shift into park, he said, "I guess that's why you married me, because you like Texas." Maybe, I thought. Living in Utah, meeting mostly graduate students, everyone else a Mormon theologically required to try to convert all non-Mormons, me included, I'd felt relieved to meet someone who liked the blues and good tequila. A slim foundation for marriage, however. *Who giveth this woman to this man?* "I sure do," my dad had answered. He'd bought and sold a lot of used cars in his day. He meant like a title transfer. He didn't want to be responsible. When he left my mother, he'd left father-feelings behind. Then my mother took off with the first man who noticed her—gone too. My husband looked rueful in the cab of the truck, the expression on his face like he'd flubbed a simple catch in the last inning. He'd no doubt wanted a better family than his too—tirades, threats. He'd done his best. I had too. Neither of us had a clue.

I'd been the first person in my family to go to college, where I felt too rough-and-tumble to date classmates. I didn't know how to pronounce "Goethe." Or the names of certain wines. In Kansas, where I got my master's degree, I'd rented a house in the middle of wheat fields, and on snowy nights I dreamed about John Donne. The dreams weren't erotic exactly, but John Donne, wrapped in winding cloth as he is in the only known likeness, his voice uncannily like the voice of the professor who taught me John Donne, his eyes tender, told me that love is an altered state but not a hallucination. Love is alchemy. *No winter shall abate the spring's increase.* I wanted love like that. Yet things I cared about—words, finding precise words to describe complex experiences—made me ill-suited for men I met as I waitressed or went to clubs. I'd changed social classes and educational levels fast. When I met my second husband, he'd been my equal, sort of. A few years later, he wasn't. Whose fault was it? I maxed out a credit card with a $1000 advance, which I gave him, and a gas credit card I'd cancel later. He drove away forever.

Fall came. New people flitted in and out of my sphere. I didn't keep close track. My job was easy as long as I focused on the students, didn't worry about office politics or where I fit in. At home, I taught myself how to use kindling—how to start a fire and stoke it.

I met my neighbors, Lauren, a half-mile north, who had a husband and a seven-year-old son, Nathan, who'd sometimes wander over. One day, hands cupped over his ears, she said, "He has a crush on you." I said, "No, everywhere I've lived, neighbor kids visited me." A kid visits for maybe an hour. A parent's too busy overseeing a child's entire life to listen the way I could—responding to every kid-opinion or knock-knock joke.

Clara Mae, my elderly neighbor a half-mile to the south, was starved for conversation. One day we climbed three flights of stairs to a deck she'd built on top of her house so she could see above the dense trees, which made her feel oppressed, she said. She handed me a glass of wine. "But humans aren't always better company than trees." She told me she'd been born on Galveston Island in 1929. When she was a little girl—she showed me a picture of a picket-legged girl in a pinafore dress, her hair cut in bangs—her father used to drive her through the red light district on Saturday nights because he wanted her to know it existed. "Why?" I asked. "Oh, he was marvelous," she said. "He wanted me to understand some people are too unlucky to live any other way." Clara Mae also knew old songs and liked to sit on her aerie-deck and sing: *I wish I were a maid again, oh, but that can never be.* "'Maid' means 'virgin,'" she said. "You know that, right?"

I had a neighbor in back, not far as the crow flies but more than a mile by road—he had a big house, outbuildings filled with un-documented workers. One day he came to my back door, knocked, introduced himself, "Ronnie Larkin." He asked if I wanted to hear the history of my house. "I guess," I said. I had a rag in my hand. I'd been cleaning. "That fool got the land cheap," he said, "and he built his house so he could look at my creek. I planted that row of hack-berry trees, which grow fast, to show him not everyone can have a creek view without paying the taxes I pay." My window faced a row of spindly trees. "There's a creek behind those trees?" I asked. He nod-ded, eyes puffy behind his glasses. "I'm a good neighbor, though." He turned and went back home.

One Saturday, I was stacking firewood. A car pulled up and a man and woman got out and introduced themselves, my landlord and his wife passing through, and they thought they'd stop for a visit. The woman said, "There's two of you, right? Where's the hubby?"

I paused and shook my head.

The woman said, "That little gal who showed the house said so, by golly. What happened?"

I said, "He went back east. He'd been out of work a long time and..."

The landlord said, "He didn't have a job!"

The wife patted my hand and said, "Adios to that. And don't look back."

I didn't look forward either. If I had, I'd have realized a cabin in the woods outside a village wasn't the optimal location for a single woman. *A woman has her needs.* Someone said that on a talk show once. Anyone newly single who vows they'll never again want romance is like someone who's had the flu saying: I'll never eat again. Yet with two failed marriages under my belt, I wanted romance on my terms, maximum pleasure, minimum risk. The flattery of first, second, third dates. Infatuation. Sex. This is a man's province. A woman who wants sex without vows or future plans gets called names. So I'd be breaking rules. But I wouldn't hurt anyone, except myself maybe. Still, in the recesses of an unchanging idea of who I hoped I'd be, an incompatible wish: I wished to be a mother. I'd always wished to be a mother. If I built four walls and kept all trouble outside—if I nurtured and protected someone else—I'd become a better person myself.

I knew that motherhood wouldn't be a simple way of extending my love and getting it back, though I'd get some, a windfall. It was pledging steadfastness to another life. Did I think could? Every potential parent worries, I figured. Besides, anything worthwhile I'd wanted—to be a professor, which required multiple degrees; to be the author of published books—had required a leap of faith in my current abilities. If it's important, it's bound to feel scary at first, and it gets easier after you get started, so I thought.

In any case, I'd need a man. My list of husband-prerequisites was more grandiose than when I was a girl reading fairy tales. I'd marry a handsome man with a job I'd admire, and he'd see my ambition to write as praiseworthy, help raise our children and, once the door was locked at night, take my breath away with the way his hands moved, the words he spoke as he stripped me down to desire, took me from daily responsibility to a white-lit moment. I'd marry a prince. But men I met didn't make sense, not a living either.

The only man who'd asked me out since I'd moved to Texas was a man who changed the oil in my car. And someone at the hardware store who handed me his card and said he'd trim trees in my yard if I'd date him. Twenty miles away, on campus, I had three single colleagues, all women. One was still saying *he said and then I said* about someone she'd split up with nine years earlier. And Tess, kind, jolly, older than me, lived forty miles north, in Austin. A third had turned asexual, channeling her energy into good works. In an unguarded moment, she confessed to me she'd given up, but her body had not. "I have these dreams," she said, "enormously sexual and pagan, like in an A.S. Byatt novel." The dean, a woman, a grandmother, lived in Austin too. She asked, "Do you have a boyfriend?" I said no. She said, "Well, you won't find anyone single in this county."

I couldn't have children alone, I thought. Not until I paid off my debts. Not in a cabin with no heat but a woodstove—red-hot, a child-hazard. I have time, I told myself. All the same, I stared so long at babies in grocery store shopping carts that parents either stopped to chat about how perfect their child was, or they moved away fast like I was a kidnapper.

A few months later, I was coming back from a professional conference, the plane landing in San Antonio, fifty miles south. I had a long drive home that night, and then I'd need to start a fire and warm up the house. An old woman in the seat next to me said: "I'll bet you have a nice young man waiting." I looked up, surprised. She repeated, "I'll bet you have a young man waiting to drive you home." I shook my head. She raised her eyebrows. "I'm single," I said. She said, "You can still have a man." I explained I was getting a divorce, and new to Texas. She asked where I lived and worked. As we deplaned, she said, "You need two things. A gentleman friend, not a husband. Never let him move in or spend your money. But someday, come nightfall, you'll want a man's company."

I shrugged. "True."

"And," she said, "get out in that backwater town, get to know some old people. Suck up to them. They'll sell you a house on land contract, nothing down, and you won't pay more than you pay for rent." I tried picturing myself befriending elderly people who had a spare house— it seemed unlikely. I went to work, home again, graded papers, did chores. I'd hardly met anyone. I had my most personal chats with strangers, this woman, for instance. I said, "I'm not the sucking up type. But I will take your advice about the man."

I drove home, through the snarl of freeway, up I-35, then a short-cut across Purgatory Road. I anticipated hills, dips, the way the road would curve. I'd settled into a cadence. My future would be fine. But this wasn't it, I thought, as I opened the door to my dank cabin with its stained carpet I'd hidden under my great-aunt's Oriental rugs. I'd stay awhile and pay off bills—hard to ignore as I sifted through mail. Mail used to be a continual shock, repeated bolts from the blue: some new creditor my ex-husband had failed to mention, or the IRS, which had spent years tracking him, levying yet another penalty. My bills were current, I reminded myself, if numerous with vast balances: bills I didn't mind paying, student loans, which had given me my life; bills I did mind paying, bank notes for my ex-husband's pie-in-the-sky ideas. I haven't been so squeezed always, I told myself. And I won't be. Then I saw the envelope. When I paid rent, the landlord sent a receipt. This time he'd added a note. "You seem nice. We want to sell you the house."

Homemaking

Five years later, carpenters sawed a hole in the wall. I was in my bedroom at the other end of the house, trying on clothes, trying to find the right look for the appointment I had scheduled that day. Effort that led to accomplishment is a way of ignoring botched goals, I thought, a Plan B that evolves as Plan A fails. Just then, my aimlessness felt like sartorial aimlessness. I had two looks. Professor, black clothes covered with chalk, worn with boots in winter, sandals in summer. Cheap clothes look less cheap and more stylish in black, you see? Or my Saturday night look: siren. I needed something else now. My mother's dictates, long repressed, surfaced: Look inexperienced. If you can't, look like a matron.

I put on a slinky dress, a drab cardigan over it.

I stepped outside, over coiled power cords, to talk to my carpenters. I turned passive when I spoke to men. *You decide.* And I always felt like I was impersonating someone better prepared. If people knew me, I thought, they'd ignore me, cheat me, roll their eyes. My lead carpenter looked like Gregg Allman, and he'd hired his brother, Brent, who looked like Duane Allman. He'd also hired his son, Sean, who looked like a teenage celebrity heartthrob too young for me to register. The carpenter who looked like Gregg Allman was named Greg. He said, "I'll set plywood over this hole before I leave tonight."

I said, "Will you nail it shut?"

"Wasn't planning on it. You scared?"

He meant there'd be no way to lock up. Something sifted from the sky into my hair. Sawdust. Sean leaned from the top of a ladder, grinning. I asked, "Will this hole stay open all summer?" Greg said, "I'll get locks eventually. I need to level everything first."

"Fine." I was hard as nails, I meant.

I got my teaching job, first in North Carolina, then in Texas (low pay until you get promoted), because I'd sold my first book to a small press. Then I sold a second book, and paperback rights to my first book, to a big press. I'd come back from a writers' conference where an editor heard me read, then asked for manuscript pages to take home in her briefcase, and a month later I had a contract. I used the money to remodel, turn my gloomy cabin into a snug cottage. Then I sold a third book for a sum so generous I could add on new rooms, buy a new car, adopt a baby. If I spent carefully. What I saved on the house I could use on the adoption. I paid an ex-contractor I used to date to teach me to be a contractor, since I couldn't afford one. I gave him $1500 for drawings and a materials list.

First, I'd solicited carpenter bids.

Greg and his brother had just moved here—to this everyone-knows-everyone town. They underbid other carpenters. I told Greg I was adopting a baby, who might arrive suddenly. He said he wished he'd spent more time with Sean when Sean was little. He lived his formerly-toxic life one day at a time. He quoted Chief Joseph: "I cannot go the old way." I still drank when I was mad or tired, but I didn't have time for it. I'd spent the winter teaching and writing. I wanted a child, a house big enough, a car safe enough.

All summer, I worked on the add-on.

I painted, inside and out, sanded and finished woodwork, did electrical trim. I refinished used furniture for new rooms. I loaded the CD player with rock and roll. I made biscuits and coffee. I collected bids from other subcontractors who'd ask about my floor plans, my square-footage, my life. The roofer handed me a bid and said, "Talk it over with your husband." I said, "There is no husband." He looked panicked. "No boyfriend either?" The plumber said, "If you don't mind my asking, is there a reason you aren't married?" I said, "I'm not opposed to it. I'm divorced." It's a small town with a finite number of roofers, electricians. How I answered could affect the quality of work, or price. The tile layer said, "I don't get it. You kept your figure. You cook like this." He waved at a tray on the porch rail. I'd made cinnamon rolls that day. I hoped home-cooked food would foster good craftsmanship—I didn't have the sternness or know-how to achieve this the usual way. And I was proud of my cooking. My mother's meals had been well-seasoned with fresh ingredients and attractive presentation. She'd taken Home Economics to heart. The times she'd looked most in love with my dad—blushing demurely—had been as she'd serve up food and he'd say how lucky he'd been to marry her.

Greg and I got past small talk fast. Once we were unloading two-by-fours, and I stopped to call a social worker to schedule my home study—the first step after you've filled out adoption paperwork. A social worker comes to see if your physical habitat is appropriate for a child, inspecting each nook and cranny, and she interviews you there, with your guard down. When I'd hung up and come back outside, Greg mopped his face with a red bandanna and said, "I like how you get things done even if you go against the grain."

But the day he was sawing the hole in the wall, I told him I'd see him later on. "I have that appointment."

He nodded. "Let go and let God."

I got in my new four-door sedan with good safety ratings, and sped off to San Antonio.

An hour later, at the adoption agency, case workers came out from behind their desks. "Hi, Debra," one said, "is your semester over?" Another: "How's construction going?" Another, "Where'd you get those sunglasses?" I said, "New York." This sounded cosmopolitan. In fact, I'd bought them at a kiosk as I'd changed planes on the way to somewhere provincial. The adoptive parent liaison, Marla, said, "Nice shoes." I'd worried too much, I thought. In a city, a mother could be gaudy. Marla and I looked at forms I'd filled out. She said I was open-minded about race. "Good home study," she added.

In the old part of my house, I'd cleaned windows, ceiling fans, closets. I laid out blueprints for the add-on, barely underway. The social worker had glanced around, then asked for a specific way my life would change. I'm good at Q & As. She said "specific," so I said: "I won't be able to grade papers late at night. I'll work in the day, with interruptions." I felt anxious. *Waiting not to rid my soul of one dark blot.* "How will you handle a tantrum?" I'd sit near, not too near, wait it out, I said. I wondered when she'd get to the past, my hard-drinking father, intermittent mother, my own divorces. Broken homes. I once saw a house split in half by a storm. A tree had landed on the bed. The exposed bedroom looked naked. Would my patched-up past break open? The home study was a test I didn't want to pass unless I should. "It's as if I'd specialized in unemployed men," I said, "though my father earned a good living, but not my stepfather. Yet those dead-ends turned out to be helpful," I added, "in that I had to make my own way, so there was no reason not to risk it, go for a PhD. It was a long shot, the idea I'd be good enough." The social worker stared. "Look. You accomplished a lot. Stress the positive."

At the agency, Marla flipped through the photo album she'd asked for. I'd had Clara Mae come by with a camera. I'd gazed into the lens, making a healthful salad here, stirring a roaring fire there. I'd sorted through old photos for every picture of me with a child—children of friends in grad school sitting by me on sofas long ago left for trash. Marla said, "Your letter, nice, the first paragraph." She meant the letter that begins: *Dear Birth Mother.* I'd thought about the person reading it. *This terrible and difficult time.* I tried to imagine—carrying a baby, feeling so wrong, so imperfect, I'd let a stranger take over.

Marla said, "You'd be surprised how adoptive parents don't understand. They think it's this joyful handover. There's hardly any press about how birth mothers feel, or suffer."

I nodded.

Marla said, "You're interested in babies other clients won't take. It won't be long."

Late that night, I stared at the door-sized maw that led to the add-on. Plywood leaned against the hole. The bottom gaped. In the past, I'd moved so much, rent house to rent house, I'd grown fanatical about locks, doors, windows. I liked window shades—cheap, essential—because I understood the optical fact of lit, indoor rooms and, outside, infinite camouflage. I used to go for walks at night and stare at a father in a striped chair maybe, a mother in a red sweater feeding her children at the table. Nice wallpaper, I'd think. I envied family life, lamplight fastening down the night. But I didn't want people looking in at me. I used to dream about my doors or windows being kicked open, and I'd wake, related to no one, the streets full of strangers. But sounds outside here were deer, possums. This hole, no problem, I thought, as I pulled the shades down, locked my real door.

Daybreak, Greg's truck would rumble up. I'd move the plywood aside, step through the hole to the living room-to-be, the child's bedroom and bathroom adjoining; an unfinished stairway curved to a loft. Then Brent and Sean arrived. And, today, Clem, who lived in a tent. Greg had suggested Clem for basic plumbing and wiring. He'd be cheapest. Greg gave me Clem's ex-wife's phone number—Clem had plumbed and wired her house. She'd told me to give him a big meal once a day. He was licensed, safe, but a drunk. Tell him obvious stuff like, yes, I want a light there. Use someone else to install fixtures because he didn't like using a level. I told Clem his ex-wife spoke highly of his work. "She hurt my heart," he said, handing me his plate. I'd gone through ten pounds of flour in a week, I thought. He said, "I don't see why you're adopting a baby when you can have me for free. I'd be less trouble." It was a joke, maybe. He crawled under the house.

Then the guy who'd lay a new line to my septic tank arrived. He was tall and handsome. Clara Mae once told me that if I look at a man and can't look away and he can't either, he feels the same. "Not that instant mutual magnetism is helpful," she added. "It's led me down the primrose path a few times." As I talked to the septic guy, I put on my all-business face. We surveyed the land, me holding a stick on a string as he stared through a meter. He yelled, "To the left. Good gal." Then he stepped into the old part of my house, glanced at an antique sampler: GOD BLESS THIS HOME. I like its kitsch look. I also like its sentiment. I mean that I can't tell if my decorating style is an ironic comment on retro domesticity, or if I'm retro, domestic. He told me about the winter of his divorce, staying in a hunting shack. He lay on the floor, praying. When he stood up, his pain was gone. "That's why I'm born-again," he said. Then he sat down, did some math.

I went outside, poured paint, climbed the ladder, and thought how the idea that men won't talk about feelings is wrong. They won't talk to a wife or a long-term girlfriend because then she knows too much forever. But, to a woman a man is alone with a few weeks never to see

again, he'll talk. Talking is also permissible during first-phase woo-
ing. Men I'd hired treated me like a date-substitute, I thought. GFE,
girlfriend experience, a prostitution term (it costs more). I was doing
the paying, but the dynamic is the same, lonely men talking to a lone
woman. Greg had told me about his divorce. Before he got sober he
was useless, and Sean's mother left him. When Sean was a teenager,
she'd called, said: take him, make him a man. Too little too late. Sean
moved out of Greg's house to Brent's. "Who am I to tell him not to
drink?" Greg said, his eyes troubled.

As I painted, I thought how pent-up desire is noticeable.

I'd recently seen my friend from graduate school, Jack Creeden.
Jack and I used to sleep together when we were in our twenties—
we'd fight and make up, fight and make up. But now he was my
oldest friend. He'd lately taken a job in a dull suburb. I saw him at a
professional conference, and he told me he hadn't had sex in years.
He'd looked pale and stared at women he didn't know. "This can't
be healthy," I'd told him. I still subscribed to the idea that you have
sex regularly, or you get starved for it and tip headlong for the wrong
person—better to have no-strings sex with the wrong person and
move on fast, I thought. I'd also noted, a curious fact I hadn't made
sense of yet, that I'd never liked sex when I was married. Of course,
when I was married I was mad or scared. But I hadn't been prepared
for the ferocity of desire once I was always alone—the idea I might
never have sex again, not if circumstances didn't change, acting on
me like aphrodisiac. So I had fleeting, extricate-myself-fast affairs
when I traveled. Or I slept with men with whom I had too few shared
interests. Sleeping with men I didn't mean to keep, chattering away
afterward, happy, leaving the future undescribed, I felt indulgent yet
frugal—this moment, like canned beets on the shelf in the time of
famine, would last me.

But if you have sex with a man you don't want, he'll want you.
Economic law. Demand increases as supply wanes. So sometimes an
affair lasted too long and ended badly, bungled etiquette—e.g., Dan,
the ex-contractor, my "boyfriend" for a few years. We'd run through a
list of alternative names for what we'd been to each other. "Partner"
wasn't accurate. "Lover" sounded pretentious, or indiscreet. "Gentleman friend" sounded as if I'd depended on the kindness of strangers.

At any rate, I couldn't picture a future with Dan. And yet he wasn't mean. So I'd procrastinated, waiting for a deal-breaking, tooth-and-nail last fight, which never materialized. We fizzled out, mutually bitter.

And now I'd set sex aside because I didn't see how I'd have it when I was a mother. I'd expected sex to come up in adoption agency interviews: did I plan to date? had I puzzled through the logistics? No one asked. Yet I'd thought hard and decided that mothers do have sex but with the baby's father, not applicable. I could remember meeting only one sexy mother ever, Ginger, who lived next door when I was a kid, and she suntanned in a black bikini. Ginger's baby didn't smell fresh, my mother pointed out. His head was lopsided from lying in the crib too much. One of my aunts wore false eyelashes when she competed for Miss North Dakota. Then she married, had kids, toned down. Sex leads to motherhood and goes underground. I wasn't about to buck tradition, instinct. My sex à la carte plan—defunct now. I didn't live in the world's dating capital, besides.

The septic tank guy came outside. "So what do you do in the evenings?"

Sean had taken down my TV antenna. A hole was in my wall. I felt unprotected, tongue-tied. Yet I couldn't be rude. He was working for me. How would I change the subject?

"Do you always wear dresses?" he asked.

I wore old dresses to work in—stained with paint and polyurethane now. They were cooler. I was about to say as much. Then I heard my phone ring. "I've got to get that."

He nodded. He'd start work Monday, he said.

I got the phone. Marla. She needed another adoption form filled out, I thought.

"A birth mother has selected you, and her due date is soon," Marla said.

Where?

When?

Marla laughed. "This is the fastest this ever happened. She saw your materials and said: I like the lady professor in the yellow house. Her baby is due in three weeks. Here's the catch. She was visiting her brother here. She lives in Philadelphia. The baby wasn't planned. She was raped. She has children at home. You'll fly up and bring it back."

I calculated. Plane ticket, no notice. Hotel. Rental car.

On the back burner, this thought, glowering: rape. The baby could never know. I'd hoped for a birth parent story not so appalling I wouldn't have to hide it. Too much to want.

"She doesn't believe in abortion," Marla said. "She's been in a deep depression. Finally she called her brother who's stationed down here. She wants to talk to you. Call her."

We hung up. I ran outside. I told Greg, "The baby will be here soon."

He stood, flummoxed. Then smiled. "That's great." I noticed a blowsy-looking woman next to him. "This is Delia," he said. "Delia, this is Debra." He looked flummoxed again. "Delia wanted to meet you since I talk about you all the time." I understood. Single, not young, not old yet either, I was used to clarifying I wasn't the other woman, homewrecker. I said, "Greg always talks about you too." She nodded, appeased.

I talked to the birth mother that night. Her voice was quiet, careful. After a minute, I said, "What would you like to ask?" She said, "How do you feel about a child of color? Are you racist?" Well, I thought, everyone is a little. Or religionist. Biased toward good looks, or certain nationalities. I couldn't say that. Everything else was a cliché. I told her I'd taught in North Carolina and had changed the textbook in order to teach more black writers, to fit the student body. "When civil rights happened I was a kid," I said, "so I saw it on TV. My gut feeling was that the cops with dogs were the bad guys."

Silence. "That's fine," she said. I'd sounded oblivious, I thought. Or obvious.

But the adoption was on, Marla told me by phone the next day.

Then my mother called from Arizona. Her second husband had just died after a long marriage during which he'd kept her sequestered. We'd stayed in touch by phone—that's how we talked for seventeen years. She'd seen my sister and brother in person, but only because her husband had visited his own relatives in Wisconsin. The lack of contact was her fault, I felt. Or he'd coerced her. I was too confused to sort it out. And anger got you nowhere—I wanted to move on, forward. I'd listen to her on the phone and understand: I'm the dead husband stand-in here. We were strangers now, except I remembered the gentle, half-sad woman she used to be. I used the same conversational techniques I used when troubled students came to my office and told me they were worried about their whole life. I'd nod and murmur. I cared. But I couldn't fix anyone's whole life. My mother never said much when she called, except that her dead husband had depended on her because she was so helpful and giving, and so she'd never made friends.

I'd suggest ways to meet friends. Or I'd say, "Transitions are a hard time." Then I'd say it in reverse, and she wouldn't notice: "Hard times are a transition." We'd had this conversation yesterday, the day before. Today, I told her about the baby. She got excited. Layettes, she knew. Formula, bottles, diapers. "I'll be there in two days," she said.

When she arrived, we moved the secondhand crib to my study, put a pallet beside it. She went to Target. That night she packed a diaper bag—sterilized bottles in Ziploc bags, canned formula, size-zero clothes washed in Dreft. She'd bought a pale green tiny sweater because the plane would be chilly. She helped me pack my own suitcase for the hospital.

I'd be going to the hospital in Philadelphia.

We waited.

She washed curtains. Reorganized the laundry room. Hounded the carpenters. Woke me to look at her scalp. Did she have skin cancer, did I think? She quizzed me about my ex-boyfriend, Dan: why did we break up? I tried to answer. I remembered a day I'd been teaching the History of the Novel and left class all excited about the idea that the individual's relation to social institutions—a reverent, loyal relation, or an alienated, cynical relation—dictated the shape of plot. Dan was waiting at my house with a bottle of wine. I left campus. And I left one world for another. I couldn't explain to Dan why this idea stirred me. I couldn't explain to myself. Either you're interested in the history of human beliefs, a view that takes you outside a moment, a generation, or you aren't. I'd have to think of something else to talk about, or he'd turn away, miffed. "We didn't have much in common," I told my mother. "I couldn't talk to him about my work." She said, "I guess you're too smart for me now too." She kept on—how kind he must be because he'd drawn up plans for my add-on. I said, "I paid him, Mom. He needed the money."

One day, she and Clara Mae sat on the porch, watching a female cardinal build a nest, a male cardinal bringing twigs and string from afar, and Clara Mae said: "That's like Dan in west Texas who helped Debra get her nest ready here." She didn't add, as she sometimes did, that at least male animals kept transactions between the sexes honest: sperm, a little drone labor. She didn't know my mother well enough. My mother looked delighted. "I wouldn't have put it that way," she said, "but that's it exactly. Dan sounds so nice." I passed by, carrying PVC pipe. He'd come by in a few days—he had business in town, and he'd stop and look at the add-on. She'd fawn, flatter. To hell with the bird analogy, I thought, this pathetic fallacy, this projecting human longing onto the natural landscape, like I'm Snow White here and birds will tie ribbons so my dream comes true. Then my mom told Clara Mae, "Tell you the truth, she's too picky." I gave her an evil look. It had taken grit to get picky enough. Not that she'd know. Once she said: "We didn't have the idea of 'co-dependent' when I was young. 'Co-dependent' meant good wife."

Late one night after swift phone calls—"I know my timing, I've already had children," she said—the baby was imminent. I'd leave for Philadelphia the next day. I lay in bed. How would I find the hospital there? Where would I sleep? How would I sleep? How will I learn to feed a baby? Finally, knowing there was room on a flight at 5 a.m. and I could worry on a plane as well as at home in bed, I left a note, headed out. I bought the ticket, stood in line. I held the car seat, the diaper bag my mom had packed. I was about to board. The gate was closing. I heard my name. "Debra Monroe, come to the white courtesy phone." I stepped out of line. The message: call home. I did. My mother said, "A man from Philadelphia called and said that girl found a family up there with two parents. She had a boy—no matter now, though. You're supposed to come home."

I drove back to my little town, then up the cedar-lined road to my house.

Construction—loud, buzzing, yowling. Greg looked at me. "False alarm," I told him. I went inside. My mother cried. She said, "Ever since I'm a widow, I can't accept sudden change." I thought if she were a stranger and I didn't loathe her dead husband, I'd feel pity. Also, that years of anticipating his whims and bad moods had damaged her nerves, no stamina. I put my arm around her thin shoulders, con-

vinced her to take a nap. But the next day disgust at the anticlimax
had replaced her sadness. She drove back to Arizona.

A new plumber had come to install the bathroom fixtures. He told
Greg he couldn't install the bathtub/shower unit because Greg hadn't
built the furred out wall to close it in. Greg said, "Yes, a bathtub/
shower needs a furred out wall." He turned to me. "Am I your mind
reader? It wasn't in your plans. I guessed you wanted an old tub, some
antique."

The plumber said, "You two need to work this out. And call me."

Greg turned to me. "I respect you're trying to build this house on a
shoestring. But I didn't draw these plans, and I don't want to be rude,
but they're a little fucked. As long as we're on the subject, the space for
the stairs is too steep. It's not code. Realize, my reputation is attached
here. I don't want word getting around I don't know what I'm doing."

We were fighting. Sean stared at us.

"It's not your fault," I said. "Please. I'll fix everything."

I wondered that night: Had Dan drawn bad plans? Did he always
draw bad plans and that's why he was an ex-contractor? Or was the
furred out wall a given—too basic to draw—and Greg didn't know?
Could I return the bathtub/shower unit? Where do I get an antique
tub? My worries heaped up. What if Greg quit? Housework helps
me purge panic, so, stepping around the old part of my house piled
with baby gear I didn't need yet, furniture for half-built rooms, materials for construction still pending, I swept. Why had I thought I
had enough skills to build a house? I mopped. Because I took Shop
instead of Home Ec. in high school, big deal. I took Shop because a
friend and I used the lathe to make bongs. Besides, my mother had already taught me cooking and sewing. I scrubbed a shelf. I ran bleach
down the kitchen and bathroom drains to keep pesky drain odor
away. I need a real contractor, I thought. Yet I couldn't afford one, unless I gave up adopting. But a baby was my reason to build. I wasn't
getting younger. The phone rang.

Marla. "I know it's late, and I wondered whether to call, but I have
to see how you feel. I honestly don't think this birth mother's for real.
She might be trying to flip someone out, the baby's father. It's a two-
year-old. She says she wants to put her up for adoption."

A daughter whose mother doesn't want you even after she knows you?

Who'd get over that?

"The baby has been with relatives all along. That's why I think it's dicey."

I called the birth mother the next day. The child's name was Tamarinda. "What does she like?" I asked. The birth mother said: "Tam? Tam likes toys, I suppose." Be concrete, I thought. I said, "What are her favorite foods?" The birth mother said, "Hmm. That's a hard one. French fries." Finally, we hung up. I called Marla, who said, "I was about to call you. The birth mother doesn't even have custody. I guess she thought she'd get money. We'll be careful before we contact you now. You've already been through a lot."

I went back outside. Greg, Brent, and Sean were in the driveway, looking at the sheetrocker's rickety truck. He'd come by to get paid; good riddance, this man who'd hammered a nail in my new woodwork to hang his shirt on. His crew had hung and taped the drywall. Then he'd fired them and sprayed plaster himself, telling me, "All Mexicans want is money." In exchange for labor, how unusual, I thought. I'd taped newspaper over woodwork, the stairway, the banister, everything I didn't want plaster sprayed on. I forgot the open fuse box. This guy sprayed it. I told him, "I was in the next room. It would have taken me two minutes to cover it." He'd said, "It's not my fault you don't know what's up." So I'd flipped off the main breaker, cleaned each fuse with a toothbrush and razor blade. When I was done, I cleaned up his sandwich wrappers, his Coke cans, Skoal. I found a plastic jug, half-full. I thought it was chemical—I shouldn't put it in the trash. I took the lid off. Pee. He'd been too lazy to walk twenty feet to the woods.

Brent and Sean were laughing as the sheetrocker fiddled underneath his truck.

Greg glanced at me. "Rough night last night?"

Brent told the sheetrocker, "Stick your feet through the floorboard and run like Fred Flintstone."

The sheetrocker: "Shut the fuck up, patronizing motherfucker."

Brent said, "Nice hanging out here."

Sean laughed harder. He gestured for me to look. The sheetrocker's torso was under the truck. His hips and legs, not. He wore shorts.

"Chrissake," Greg said, steering me away, too late. I was struck by the fact a man's genitals are attractive if you want to see them, ghastly if you don't. My mind flits around if I'm tired. I also thought: someone somewhere loved this man at least once, probably. "You," Greg said to Brent and Sean, "work. You," he told the sheetrocker, "get this junk-heap running or call a tow truck."

We went inside.

"Every night," I told Greg, "I scrub and scrub, piles of scraped-off paint and sawdust and whatever in the bath water, and I think I'll be filthy again the next day. Being clean is temporary. But dirt is without end. Still, you take a bath every night anyway."

Greg looked at me. "Are you talking about dirt, exactly? You sound depressed."

"Late at night things look bad," I agreed.

The contractor who'd do the wood floor pulled up in a van with a fisher-of-men logo. He shook my hand. He wore a wedding ring. After preliminary chitchat with me, he talked to Greg like Greg was the husband in charge of dimensions, cost, and I was the wife in charge of aesthetics. Did I like yellow oak? His assistant, standing by while the boss talked to Greg, asked me: Was I married? Divorced? "Misery loves company," he said. "My ex-wife took everything. She took my horse. I'm a rodeo cowboy. How can I work?"

"Brutal," I said.

After the floor contractor left, Dan pulled up. He stepped out of his truck and smiled.

I could smell his aftershave. I'd emphasized months ago I was done sleeping with him, but he likely didn't believe it yet because when I had slept with him he was gone all the time. He'd say: "I get so much out of a few days I don't need to see you for a long time. I'll be the love of your life if you let me." We did it his way and fought because it seemed like I was available if he wanted me, and not vice versa, and did it my way and fought because he didn't like answering to anyone. "Absent father complex," my mother had said. "You're working through the past, dating a man who's unavailable." I likely had an absent mother complex too, but she didn't say so. She worked as a bookkeeper for a psychotherapist and had turned into a causality fundamentalist. Every effect had one cause.

I told Dan about the bathroom. He went inside. He and Greg faced each other. They're tall. They shook hands, shifted this way, that. They stepped into the bathroom. Sean and Brent stood in the bathroom door, listening. I tried to listen. All I could hear was muffled scraps, words, tone. I heard them say *she*, loud, louder. She thinks. Said. Wants.

Dan came out. He had to be somewhere, he said. "I see you've got everything arranged the way you want." He got in his truck, gunned it, gravel spitting as he drove off.

Greg said, "I didn't realize yesterday it was your boyfriend who drew the plans."

"Ex-boyfriend," I said. "He's a little territorial."

Greg nodded. Then told me he'd build the furred out wall. He'd show me how to sheetrock it myself. He'd put my door on, not the door with plywood that led from the old part to the new living room, but an outside door I'd be able to lock. Soon, next week. "What about my TV antenna?" I asked. Nights alone in my perforated house made me tense. Greg said, "Have Sean put that up tonight. Pay him a few bucks. Keep him out of trouble."

Sean climbed out of his beat-up car and handed me a bag. "It's my birthday."

I pulled out two bottles and set them on the porch rail. Tanqueray gin, tonic. "Happy birthday," I said, "but neither of us is having a drink until we're off the roof." We put the antenna up, guy wires in position. We went inside and plugged in the TV. It worked, but I'd have to lurch through mazed furniture and baby gear to sit in a chair and watch.

Sean put ice cubes in glasses. "By the way, how's your mom?"

"Fine." We'd talked by phone. She was lonely again. Because we'd bonded over the first baby, I'd told her about the second, the two-year-old. The might-arrive-any-day baby seemed to be our only topic. Every other conversation got too near the fact she was pretending she'd never been in a weird marriage that caused her to ignore her grown children, and I'd decided it was easier to pretend with her than force the fact out of its recesses and make her explain, apologize. She couldn't, I figured. She hadn't admitted to herself she should have tried to see me. This is what she needed to believe—our reunion wasn't a reunion. On the phone, she'd asked me if maybe I was using a dodgy, desperate agency. I said, no, it was birth mothers who were desperate. She said, "I saw a movie on the Oxygen channel. That girl was proud to give her baby up." I told her movies aren't real. But I wondered if adoptive families with two parents found birth mothers in easier situations—girls whose youth minister or guidance counselor helped them decide adoption was noble. She'd said, "I'm too high-strung to help you," and hung up.

Sean pointed at a rocking chair. "Some of your stuff is nice. Some of it is crap."

I said, "Tomorrow I'll come over and critique your furniture. And Brent's." I could imagine. Sean smiled at me. I said, "I suppose a beer can collection is part of your decor?"

Sean said, "In fact, it is." Next he paused, on the verge of speech, but he didn't speak. Then he said suddenly: "So you're going to adopt a black baby and bring it up in this town. Have you thought that through—what you're putting yourself and the kid up against?"

I was surprised. Did he think he was some talk-show host? "Does it bother you?"

He looked like he didn't know the answer. "Probably not," he said. "But you can't say that about every person who lives out here. Times have changed, but not that much."

I'd thought it through insofar as I could. We wouldn't be up against Jim Crow attitudes, but our lives would be complicated. I'd made my decision, but the child who'd grow up in my mostly white world wouldn't have a choice. Yet none of us gets to pick our parent, I thought. Was having a mother of a different race an especially onerous condition to impose on a child? I knew raising my child would be hard, but I didn't know the specific ways, and wouldn't until I was in the midst of it. "I hope you're wrong. If you're not, I'll step up."

He shrugged. "That's just my two cents. Kudos to you for having the balls, pardon my French." Then he leaned in. "Admit you've noticed the chemistry." Before I could ask—and I did think he meant how he got along with his uncle, or how the three of them worked together—he said, "You felt it too, that day I was on the ladder. Our eyes locked."

I choked on my drink. I'd tried to be nice to everyone. Except the sheetrocker. Sheetrockers are trash, I thought. Already I was a little drunk. But why? Why smile, cook, soothe ruffled feathers? I needed labor. They needed money. Reciprocity. On the other hand, houses were going up all over. They could refuse to work for a woman with no contractor—likely snafus, missing furred out walls. Or do shoddy work, fritter away my dream.

"You walk around, pathetic, saying 'yes this is okay, that's all right, hope you're doing fine'." Sean said this last part, hand on his hip, falsetto. "You have self-esteem problems."

I was pissed off. Knowing you don't have enough doesn't mean you get some. "Where do you get off telling me that?" I said. "You don't strike me as a self-esteem paragon."

He blushed. "I lack it. My mother said. So I can see you do too. My mom is a class act. So I'm attracted to older women. I told my uncle you're hot. He said to go for it."

"He said that? That I seem available?" I was furious.

"No. He was supporting me, saying be proud of what I've got. You find me attractive?"

"I never considered it. Really. Your dad is cute."

He slammed his drink down. "I don't need this." He stumbled, rushing out the door.

I thought I couldn't work with an angry man. I ran after him. "Sean, Sean," I yelled in the dark. He must have stopped. I bumped into him. I smelled his soap, also a human smell, sweat, skin. I sagged into him for a minute, his unseen body a container for any idealized attraction without obstacles, obstacles as in: he'd be impossible to talk to the morning after. In this one-horse town, everyone would be. Still, I'd been alone all summer, carpentering, weathering the news the baby is here, yes, and, no, the baby isn't. But, I thought, if staring at a man and he stares back means this inconvenient feeling is mutual, then both of us hanging on in pitch darkness was worse, and I knew instantly my plan to live without sex until the baby grew up and left home wasn't practical, not that I wanted to have sex just then with a twenty-year-old. Sean, smart-aleck, said: "You like me."

"Not like that." I ran inside.

I drank gin, another drink, another. I woke in a chair, people on TV murmuring about bilingual education. My head pounded. The real door was locked, window shades pulled down tight, the night sealed away. But the door-hole gaped like it had all summer, plywood tilted against it. For a few weeks in June, a frog had hopped through the crack at the bottom—he must have seen light from afar shining on my tiled floor. I'd take him outside. He'd come back. Finally, I put him in a Tupperware dish, drove him miles away. But that night I drank water, went to bed. Lying in the dark, I got scared the way I did when I was a student in cheap rental houses and never read the paper because there was always a serial rapist somewhere—a paralytic fear, all eyes shining in the dark shine for me.

How many near-strange men, my subcontractors, knew I lived alone with a hole in my wall? I went through the list, methodical, compulsive. Then I heard a noise, something being slid. I lay there, frozen. Then stepped out of my room, flipped the light on.

A pile of shit gleamed in a clear space on the floor.

Ten feet away a ferocious fat raccoon, maybe thirty-five pounds, reeled on his hind legs like a baby grizzly, flexing his claws, baring his teeth. I had two options, to stay closed in my room all night and let him roam, or run him out the way he came. I threw shoes at him, every sandal and boot I had. Then I started in with books. *The Collected Poems of Theodore Roethke. The World We Have Lost. Seven Old English Poems edited by John C. Pope. The Norton Anthology of Short Fiction.* He ran out the gap. I cleaned up his shit, his scat, my shoes. I picked up books, bent, battered, and went to bed.

Nice if my courage had arrived that night. But it would take six more years, another set of incursions: chainsaws, hatchet jobs, scalpels, lawsuits, mortal risk. I'd survive it all and turn out smarter. Protective, not paranoid. I'd get clout. Meantime, I spent the interim faking clout. A few weeks later, I cooked a good-bye lunch for Greg, Brent, and Sean—with fifteen years less experience at feigning confidence, Sean had been standoffish since his birthday. A subcontractor was laying carpet in the baby's room, and the three of us sat at a table outside, under the trees. I served pasta with tomatoes, brie, fresh basil; homemade bread; fruit salad. Sawdust blew in and dusted the food like sugar or parmesan cheese. Brent said, "This isn't the first time I've ingested sawdust."

Greg asked about my weekend. I poured iced tea. "Same old."

I'd spent it near the phone. Saturday, a case worker named Nikki had called me because Marla was on vacation. I'd met Nikki at the agency. She had a kind face. She was single. She'd adopted three hard-to-place children. Marla had told Nikki not to call until she was nearly certain. A newborn baby boy lay in a hospital thirty miles away. The birth parents were seventeen. Nikki, calling from her car, told me to stand by. I was watching reruns of *Lawrence Welk*—perky yet lulling—when she called again: "I'm sorry, Debra. I got there and found all three lying together in the hospital bed, mother, father, baby, the mother and father crying. They have no home, no money. But they can't do it." A new sad story. "That's fine," I said. I didn't want some woman's baby if she did.

I'd missed the segue into the next part of the conversation, Greg's weekend. Sean said, "What else did you expect from her, some ex-stripper you met at Narcotics Anonymous?"

Greg stopped eating, fork poised—the look in his eyes was like he meant to ride out his last days alone, everyone else fend for yourself. I thought of the Allman Brothers, how Duane died young and fierce and Gregg got old, little. I'd seen a picture.

Brent said to Sean, "Take it easy, dawg. That's your old man. Respect."

Then the carpet layer called to me from the new front door that you could lock. But it sat open, windows too, to keep the breeze moving. Then he stopped yelling and stood, resigned, shoulders limp. I said, "Are you hungry? Would you like some lunch?" He shook his head, brown eyes beaming out sadness. I imagined them filling with tears. He was recently divorced maybe. Or he lived far from people he loved and felt homesick. Greg asked him, "What do you want?" He called out, "I am not from here. I am from Ohio. I'm not used to laying carpet without air-conditioning. Turn it on, please."

Brent said, as we carried my refurbished furniture into the new part of the house, "He needs to take a cue from you who worked in hundred-degree heat all summer. He should have seen you in your red dress, running the power-sander up and down the stairs." Sean, holding the other end of the baby's dresser, said, "I remember that dress. Nice change from the black. You had a purple bra strap showing, I recall." Greg, carrying a chair with one hand, floor lamp with the other, shook his head. "I didn't raise him. You can't blame me he has no manners." He thought a minute. "Maybe you can." Brent and Sean set the dresser down. Brent slapped Greg's back. "Lighten up," he said. I wrote Greg a check. "Call if you need us," Greg said, staring in the rearview, backing away.

For a few days, I hung curtains, arranged sofa pillows. I unframed an old print, angels carrying babies down from clouds, and used brown watercolor to wash over one of the curly-haired babies' faces to make it black, and a stylus with ink to make its hair kinky, ethnic, then re-framed the print and hung it over the crib. My semester started in a month. Days loomed. I called the book page editor of a newspaper in Austin and told her I was available to write reviews. She promised to send me two books the next day. "Did you ever contact that young man I tried to fix you up with?" she asked. This had been months ago. I'd phoned him then, but I'd been finishing my book, making house plans.

I had time now. I called him. His name was Will.

We decided to have a date at my place—hour commute, one-way—and swim in the river. I had yearnings about steadfast love, fatalistic qualms too. Will was educated, so we'd likely have something in common besides desire. Yet I worried that while I talk about books for a living, on weekends I talk about nail guns, septic tanks, or growing up in the north, going to bars on a sled towed by my dad's snowmobile, watching him drink, or creepy things my stepfather said. When Will arrived, we said hello. I showed him the house, the old part, the new. I showed him the baby's room and said my adoption papers were filed. This must be the strangest blind date he's had, I thought. Will stared at the sixteen-foot living room ceiling. "How did you paint that neat line between the wall and ceiling?"

"It helps not to look down," I said.

Later that night, we ate mangos on the porch. Try to act interested, I thought. I do want a man who talks about books, ideas. But he couldn't use powers tools, and I could. Will leaned close as if to kiss me, and I sat up straight. "Do you think the baby's bedroom, all set, curtains hung, pictures on the wall, seems like some shrine to dashed hopes," I asked, "like Miss Havisham with her wedding cake?" He laughed. It was nice not having to explain who Miss Havisham was. "No," he said, "the whole place looks homey."

We said goodnight.

I took a long time washing up dishes. I finished the wine.

The next day I had a headache. How can I stand this? I thought. I sat in a chair. The phone rang next to my head: Marla. "Debra," she said, "can you get in your car and come now?" I was confused. It was Sunday. The agency was closed. She said, "To the hospital." She burst out laughing. "This baby is lucky. I have to confess you've been one of our favorite clients. All of us are rooting for you. Your work ethic. You've been kind to the birth mothers. Your interesting career." Me? I thought. She asked, "Are you ready?"

I went to the baby's room, got the diaper bag my mom had packed for the trip to Philadelphia I never took. I opened drawers, pulled out sterilized bottles still sealed in bags. Diapers, undershirts, blankets. I went out into the world—to San Antonio at least, a city.

I came home several hours later with my daughter.

I unlocked the door and set the car seat down, so weighty now, put to use. The door stood ajar because I was going back out to the car to get my spare case of formula. The window shades were up— black, opaque windows. Nighttime went on and on outside. I looked at the clock. Someone else would have to worry about unknowable catastrophes that might intrude, I thought. My daughter would wake soon, hungry. I stared at her, this flesh, this life, this better chance. My wishes for her enchanted future stacked like bricks and lumber into a sturdy dream. I'd be her mother forever, and this would make her happy, not aggravated. She'd go to work each day, confident. When she became a mother herself, she'd feel prepared, deserving. When she spoke to men, they'd always listen. Her eyes blinked open. I'd be there, she seemed sure. I had to keep her sure.

A History of Fear

A long time ago, when I was still in Utah and not yet married to my second husband, a doctor with a blunt bedside manner stood over me doing an ultrasound. "Three months, you're out of your mind," he said, "this fetus isn't even six weeks yet." I lay there worried I hadn't worried enough to have kept the baby alive: life-to-life incessant worrying. The doctor left. I got dressed. The doctor came back and told me the fetus was nonviable, had been a long time. He gave me pills. As we know, I'd wanted the baby. I didn't want the father. He turned out nonviable too. No one knows me, I thought. I was poor, a student. The baby I'd carried had seemed superfluous to the doctor but not to me. As I left the hospital, I stumbled into the cardiovascular annex, a tunnel with electromagnetic current, and my one credit card got demagnetized. I tried using it, *invalid*. A wave of grief, illogic, hit me: I'd been culled. This memory dredged up years later, that Sunday afternoon Marla from the adoption agency called and said to come to the hospital in San Antonio now. *Now.* This time, I wanted direction, the right way.

The hospital in San Antonio was a labyrinth.

The people I asked were hospital visitors too, shouldering huge life changes. They looked dazed, exhausted. Or, as I got closer and closer, elated. Finally, I stared through a plate glass window at Plexi-glas cribs. Two held bald, white babies. A third held a black baby with thick hair. A nurse tapped on the window. "Which are you here to see?" she mouthed. I knew the baby was black, a girl. I pointed. The nurse held her to the window. She said, "She has beautiful lips." Or so I thought she said. Were lips something people noticed about new-borns? The baby would feed better maybe? The nurse spoke again. I didn't understand. She walked to a desk and, holding the baby with one arm, wrote a note, held it to the window: *Are you the case worker?* I shook my head. She put the baby back. I sat in a chair and waited an hour, another hour. Then the nurse came out from behind the glass and said, "Why didn't you tell me you were the adoptive mother?"

I said, "I'm not yet. The birth mother could still change her mind."

The nurse said, "The case worker is on the phone. She wants to talk to you."

On the phone, the case worker told me the birth mother wanted to give the baby up. At first, the birth mother had said she didn't know who the father was. Then she said she didn't know where he was. "We insisted she find him," the case worker said. "He doesn't want to sign. On the other hand, he's seventeen. Go to her room. Get to know them."

I wanted to do this without feeling like a shark, a smooth talker.

A baby. My ideal. Mine. Yet if no one wanted the baby, she needed me too. But I don't trust people who tally up their own good deeds, so thinking about how I'd be good for the baby wasn't right. And I never lost sight of the woman who was already a mother but out of luck, and options. Obsessed by these gradations—most right, least wrong, most kind, least cruel—I knocked. She sat in bed. He sat in a chair. He exhaled like a tire going flat. I guess she'd told him to stop talking, and the tactic he had left was sighs.

"This is my first baby," he told me. "I'd wanted us to raise her." The birth mother glared. She was older than the baby's father, the case worker had said. She already had a child. She hardly knew him though she'd slept with him. She said, "There is no *us*. You don't know what it takes." A minute passed. Silence. I told her I'd brought pictures of my house. "This belongs to you?" she asked. "It looks real cute." She said, "I'm staying with my mom, but when I get out of the hospital she'll throw us back out. My other little girl can handle it, but I can't take a baby on the street." She looked away. "What I'm doing is bad. But I didn't kill it." The birth father jumped, startled.

Later I told the case worker what the birth mother had said—she didn't kill it. "At least she didn't have an abortion, she meant," I said. The case worker raised her eyebrows. "I hope." She pointed out that the birth mother couldn't afford a doctor's visit.

The birth mother said, "Please, if you can't ever keep her, give her back."

I said, "I've never wanted anything more than I want to be her mother. Nothing will happen where I can't take care of her. Unless I die." Unlucky talk. "I'm healthy," I added.

She said, "You hear about these kids going home to home, lost in the system."

I said, "That's foster care—when the government takes an abused child. Foster care is temporary. Adoption is permanent. I've never heard of an adopted child who didn't stay with its family." Usually the agency explains all this. But the birth mother hadn't phoned the agency until her labor started and she walked to the nearest ER. The case worker had faxed papers to the hospital. They sat on the night-stand, the blanks still blank.

She turned to the birth father, asked if he wanted to see pictures of my house. He sighed again, his whole body. She lost her temper. She yelled at him, "You are in a fantasy."

I have a rule: inertia on purpose (no doubt, a deferential byproduct of having spent years living with hotheaded people). Because what if a ripple I cause swells into a mishap, calamity? I also felt like I was eavesdropping. I worried about all of us. I said, "I hope you'll decide to trust me to raise your child, but you need privacy to make this decision." I went to the waiting area to stare through the glass at the baby, but the nurses invited me to their lounge. "Too bad you don't have some relative or friend to sit with you now," the nurse said. I was too rattled to pray for specifics. So, silently I went through the Lord's Prayer, which covers food, shelter, forgiveness for even unconscious sins, and the reminder we can't wangle outcomes. Thy will be done. Some people think the word *amen* is transformative—Amen, and the future is here. But you can't handpick it.

The case worker got to the hospital and went to the birth mother's room. The birth mother told the nurse I could hold the baby. The birth father said I could hold the baby too, but he hadn't agreed to sign. I'd be holding a baby that might not be mine, the nurse pointed out. Would I risk it? I held the baby. I fed her. I touched her minuscule face. I was a humming machine, worrying yet not worrying. Like listening to Muzak and you're on hold—business is getting done even if you can't see it, hear it. Having prepared for months (years I'd dreamed this moment), to love a baby that didn't exist, or if it did, it was in someone's body I couldn't guard or supervise, my daydreams had felt like pleasure until they got too detailed and scared me. Longing triggered my own doubts too. Who was I to deserve being a mother? I distracted myself, anodynes of chores. I fed her again. Newborns eat every three hours. The nurse walked in. "The birth father signed the papers," she said. The case worker came in, confirmed this. Amen, and I'm a mother.

I made birth announcements by phone. A nurse took pictures, my daughter's speck of a head in my crooked arm, phone jammed under my chin, credit card tucked between two fingers, the same look on my face I see in every photo taken those weeks: thrilled, astonished. Did the nurses understand they were sending this baby home with a rank amateur? Still, I called my friend, Sofia, in Florida. She's a writer, a mother. She'd married a good man on her first try. I'd met her and her husband, John, at the conference where I sold my second book, where we drank Bloody Marys all day, and I'd liked Sofia at once, with her punk rock fashion-statement, her obsession with good food and good manners.

I called Jack Creeden in Georgia. Jack got married in Utah, like I did. After I left, he and his wife had two babies and, when the babies were little, Jack and his wife divorced. He could have stayed, teaching for a low wage, but he got offered a real job, and now he saw his children for Christmas, spring break, all summer. Never enough. He hadn't realized his ex-wife, who wasn't maternal, he'd said, wouldn't get tired of the work and worry and, after awhile, relinquish custody. Jack was a walking-talking void, I thought, a hole where his kids used to be. He asked me for details about my baby: How much does she weigh? How long is she? He remembered the weight and length of his own babies. "Great, Debra. I can't wait to see her," he said, animated, a little plaintive too.

I called Clara Mae. I looked at the clock. I knew she was already in her bathrobe, sipping wine-from-a-box. "Is she it? This one's for real? You're sure you're already her mother, and no one can change their minds again?" I answered, laughing, "Yes, yes, yes."

I called my friend Shen in Utah whose children were grown, and she loves babies inordinately; she hung up to buy a plane ticket to Texas. On a whim, I called Will, the man I'd been on a date with the night before. He said, "Debra. I was about to call *you* to say I had a great time." I said, "I'm at the hospital. I got my baby." He said, "What?" I said, "You remember, I showed you the baby's room and said I didn't know when I'd get the baby." Tentative, he said, "Yes?" I hadn't said exactly that. I'd implied the empty baby's room all decked out seemed eerie since the baby was an intangible glimmer, an aspiration. "Congratulations," he said mock-hearty, every trace of want-to-see-you-again gone.

I called my sister in Wisconsin, and I asked her to tell the rest of my family. It turned out my mother was staying there. Since her second husband died, my mother, lost, lethargic, wandered from relative to relative. My sister once said about going to a therapist: "But you'd have to start all over, describing what you've been through. Why not call a sibling?" That night on the phone, she told me my mother was at a golf lesson, a hobby to get her out of the house, around people her age. My sister asked the baby's name. I told her the first name, *Marie*, which I'd picked out twenty years ago, but I'd added my mother's name, *Arlene*, as a middle name, a link to make my mother and me umbilical again, connected. My sister said, "I can't wait to tell Mom." I agreed: "It can only help." My mother worried she didn't belong in her kids' lives anymore. She didn't, yet.

Then I went home and worried like every new mother.

A steep learning curve, exhaustion and dread.

I woke the baby to make sure she was breathing. She cried, and guts I never knew I had twisted. I dwelt on worst contingencies. A moment's carelessness: her head splitting like a melon. If she fell from a boat, she'd plummet. Not that I went on boats. During the well-baby check-up, the pediatrician showed me the Heimlich Maneuver. Hold the baby on her belly, one hand clutching her jaw, strike her back with the other. The doctor said, "Better to break a rib, get the obstruction out, save her life." I pushed away the thought my baby could gasp, lose air. I spent the Heimlich lecture controlling my facial expressions, trying to seem neutral, attentive. This piled-on fear mixed with bliss.

But I didn't have skills.

I didn't understand nipples, for instance. A real mother has her own ever-adapting nipples. I had the manufactured, rubber ones. I'd been doing fine with rubber nipples for weeks when, for two nights and a day, I tried to feed my daughter and she pushed the nipple back out and screamed. I'd been awake thirty-six hours, trying to get my daughter to eat when my neighbor, Lauren, who years earlier had adopted Nathan and hence used bottles, not breasts, dropped by. She was in a hurry because she's the family breadwinner and the agency where she worked was having budget cuts and she didn't know if she'd survive the downsizing. "But I wanted to check on you and Baby Marie," she said.

She told me, first, that I had my dress on inside-out. Also: "It might be time for a new nipple size." She explained that there's one set of holes for newborns, another for older babies, another for babies older than that. I used a needle to poke a bigger hole in a nipple. Too big. The baby gagged. I poked another. It worked if, feeding her, I'd stop, start, and stop. I got enough food in her to put her in the car and buy new nipples in San Antonio.

Shen was arriving from Utah that day to see the baby—her plane landing in San Antonio. I couldn't find a parking space. This was before ordinary people had cell phones. I drove round and round. I pictured Shen waiting for me patiently. When we first became friends, her children were in middle school, and we'd spent hours in Shen's minivan, waiting for her kids to emerge from school, tennis, soccer practice, chess, dance team.

She'd had been standing by the baggage claim over an hour when I finally pulled into a spot, unhooked the baby's car seat—a bucket with a big handle that works as an arched safety device, as armor, and the baby gets strapped in underneath like for a roller coaster ride. A car seat is heavy but designed to be carried with one arm. I switched from my right to left and back again, then hugged the car seat to my chest. It was blistering hot—over a hundred degrees, asphalt radiating heat. I was wearing a pink dress with white shoes because I was representing my daughter. But those white shoes never fit well. I walked faster, and I encountered a curb. The car seat left my arms, airborne. I ran under it this way, and that. I caught it. Or it landed on me. Then it bounced, skidded, stopped. I held my breath as I crawled across the parking lot to check on her.

Marie was sleeping. She opened her eyes.

Security guards came running. I was holding the car seat to my chest again, my heart. "She's fine." I'd said this louder than I intended. Was I screaming? Would they take her from me? One said, "We know the baby's okay, lady. Those seats are built to withstand crashes. What about you?" I was bleeding, my chin and knees. I stood up and hurried away.

I found Shen. I asked her if she'd been this bad.

"Bad?" she said.

"Inept. Useless."

"Oh that," she said, "of course."

But I figured I hadn't learned something basic. My brother once said, disgusted about a dog who'd abandoned her puppies and he'd bottle-fed them: "She's a terrible mother." We never said this about our mother who'd been attentive when we were little and, when we were older, after our dad left, attentive to the point of intrusive, a nuisance, a sorrow, a tagalong. Then she married that man so mean that, in her earlier incarnation, she'd never have let him near us. She said by phone, "I raised you. I'm all done." So I never said she was a bad mother because when we were young she wasn't. And then? Having endured a first bad husband, she couldn't detect a worse one when he showed up later.

I was repressed-but-angry about my own mother, I thought. So I might be too controlling. Or lax, careless. Even the process of adopting—studied in an office by one social worker, then in my house by another—magnified potential flaws. Most expectant mothers don't ask people to assess their normalcy, their medicine cabinet, their closet, their beliefs. Then I waited for a birth mother to choose me, knowing she could choose a mother with more money, more religion, a husband whose income let her stay home. I worked full-time; I had to. And I'd failed at husbands too. I might fail at family life, period.

During the adoption agency screening, I'd dropped hints. The questionnaire had asked: "What word best describes your relationship with your parents?" I'd tried out "long-distance," "interrupted." But went with plain old "divorced." My mom and dad were divorced. And this also applied to my relationship with them. If someone doesn't want you, you leave them. I'd thought the antidote to my lack, family, would be love restarted, a child. But I was lucky my mother didn't leave when I was a baby, I came to see. According to a book I consulted again, again, *The Mother of All Baby Books*, love—the desire to get it, give it—is like spelling. You learn good spelling early. Or you never do.

The official word for love is *bonding*, if you're good at it. *Attachment disorder* if you're not. Attachment disorder apparently means you give your love away like party favors. But you have trouble giving your love for keeps to people who matter. You can't tell who these people are. A stranger closes in, and you're wide open: a sitting duck, easy target.

After Marie and I settled in at home, the social worker assessed us. "Mother and child bonding fast," she wrote. She underlined bonding. Baffled, I asked how she knew. "You and the baby continually touch each other," she said. "Maybe you didn't realize you were stroking her leg with your thumb as you described her schedule." Then the social worker did a bonding test. She held a doll. Marie grinned, thrashed, lunged to hug it.

She didn't have attachment disorder yet.

Once, my colleague, Tess, years older than me, and childless, said: "Jesus, how do you know what to do—when she needs to sleep, eat, burp?" I considered it. "She makes a specific noise for each." Marie communicated. She'd cry to let you know she needed food, a diaper. But she didn't waste crying. If I couldn't get to what she wanted because, for instance, I was in thick traffic and murmured over the seat, "You poor thing, I'll pull over soon," she'd stop. Despite my classic new-mother neurosis (and I didn't have hormone fluctuations to explain it), I saw Marie knew how to calm herself and would likely become a stable child and after that—after I was dead, done—an adult who suffers like all of us but realizes happiness comes in swift instances and not to squander it.

But still. In the church vestibule one Sunday a little girl said to me, "My brother is in a wheelchair and won't walk or talk the rest of his life." I looked around. I didn't see a wheelchair. I glanced at her mother. "Home," she said, "we don't bring him to church." I blurted, "I'm sorry." The woman shrugged. "It was long ago. My daughter is just now going through a phase where she talks about it." I worked to conceal my emotions. Recoil. As if what they had were contagious. Cold curiosity. I wanted details to guarantee it could never happen to us. I clutched my daughter close. The woman said, "I was at work. He choked on a peanut butter sandwich. The daycare worker didn't notice. Two minutes, no oxygen to the brain." My heart started beating again. I said, "Two minutes that changed your life." Her eyes shut. She opened them. "You have no idea."

A few weeks later I had to go to a meeting at night where everyone was rich—the university hoped these people would donate money for a museum. My babysitter had been frosty and firm: she wasn't available at night. The university's maternity leave is five weeks unpaid, nothing I could afford, so I used a babysitter when I was in class, ten hours a week, then read and graded papers as Marie napped beside me. When she turned two, I could enroll her at the Baptist preschool, the only preschool in town. But first I had to go to this meeting to prove motherhood hadn't changed my ability to be savvy, a warrior, a breadwinner, father as well as mother. My job was stable. I was tenured, promoted to the highest rank. So my anxiety about work was irrational, a side-effect of my monomaniacal focus on Marie—surely I'd failed to notice the sky falling somewhere else. I got us both dressed and put a ribbon in Marie's thick hair. At the meeting, a woman said, "How nice you take in foster children." She was a potential donor, so I couldn't correct her in an offhand way. A man standing nearby said, "It could be her own."

"Yes," I said.

The man said, "Does your husband work for the university then?"

A leading question. What he meant, I thought, was: if you've married a black man, surely he's educated; that would explain it. Or it was a way of asking if I'd married at all. If the baby's father didn't work for the university, then who was he? Where was he? People who assume she's my biological daughter are always white. Black people can tell by looking she's not biracial. I sound testy, but this man and woman were from a stratified life, a sealed-off layer. My daughter and I were weeds in the hothouse. We didn't belong. "I'm not married," I said. The woman's eyebrows shot up. "I adopted her."

The woman said, "I should think that's very impractical, with your career."

The man said, "I was thinking how lonely. No one to share the child's milestones with."

I didn't answer. I listened to the meeting, the grant proposals we could write—I could, that was my role—and let my daughter gnaw on my finger, a combined pacifier and teething ring effect, except it was me, security. The woman who'd called her a foster child stood. "Excuse me." Everyone stopped talking. "Of course you know you've put your finger in the baby's mouth," she said, "but if you saw her face now, you'd see she's choking."

She wasn't. She was gnawing. But the meeting was over anyway.

I didn't dwell on it. I was preoccupied with sleeping. First, in the same bed with Marie, which she seemed to dislike, whimpering. Then near her, her cradle beside my bed. When she wanted to be in the wind-up swing, I dozed on the floor. I slept roaming and peripatetic for months. And I took Marie with me on my book tour. Apparently, I made this look easy because in all the newspaper photos I seem cheerful, assured, and so does Marie. I flew back and forth to fifteen cities, and home again, home again. I rescheduled a few classes but didn't miss any. Once I went to teach with a spit-up rag on my shoulder. An older student, a mother, raised her hand to point this out. In the classroom, I thought about teaching, but mostly I thought: My baby is not with me. How is she?

Lauren pointed out, "Well, she breathes too loud, labored." Lauren went on: "Listen, motherhood is a series of emergencies. You rise to the challenge over and over, and then calm down and go on, business as usual." She gave me a lesson in croup, how to listen for the distinctive cough, a sound like a seal barking, then dial 911 and take Marie into the bathroom with the shower on hot, high, until the ambulance came. I paid attention, eyes wide. Marie never did cough like barking seal, though. I got used to her huffling breath at night, white noise, like a fan you run to keep sounds from waking you. Marie was allergic to dairy, didn't do well on soy. She was congested. She vomited. I took her to the doctor. Babies vomit, he said. Marie was small, her tonsils huge.

Nothing to worry about yet.

When she was six months old we appeared before a judge who'd met with the social worker—adoption confirmation hearing—and the judge asked: "Have you changed your life?"

I searched deep.

I'd changed my house. People who didn't understand my preoccupation fell away, and my only new friend was a single mother too, Jana. I met her at the grocery store. She had a tattoo of a pink mermaid. We had same-age baby girls in car seats propped in shopping carts. Jana had a four-year-old, Noah, who looked away when I said hello. He was autistic, Jana explained. She smiled at Marie. "You all aren't from here," she said. I said, "Not originally, no." We traded phone numbers. But mostly we talked by phone because we didn't have time to hang out. I had my job. Jana did too. She was a massage therapist. And Noah's schedule was difficult, his special therapies. Me, I didn't take even a shower without putting Marie in a strapped-down seat on the bathroom floor. Weekdays blurred. Weekends—my outing, recreation—I went to Walmart, locked Marie's car seat into safe position in the cart and wheeled through bright aisles, staring at other mothers and babies as I bought formula and diapers. "I did, your honor," I told the judge. " I do." I got goose bumps. Adoption was like getting married, only permanent.

One day I was explaining this—how I'd changed my life, my love going to the baby now and thus unavailable—in a cafeteria-style restaurant to a man I'd dated a few years before the baby came. He was getting older too. He'd run into me one day, looked at the baby starry-eyed, asked to hold her. He wanted us to try again, he seemed to be saying. But I wasn't paying close attention because I'd been tearing food into tiny bits. "Well?" he asked. I said, "I'm tied up with the baby." I looked at her in the high chair where, a second earlier, she'd been smiling, mucking around with bits of bread and red Jell-O.

Her face seemed stuck, eyes wide and startled. She made a noise, *ack.* I stood. I slung her over one arm onto her belly, my hand clutching her jaw. I used my other hand to hit her under her ribs. Thwack. Nothing. Thwack. A piece of bread flew out, and a stream of Jell-O. "So you see," I said, gathering her up, the diaper bag too, "I'm not in a position to do anything besides take care of this baby." I was wearing sandals, I remember, because as I drove home my foot on the gas pedal was sticky and translucent red.

I told Tess I'd done the baby-Heimlich in Luby's Cafeteria, and she said: "Are you sure she was actually choking? Maybe you felt ill at ease, and you're sleep-deprived as well?" I told my babysitter, a grandmother who, over the years, had tended dozens of babies. She said, "I'm always taking chewed food out of her mouth. She can't seem to swallow."

I watched Marie sleep—listened to her sleep, a sound like a valve opening and closing—and thought how, first of all, I felt incompetent. One worry. Second, she was a baby, which is to say fragile, and her prenatal situation had been less than ideal; she wasn't robust. A different worry entirely. But I couldn't separate them. Probably every mother doubts her worth. Perceived failings come to the surface because it's not your life you might ruin but a life depending on you. My friend, Shen, who'd visited when Marie was newborn had said she loved the newborn phase most. "Symbiosis," she'd told me, "the baby so utterly dependent." Dependent, pendant, pendulum. Variations on a single theme, I'd thought at the time, my baby in a Snuggli stomach-carrier hanging from my neck.

Before I was Marie's mother I'd loved babies only abstractly, their stout bodies, the gummy, uninhibited way they smile at something ordinary—a dog, a branch, a cloud, the sky. Because babies aren't from here. They're from the other side. They've recently arrived. Earth thrills them. In my halcyon, undaunted, pre-motherhood days, I'd been at a conference, and I offered to hold a stranger's baby while she went to a panel discussion. I sat in the hotel restaurant, and a famous writer sat beside me. He started talking. The baby wheezed. She'd chewed on a napkin, and it dissolved in her mouth. I cleared the wad with my finger, put other napkins out of reach. The writer, who was a father, said, "Babies gravitate toward danger. Then they grow up and can still find a thousand ways to die."

I knew.

Children could be run over by their own school bus. They could have cancer, recover, then die from side-effects of chemo. A pedophile could steal them. They could drown, crash, freeze. But for some reason I was obscenely fixated on keeping airways open.

Love is breath, I decided.

Life-to-life, breath-to-breath, my attentiveness: *vital.*

My daughter wouldn't get enough, I worried.

Yet she must have. Time passed and passed. She was alive. Undersized but beautiful and always happy. She was eighteen months old and walking. On one of those sunny winter afternoons when the midday temperature is balmy, I took her to a fancy playscape in San Marcos, twenty miles away. I sat on a bench as she kneeled in a pile of sand. We'd better leave at just the right time, I thought. When the sun sank, the air would turn suddenly chilly—wisps of twilight hanging low and frozen above the trees. Now Marie was crawling through a long tube of plastic coiled to look like a snake. A tunnel, I corrected myself. I waited impatiently for my next glimpse of her, her reappearance at the other end. The child, not the mother, should be working through object-permanence fears, I thought. She's supposed to be having separation anxiety, not me.

I wanted to keep her in a bunker, confident I'd fend off evil. I also wanted to give her freedom to explore, go far, find her way. Likewise, I wanted to let strangers who wandered up to admire this extraordinary, unexpected child whom no one believed belonged with me say what they would: so pretty, all that hair. I wanted to nod, agree: yes, perfect, flawless, charming, my daughter. But they were strangers, so I had to shield her. I sat on a bench, waiting for her to come out of the tunnel, and I thought how she'd passed through someone else's birth canal. I'd skipped labor which, as some theologians say, is the price we pay for our imperfections. My labor would be psychological, I thought.

A man sitting near me on the bench in the half-light spoke. "I take it you did an international adoption too." He pointed at a girl, maybe ten years old, on a swing. She was twisting the chains above her into in a tight coil, letting go, then screaming as she whirled. "We got her in Romania last year," he said. I nodded. Then I told him my daughter was born here, in San Antonio. He asked, "How old was she when you got her?" She'd been newborn, I said. He sighed. "Then you don't worry about attachment disorder."

The temperature was falling. But I had to know. "Pardon me?"

Marie reappeared at the tunnel's end.

The man said, "One symptom used to diagnose attachment disorder is whether the family is always angry. Well, we passed that test. Our whole family is always angry." He said his whole family had just come back from a month-long, attachment disorder, in-patient therapy in California. He shook his head. "When we first decided to adopt, it sounded so right. We wanted to help this child with no one, no home. But now my son is terrified of his new sister. My wife, who spends the most time with her, is at her wits' end."

I remembered footage of a Romanian orphanage I'd seen on TV, thirty or forty kids, one caretaker. When the food arrived, children moved in like a flock, a herd, squawking and flapping their way to best portions. I said, "How did you know she had it?"

He said, "In a nutshell, when a child has tried to attach over and over, but, for whatever reason—the death of a parent, both parents, trauma, neglect—has learned that love is painful, the child develops skills to keep people from wanting to love her, so the child won't get hurt again. Our daughter uses her God-given talents to make sure people won't love her. Our challenge is to keep trying, but she doesn't want love, not yet. Not anymore."

I picked up Marie and pushed her arms into her little parka. I shivered, thinking about my first boyfriend, a motherless boy from the Ojibwa tribe I used to sneak out of the house to see. And my college boyfriend was already dead, drug abuse, car wreck—I'd loved him because I understood him. When he was a kid, his father locked him in the basement for weeks. Then his father ran away, taking the other son. My boyfriend and his mother never saw either of them again. Someone had to love this person, I thought. If not me, then who? In graduate school, I had another boyfriend. One of his roommates once said, "He acts like a jerk to make sure people won't like him, so he can reject people before they can reject him first. And it works." And my second ex-husband's mother once told me, her eyes welling with tears: "It might not seem like he loves you, but he tries."

I wanted to ask the man if he'd ever wondered before he adopted whether he'd be a good father. Viable. But of course I didn't ask. He'd had his own child first, and a spouse.

The man called for his daughter to get her coat. Time to go, he told her.

I asked, "Can people get attachment disorder without war or violence?"

"For sure," he said. "You meet people every day with mild to moderate varieties. You know the type. They can't commit. Or they fall in love fast, or out of love just as fast."

Love-phobes, I thought. Or was it more complicated than that? There didn't seem to be a cure. I was semi-expert on the subject, I thought. I'd done all that primary research. Too bad I didn't have something to show for it. I couldn't put it on my résumé. Secondary Research Interest: Men with Attachment Disorder. Marie and I walked through the dusk to our car. The man helped his daughter into theirs, clicking her into her seatbelt, and he called across the parking lot, "For some people, love and fear feel the same."

I drove Marie and myself toward home, my sense of what love is and how it plays out in a state of shift: plate tectonics. I fell in love fast, I realized. But not out. I stayed too long—long after loyalty made sense. Why? When I was young, I'd had a doting mother and a fun-loving dad. That's how he used to seem. He was dreamy good-looking and played ragtime piano so fast you wanted to dance, though he couldn't read music. My mother had milk-chocolate eyes and dark hair she wore permed, bouffant, or sometimes pinned into a French twist. She'd wear sweater sets with slacks or skirts, or, in the summer, pedal pushers with a ruffled peasant blouse. She was pretty with a well-engineered figure, in part because of the way bras were built back then, making breasts high, angular. Once, a traveling auto parts salesman was passing through and my dad invited him to dinner, and this man drank highballs and called my mother Darlene, not Arlene, and asked her to sit in his lap. My mother was shocked, insulted. My dad seemed uncomfortable too with this explicit sexual pitch, this new view of my mother's allure.

She aimed instead at looking attractive yet demure. Once she came to my spring concert at school wearing a fitted yellow coat with small buttons like lemon drops and, around her neck, a filmy, floral scarf she'd cut and hemmed herself. The girl sitting next to me who lived on a farm and did chores in the morning, said, marveling: "*That's your mom?*" I'd smiled, proud. Yet when I told my mom that night the little girl who smelled like silage had said she was pretty, my mom just shook her head and talked about her older sister, Aunt Elinor, who had naturally curly hair, and her younger sister, the beauty queen.

Sometimes I'd wake at night and hear my mother crying or shouting. In the morning, though, she'd say I'd dreamed it. Or that we had to work to understand my dad because he'd had a sorry life growing up, his mother sometimes cooking and talking and, next, running away or being locked up in a room. When I was little, my dad was a hale-fellow-well-met. He had social aspirations. He served on the church board, the Chamber of Commerce. He wanted to be mayor one day. Then my dad's friends changed, and he did too.

He crashed his snowmobile one night, and he was in traction in the hospital for a year. People smuggled bottles into the hospital. He was taking prescriptions pills too. When he came home, he was never the same. I was twelve. I learned to work around him. I accomplished one skill to make him happy—by listening, experimenting, serving samples, which he'd critique, and trying again, I'd become the one person who could make his favorite food his mother had once made, browned calf's liver with cream-and-vinegar gravy. But now I used the answering machine to screen for his calls. If he called after 4:00 p.m., he'd be drinking. He'd pause, lick his teeth, smack his lips. I didn't answer then. If I did, he'd fight over odd facts like what year I was born, or when was Easter.

So my dad didn't influence me, not anymore at least, I decided. And it didn't seem likely that my mother, having removed herself for seventeen years after I'd left, after I'd grown up, could account for my bad taste in men. Besides, my mother had come back now. We had this prickly way of talking, a short list of topics that didn't set us squabbling. But she was here, accounted for, and we had time to turn into a family again, before this slough of questions I hadn't asked because she didn't seem ready, or I knew she didn't have answers, would hold me back, my love aptitude undeveloped. Cedar trees huddled in ditches as I steered. My headlights edged up the dark road like lamps in a shaft, a finite pool of light showing me what to do next, what's the best way, urging me forward.

Small Talk

"What is she?" a woman wearing a muumuu and flip-flops asked me in Walmart, when Marie was still a baby. Already I knew where the conversation was headed. The woman and I had something in common, she meant, but not with my daughter. This question had popped out of the woman's bank of auto-questions, questions she'd blurted in the past to strangers to initiate friendly chatter. I'm not sure—who knows?—if she'd used it to ask about a human before. The way the question was framed left a slim range of auto-answers: Irish Setter, Lhasa Apso, poodle . . . "Where's she from?" the woman asked.

"Here," I answered. "She was born in Texas."

People's comments are more polite now that Marie's old enough to listen.

But I fielded them all the time when she was a baby—even before.

Before she was born, I'd gone to a fertility clinic because I had a theoretical, not real, interest in artificial insemination—a glimpse of the road I wasn't taking. I'd spent the winter arranging to adopt. I'd planned to use the agency least perturbed that I was single. Agencies doing international adoptions don't care. But I couldn't afford an international adoption, and I didn't want to miss the first years of my child's life. Once I started looking at domestic adoptions, I knew my baby would be black. The conversation with the first agency I called went like this: "What's your policy on adoptions for single mothers?"

"No policy. But you'll wait a long time, maybe six years."

I sighed.

"Unless you're open to transracial."

I told her I was.

Impatient as a teacher with a dim-witted pupil, she said, "Do you know what *transracial* means?"

I tend to notice syllables, their connotations. But her tone threw me off. "The child will be from a different race?"

"Black." A whole other category of transracial, apparently.

"That's okay," I said.

"Can you take a baby in two weeks?"

That adoption never materialized. The agency I ultimately did use asked the same question, different inflection. The adoptive parent liaison, Marla, sat across from me in a special room for interviews. We sat on worn sofas, toys scattered at our feet. She said, "How would you feel about a son or daughter who was black?" I was used to this angle by then—countless adoption agency receptionists having explained they had more black babies than homes. I said, "I *so* don't give a damn about the baby's race." She scribbled notes.

But before that conversation took place, the nurse at the fertility clinic scribbled her notes. I had an ultrasound. I met the doctor. He asked questions, some medically necessary—for sure, it mattered if I'd had sex recently, with or without birth control. But he also asked why, if I had a boyfriend, I didn't marry him. "Because I don't want to," I stammered.

He paused. "It's wrong to date someone you can't picture a future with," he said—like Marcus Welby, medical opinion and personality assessment thrown in free, a bonus. He pointed at ultrasound pictures and said ardently, "I know I can get you pregnant." He explained I'd shoot myself up (not his phrase) with hormones. I thought: I'd spend my time and money shooting up and getting inseminated, seeded, and no guarantee I'd be pregnant. Or carry the baby. I had a history of miscarriage. The baby I ended up *not* adopting would still float into the world, homeless maybe, unloved. In my mind, it was already advent: an unhappy woman somewhere carrying a child meant for me.

I asked about the price. It would cost as much to try to get pregnant three times as it would to adopt. My mind wandered. Why make another baby when a baby was already made, en route? How odd to be pregnant, I thought, especially at work. Students sometimes ask me personal questions I tend to answer because this curiosity is clearly affectionate. Because a good teacher is more than an information-purveyor, a test-scorer. You're an advertisement for the examined life. You make it look worth living. Students would wonder who the baby's father was and say something oblique, leading: is the baby's father a professor too? But there'd be no father: just a deep-freeze, a catheter, a substance ("ejaculate"). I'd be answering that question the rest of my life, I realized. Yet if I adopted, there'd be other questions: Is your husband black? Or (this is common): Why didn't you want a white baby? At the time, those questions sounded easier to answer. The doctor got out his donor catalog. "Be selective," he said. "Choose someone with a post-graduate degree like yourself. Photos will give you a sense of attractiveness-quotient."

I said suddenly, "This baby would be white." It wouldn't have to be. Yet I'd have to go out of my way picking a sperm donor for the baby to be even biracial. For months I'd pictured my not-yet-here baby. Boy or girl, who knew? But race—I did know.

A white baby already seemed otherwordly, exotic.

The doctor looked at me, skeptical. "We have sperm donors from other races."

"It's not that." I told him I was likely to adopt, and from what I understood I'd get a black baby.

"I did a residency on the other side of I-35," he said. He meant the traditionally black neighborhood, the ghetto. "And I wouldn't touch that gene pool with a ten foot pole."

As soon as I got Marie, questions and stares were unavoidable. I've since stopped noticing or caring—we've endured trouble, scared ourselves a time or two, but the fact our skin isn't the same color isn't close to traumatic, not for either of us. But when the attention was new and Marie was little, her sense of where she fit still nascent, I understood that how I responded would help or hurt her. In most settings, she'd be the only black person, so I wanted to talk about race, but not too much (an obsession), nor too little (denial). I'd talk about it when it came up but wouldn't dwell on it. This called for moment-by-moment discretion. And as soon as she could look in a mirror, or study her hand nestled in mine—as soon as she noticed race herself, I mean—I realized that she was smiling and waving at every black person she saw: in airports or shopping centers. Or she'd gurgle and gesticulate from the wind-up swing for me to notice black people on TV. In public, when she was waving, grinning, saying hi in her preverbal way, I'd wave too. Most people waved back. In front of the TV, I'd say, "That person is black. You are. You're so good-looking." True. My daughter is beautiful. People on TV usually are.

I might have talked about race only occasionally, but through the years I thought about it a lot—more than I thought about other problems. How my daughter felt about race would shape her future, but my troubles belonged to the past, so I thought. Once I got sick, I preferred thinking about race to thinking about doctors because I figured I had more control over whether Marie would grow up proud than how I'd weather some new diagnosis.

But it took effort to find answers for strangers who approached us.

People are startled we're together.

Some are amazed we even want to be.

Where you are—rural/urban, East/West, North/South—determines how amazed.

My daughter and I have always traveled. People don't notice us in L.A. They do in St. Louis. But not as much as when I brought her home to the village where I live and the fact of her face—black, swaddled in pink—was news. Urban life, by contrast, is sensory overload. Sheer numbers make for increased odds. I've seen everything, people say. They don't pay attention; they can't. This is why gay people leave small towns for cities, and why, when a friend of mine who was single and pregnant visited me here, she noted, puzzled, that, in New York, if people noticed she was pregnant the only (if any) comment proffered was congratulations. Here, people said, as soon as I introduced her (not *who's the father?*, though that's what they meant), "And what does your husband do?"

As for the North, there's urban and rural. When my daughter was two, we flew to visit my brother in Wisconsin. My daughter and I came down the steps of a prop jet that had flown us in from Chicago O'Hare. In Chicago, few people gave us second glances. In the Appleton airport, the size of a gas station, a crowd of strangers waiting for their families saw us, stood up, mobilized. A plump man with a kind face stepped forward, natural spokesperson. "Welcome, little girl," he said. "Is this the first time you've seen snow?"

This holds true for the South, too. No one looks at us in Atlanta.

In Macon, they stare.

It's complicated in central Texas where Interstate 35—more than the state line between Texas and Arkansas, or Texas and Louisiana—separates the South from the Southwest. Demographically, the South is mostly white/black, and the Southwest is mostly Anglo/Hispanic. Austin straddles I-35. So does San Antonio. You cross the freeway, you've crossed cultures: you're transracial. The desire for the known, for community, perpetuates the divide. Race and property value are still—in many places—synonyms. The town I brought Marie home to, a cedar-chopping village turned Austin exurb and thirty-odd miles west of the big divide, is the Southwest. We never had black neighbors.

"Is that a crack baby?" A clerk asks, while I'm paying for gas.

"I'll bet it's a good story." Marie and I sit huddled together in a restaurant booth. The waitress has caught us unawares. "How you two got together, I mean," the waitress says.

The UPS man: "She looks like Oprah. No, Mariah Carey."

"Haiti, right? She's from Haiti." A man selling snow cones.

The commentary persists because we're unexpected, conspicuous.

Most children aren't adopted. Those who are likely have two parents and can be said to resemble their parents *just a little*. Interracial adoption was never illegal. But the National Association of Black Social Workers opposed it, so agencies respected that stance. But in 1996 the Multiethnic Placement Act was amended to address the fact that—because there weren't enough families with whom to place them—black children were waiting years to be adopted, while white families were waiting years for a child. Most agencies reversed their position. This is also when private agencies, as opposed to religious and state agencies, sprang up all over and, because they were committed to swift placements, considered single parents eligible. Most single, adoptive parents are women: white.

One percent adopts a black child.

I didn't know these statistics then. I did know, because my social worker said so, that black families tend to adopt unofficially: cousins, second-cousins, nieces, nephews. They don't use agencies; they don't need to. Adoption agencies are staffed pretty much by white people. Black birth mothers are wary . No one talks about it, but it's the specter of history—humans bought and sold. Giving a child to a white social worker is a last resort.

Yet black babies do turn up at agencies.

When I first met Marla, I asked her if most white people don't adopt black babies, not because they're racist, but because they're afraid of defending their child against racists.

She sighed. "Sometimes one parent is up for it, but the other just isn't. Or extended family," she said. "Maybe an extended family member is racist, and you don't want to cut yourself off from family. But you won't raise your child in a hostile context either."

In the long run, I've spent maybe fifteen minutes total staring down overt bigots, people who hate us on sight. On a trip that took me through western Oklahoma, I pulled into a Jiffy Lube, and my car was turned off, hoisted, its oil dripping like molasses, when I saw the swastika tattoo, the brute face of the attendant. I saw the same expression on a woman's face in a 7-Eleven in Austin—she glanced at my daughter, then me, then flashed what might pass for a smile, but her eyes stayed hateful and the smile was in fact a display of razors wedged between her teeth. Virulent racism is rare but, like polio, not eradicated.

At home, the attention we got wasn't unfriendly. Yet comments sometimes positioned my daughter in a category that was not merely *not-us* but *less-than*, and there was a tendency to talk about her in third-person. People do talk about babies in third-person: how much does he weigh? has she cut her teeth yet? But most of our third-person questions weren't generic baby questions, and, furthermore, lasted long after Marie could hear and understand. My heart creaked every time someone wanted to know: what is she, if she belongs with me? what are we, if we're together? I worried the nattering curiosity would make her feel estranged, strange. Could she hear it and still belong?

So we lived in a comedy of botched manners I wanted to escape or ignore. But I wasn't deaf or blind. And I couldn't serve up one withering retort after another, though I thought them, steering the stroller the other way, driving home tense, my lovely child cooing and singing in the back. Back then, I had a zinger-storehouse: answers on tap. But people who stopped to say something bungling—staring meanwhile as if we were a two-headed calf, or Chang and Eng the Siamese twins—could never be flabbergasted into changing long-entrenched perceptions of what belongs with what. If I'd tried solving the problem that way, I'd have been a rage conduit. So I tried to see the person speaking as malleable: with passion and respect, my answer might turn what's been blurted into lofty conversation. I did this for my daughter—what she'd learn as my values—not for the world.

Besides, most of the time, she'd be hungry or her best friend wouldn't share. She loves cats, she'd say. Her throat hurt. Barney is weird. And why doesn't God live down here? Neither of us thinks about race, I'm saying, unless forced. When we are, I want our experience to feel like a resolution: a vague idea there's been a problem, then an insight, however incomplete. Fruition. Instead, we got enigma and nonsequiturs, hash, rehash.

Given the actual number of adoptions with white parents and black children, a disproportionately large body of literature exists. How-to: milk allergies (black babies are prone), hair care (don't overwash it), skin care (cocoa butter). But it gets harder to implement when it focuses on culture. Attend a black church. March on Martin Luther King Day. Join a black community center. I'm a research nut, yes, and reflexively dutiful. But I had to reconsider these pat answers: silver linings, each with its own black cloud.

Attending a black church, marching on MLK Day, even finding a black community center, all fell under one rubric: driving a long way to cultivate relationships with people solely because of their skin color. If my motives were decent (I wanted Marie to know black people besides two colleagues and the stylists who did her hair), hoping someone would befriend us, not because of shared experience or affection, but to augment her sense of identity, is a flimsy pretext. Trying to force friendship in single-minded ways felt like tokenism.

The driver's license bureau, the library, the chili cook-off, were the most interracial places for miles. Sometimes I did drive a long way to attend a black church. During handshaking and talking, before and after, I was grilled. Did I believe the Lord Jesus Christ is my personal savior? Did I believe God made homosexuals? (He didn't. TV shows did.) No one embraced us in the fellowship of the bride of Christ, since it was clear I was there because I felt uneasy my daughter was being raised away from community, her own.

Marie has her own questions.

On a plane flying from Austin to Phoenix: "Do black people not fly?"

My inadequate answer: "Not too often between Texas and Arizona."

Driving through two blocks of home we call downtown: "I think I'm black here, and no one else is."

One year, in February, Black History Month, PBS running documentary after documentary, she asked: "What's slavery?" I formulated my answer. "A long time ago, people thought they could own other people and make them work for no pay." I omitted other things slave owners thought they could do. In fact, for awhile, during February, I turned PBS off at night. There'd be time enough later for her to see Emmett Till's battered corpse, the endless photo record of strange fruit on thin ropes, mob glee. Meanwhile, people used to own other people, and I'd only recently explained whites owned blacks. "Why?" she said, uneasiness flickering across her face. I said, "The country fought a war to stop it."

In first grade, her teacher talked about Martin Luther King. My daughter asked me, "Why did he die?" Again, I trimmed my answer to least horrific proportions. "It scared people how he fought so blacks could live better, so black and white children could go to the same school." She looked confused. "People used to think black and white children shouldn't go to the same school." She had a friend visiting, blond-haired, blue-eyed Marina. "Why did they think that?" Marina asked. The girls looked at each other, mutually dubious. "How weird would that be?" my daughter said. They collapsed, giggling.

My heart creaked, like china with hairline cracks. If you're careful, you can use this china forever, for breakfast, lunch, dinner, every day. It won't break. We're a family, I thought. We do so much so well. Our hearts won't break. But Marie's questions pointed to another topic in the big commentary about white parents with black children, not *how-to*, but *argument-against*: a child cut off from people who look like her, who have a collective history catastrophically different from mine, won't know who she is, will want to be someone else, will want to be me, white. The National Association of Black Social Workers called transracial adoption "cultural genocide." Another argument is she'll grow up sheltered from racism and be destroyed by her first brush with it. But I think fostering less racism for a split-second—in your house or circle of intimates—is good. The logic of the other proposition is perverse, twisted: more exposure to racism is helpful.

Yet the first argument is hard to discount. If a black mother had been available, my daughter would have fared better there. Probably. But why stop? In the daydream of Marie's best life, make it a married, stay-at-home mother, and the working father and patient mother don't lose their cool, use "time out" consistently, and monitor how much TV the child watches. When the ideal mother skips a meal, she doesn't act addled. She had stable parents herself and never wonders what long-lasting love feels like, so this mother never had a bad boyfriend—not after the baby came. And if this mother needed surgery, dozens of friends and relatives would step up to make sure the daughter didn't feel abandoned. I could go on, romanticizing the parent I'm not. Skin color is the least of it.

In a hotel lobby, a maid: "Honey, are you lost? Where's your mama?"

A mortgage company clerk: "This is your little girl?" I nod yes. I think he's about to mention how spiffy she looks, new dress, freshly braided hair. He frowns. "You sure?"

A woman waiting for her prescription at a drugstore: "I want to be a foster mother too."

"*That's* your daughter?" An airline employee, taking boarding passes.

The meta-question, the quirkiest, most hyper-analytical, simultaneously personal and sociological, asked by one of my graduate students (they specialize in the above): "Do you feel you've settled that looming question at last?" We were standing outside a poetry reading. I held my daughter. Euphoria surged through my veins—being a mother felt like being in love only more intense. He said, "Now are you certain you're not at all racist?"

Published commentary asks this: how to insure the adoptive parent isn't latently racist?

Expect to flinch, I'd read. Expect readjustment to your changed comfort zone. I went over my feelings with a fine-tooth comb. When Marie was a month old, two (white) east Texas men, newly sprung from the federal pen, dragged a (black) man to death. I sat in my living room watching TV, and I had the same reaction I always have when I hear the gritty details of Bergen-Belsen, or Rwanda's civil war, or Matthew Shepard's last minutes. What moral bog of a subculture spawned the witch-hunt belief that evil is in someone else, identifiable by physical traits? I realized with a start I wasn't in a white family now. Hate crimes weren't an abhorrent moral conundrum but an open wound.

Yet the fleeting, visceral recoil I'd read I'd feel—involuntary shock at Marie's blackness—never occurred, maybe because of neighborhoods where I'd lived in grad school, maybe because I'd been picturing her long before she came. But one night, when she was squalling because she wanted a bottle, her hair tufted in disarray, the look on her face a precise mix of ecstasy at the noise she'd made and sorrow at her hunger and longing, for a split-second I thought she looked like James Brown. I told my friend, Jana, whose daughter was the same age. "I guess that's unconscious generalizing," I said, "profiling." I grasped for words. "Maybe," Jana said. Jana is white. Her daughter, Zoey, is white. "But when Zoey throws fits," Jana said, "I think she looks like Marlon Brando."

In fact, the reverse happened. Marie was a short, round baby with lush hair and skin that glowed as if lit from behind. I'd been with her day and night, day and night, and then I saw Zoey the first time. Zoey's grown up quite gorgeous—like a young Britt Ekland, not Marlon Brando—but the first time I held her I had a fleeting, visceral recoil at her leanness, baldness, pallor. A few months later, I went on book tour. I'd had the ambitious idea I could take my baby along, no problem. I was in a taxi in a strange city at two a.m., dead tired, and Marie and I had been one-on-one for days. The cab driver who was from India asked me, "What age?" I answered, "Six months." He said she was pretty. I thanked him. He said, "I could not handle one of those white babies, no hair, and skin so clear you see the blue veins." I started laughing. "See?" he said. "You agree."

I did, then. A newborn baby is yours, your attachment. Her spit or sweat is yours. You see her more than you see the mirror. She was familiar: familial. Babies who didn't look like her fell into the other category: not-familiar. So it's easy to see that, for people who weren't looking at her, or looking at black people at all, she fell into the not-familiar category. Hence, the awkward comments that expressed (most of the time) goodwill but also tried to mask surprise, or, failing that, leapt for the handiest cognitive parallel.

Once Marie and I were at an airport in the Southwest, and a red-haired toddler wobbled up and muttered. Marie turned. "Mama," she said, "that girl called me whoopee."

I understood. The other little girl hadn't seen a real black person, but she'd seen *Sesame Street*, Whoopi Goldberg singing to Elmo. Adults have said my daughter looks like Whoopi Goldberg, also like Halle Berry, Cicely Tyson, Brandi, Erikah Badu, Lil' Romeo, and Diahnn Carrol (if you're under fifty, you won't know who that is). White people who say she looks like the one generation-specific, black celebrity they can conjure don't know anyone black. This happens so often I have a pat answer: "Just a little."

Everywhere, people talk about us less now. They stare less. Or not exactly. A friend who went on vacation with us last year said they still do; I just don't notice. I'm inured. Because I look inured, people don't feel so free to volunteer their first impressions. That part of my motherhood is nearly over. Marie knows who she is now, how she fits. But when she was a baby, people felt free to initiate private, white-on-white conversation with me. When she was a toddler—neither an uncomprehending baby, nor the kid she's turned into with a discerning expression and vocabulary so huge it's hard to remember she is a kid—in that brief span when she knew words but not what they implied, she had a bullshit-meter for people who made contact because she was different. A woman walked up in the hardware store, fondled her hair and said, "This town has been so ready for a little girl like you." Marie looked confused, flattered, suspicious. "Why?"

The comments are subtler now. People I don't know say: *I know you.* They never say it when I'm alone. They know of me, and my daughter. People are always asking for my email address or phone number to give to someone who's considering adopting a child of a different race. I've answered questions, sometimes passionately. Of all the prospective parents for whom I've served as transracial adoption spokesperson, only one couple has adopted. They set out from the beginning of their marriage to become the white parents of black children; they see it as a political act. I didn't have much to say to them, except, you know, milk allergies, hair and skin care. I never saw my motherhood as political. I saw it as my motherhood. But it has political moments, and I can't back down.

The moral of this story—if I have to force it, and I don't, not for the two of us—is that Marie and I fit together, but the world with its self-perpetuating divisions doesn't fit us yet, especially on the razor-sharp edge of the national divide, I-35 the South by Southwest border. The world there, its lexicon, has a vestigial old shape. Forty years ago, before Martin Luther King, Emmett Till, the entire holy war that was civil rights, we couldn't have lived there because Marie couldn't have attended school. Forget it. I'd be childless.

So we're interesting. Though it's not something I'd wish on a child, anyone's child, for most people who make contact, my daughter is an opportunity they hurry to take, consciously or unconsciously trying to make inept repairs, insufficient amends. Comments—well expressed or not—arrive with vague sadness. People talking to us are white. Their ancestors were implicated. Their ancestors might have been sharecroppers, not slave owners, but no one bought or sold them, or chased them down and hung them. Anyone with a conscience wishes none of it happened. So when people approach us, I know that finding the right answer is part of my job as mother, small duty. While I keep the exchanges brief because my daughter's heard plenty, I understand that most people are trying to cross the divide, even though gracious, prefabricated small talk is in short supply.

People instead make an instinctive first association.

Sometimes I'm almost flattered.

Once Marie and I were flying out of the Southwest into the South, with a quick stop in Houston, on a plane without assigned seating. We'd grabbed the first row, easy on and off. The plane landed in Houston. Several people shuffled on—including an adolescent girl, her plaited hair gleaming. She had on new shoes, not a single scuff, and stood so close as she looked around, deciding where to sit, that I could smell the cocoa butter she'd used as emollient. She glanced down and saw me, my daughter. Her eyes widened in recognition, and she sat next to us. "Is this your first time flying?" she whispered. I said it wasn't. She pointed at Marie, "Hers?" I said no. She said, "It's mine. I'm going to see my dad." Then she read my daughter's books to her. Most had black protagonists, or teddy bear or bunny protagonists whose color was pink, green, yellow. She turned to me and said: "Do you know who you look like?" I'd just turned forty-one. I had on a gray dress stained with spit-up. My hair has its own gray. I said, "Who?"

She paused, careful. "Britney Spears," she said.

"Yes," I answered, "just a little."

Into the Wall

Back when my phone was still connected to the wall—not mobile, and not so long ago either—my daughter knew I was tied down by six feet of cord and distracted. She'd start searching and dismantling: an experiment in the physical properties of objects (what happens when you put a bar of soap in the toilet), and in the immutability of rules (how long before the powers that be intervene). Motherhood makes you wish for God's traits: omniscience, omnipresence. Meantime, human wisdom flickers on and off like a bad connection.

Still, I knew when I said "no" to Marie I was her first impression of power, and that how it's wielded would forever after be linked to me. I'd seen my own mother as Moral Authority Personified. Her brown eyes quickened into sympathy or outrage. The cherry-vanilla scent of Jergen's Hand Cream accompanied each edict. She taught us one lesson: the difference between seeming right and being right. You learned this precept by way of housekeeping—you swept behind and under, not around. You saw it on a kitchen plaque that read: *Character is what you are. Reputation is what your neighbors think you are.*

But she was confused.

She couldn't tell love and suffering apart. I've thought about it since and decided that suffering on purpose is ostentatious. Yet love is humble (I got this from a good source).

So volunteering to be a martyr is like showing off.

She'd been my mother until I was twenty. Then she met her second husband, Bill Lyman, and it wasn't safe to visit. They moved to Arizona. She'd call when he wasn't home; she existed as my phone-mother only, a voice on the other end, our bond stretched to its utmost. I'd never seen her in this Arizona house, so I pictured her on the other end in a crevice, crawl space. This is how we spoke for seventeen years. Then he died, and she wanted to be a real mother again. And she met a man from Oregon and married him immediately.

She'd been married to her third and only good husband a few months when she called to say hello. I wasn't thinking about the missing years. Or if I felt swindled. I asked if I could cook sausage that had been in the freezer a long time. I didn't feel like packing to go to the store: baby seat, diaper bag, baby herself. In those days, I dreamed I mislaid my daughter—I washed her with a load of whites, or left her in a pile of sweaters at T.J. Maxx. Right now she was dumping scoops of Tide onto the floor. I reached to stop her, and the phone clattered off the shelf. The answering machine followed and broke. "It would be safe enough," my mother said, "but it would put you off sausage forever."

Expediency, you see. And life-long consequence.

Then she said her stomach hurt. She had a bug maybe. Later that day, her new husband called.

She was in ICU.

She raised us in Spooner—one bank, one grocery store, two strip joints, twenty bars, and the Depot Hotel. She and my father had married in North Dakota, where he attended a little college for two weeks but quit because he had a lifelong fear of dogs and had to walk past an unchained German Shepherd to get to class. It was a silly reason to quit school, my mother said once, sniffing. He hadn't listened to her advice, she added, which was to speak to the dog owner or find another route to class. Then my dad worked as a traveling salesmen—

Cooper Tires, wholesale—and they had three babies when he decided Spooner, Wisconsin would be ideal for a fledgling auto parts store. They settled there.

My mother taught us that God loved the bum on the corner with the tops of his shoes cut away, his bent toes exposed: a lesson in pain. God loved the one black man in town, Pat Cheney, who stuffed dead deer and fish. God loved the Ojibwa Indians too, also the ladies at the Depot Hotel who got paid to be a man's girlfriend, which was wrong, she pointed out, but they couldn't help needing money, and God knew it. Then the 1970s hit our family hard—all that emphasis on intoxication and self-expression. I think of the medical term express: to press out infection, disintegrated cells. My dad expressed. Our family disintegrated. My father left my mother and moved in with the chiropractor's secretary. My sister got married, instant new family. My brother married too.

I married, first time, the guitar player who was unemployed; it lasted a year. I moved to Kansas, and three years later to Utah. Meanwhile, my mother attached to Bill Lyman.

When they still lived in Wisconsin—in sin, she would have said before she knew him—I came to visit. My sister stopped by with her five-year-old daughter. Bill Lyman asked my niece: "Are you wearing panties? Do you like boys yet?" My mother said, "She's too young to think that's funny, Bill." My sister and niece left. Bill Lyman drank and pulled cupboard doors off their hinges, the phone out of the wall. He emptied a container of potato salad over my mother's head. My mother and I spent the night on the bathroom floor, the door locked. He was passed out, but we felt safer there. Besides, we had to clean the potato salad off her. The next morning he was asleep but beginning to stir, Fee Fie Fo Fum, and she stood under a pine tree, twisting and untwisting a dish towel. I'd used part of a student loan to fly across the country to see her. "Go now, hurry," she said. "I'll be okay. It'll be better this way. He's moody. You kids set him off."

I saw her one other time when she and Bill moved to Arizona and they stopped at my apartment in Salt Lake City. I was in the middle of my semester, an assignment due in two days. The first day, Bill Lyman cussed out a clerk in a liquor store so long, so loud, he got thrown out.

Then he stayed up all night—cowboy boots clacking across the floor, the clink of fresh ice cubes into his glass. The next day we went to a car wash. He leaned over the seat and said, "Do you like to do it in the carwash, Debbie? Your mother likes it in the carwash. Ready, Arlene? Big Bill and the twins are ready to go." With a faraway look on her face, thinking of the mountains they'd just passed through perhaps, or the storybook *Heidi* and how, in it, mountain air will cure you, or maybe of some song her mother used to sing, "On Top of Old Smokey," she stared at water running in sheets down the windshield, making the light hazy, and she said, "Debra might not think that's funny."

During the seventeen years of our telephonic love, our near-severance, I'd given up on calling her myself, trying to guess if Bill Lyman might not be there. So she'd call me, and I'd know when he came back. I'd have said: "We had freezing rain." *Uh huh.* "I graduated and I'm moving to the east coast." *Uh huh.* "Space aliens live near me." *Nice to have heard from you, bye-bye.* But one day—I was living in Texas (in my cabin that wasn't a house yet), saving up to be a mother (I wasn't one yet)—and Bill Lyman's heart blew out. She drove him to the hospital as he died in the passenger seat, though she wasn't sure; he could have been in a coma. Then she sat outside the ER and could tell by the nurses' whispering he was dead, yet it was the doctor's job to say so, and the doctor was busy.

She had her boss phone my sister and me.

My mother was a bookkeeper for a psychotherapist who didn't have formal training—laws in Arizona allow for this. My mother wanted us at the funeral; her boss, an ersatz shrink, told me. So we got on planes. I remember a "Ding Dong the Witch is Dead" refrain running through my head. I got to the Phoenix airport around the same time as my sister. A stranger picked us up. We understood quickly that no one dropping in with casseroles, or asking the time of the funeral, no one from the neighborhood or office, understood our familial derangement. These people weren't friends. Bill Lyman didn't need friends. Ergo, our mother didn't. Besides, in our truncated phone conversations, she'd described everyone she knew as nuts. "Nadine needs more therapy than patients she bills for eighty bucks an hour." Or this: "Our neighbors, Arturo and Lidia, are saving for a rainy day, but they don't have the sense to come in out of the rain." What did I think? These weren't her ideas. Not her figures of speech. Not her ethics—generosity—either.

How did she look?

The same as when she was our mother who'd symbolized grace and beauty, except she was too thin now, had a bad haircut, cheap clothes, and her face contorted with panic that her meager sense of purpose, the kingpin of her hangdog home life, was dead.

My sister and I started sweeping, cooking, making phone calls, picking out clothes for Bill to be buried in. We were playing roles—gracious stepdaughters and steadfast daughters. We masterminded a funeral to help our grief-struck, windblown mother.

Some people we met were neighbors. Bill Lyman had worked for others, bulldozing the desert into gardens. A few were undocumented workers he'd hired. Most were Mexican-American, with less of a death-is-a-rude-subject complex than we had. "Your mama is lucky to have her girls with her now," Lidia said. My sister and I nodded. "When did you have your last family get-together?" Lidia asked. My sister and I glanced at each other. My sister's answer would have been complicated. She lived in Wisconsin, not far from Bill Lyman's kids, so my sister had seen my mother for about an hour every other year. Before my mother and Bill Lyman left Wisconsin for Arizona, my sister had gone to their house, sometimes bringing lemon bars and a thermos of coffee, other times to get her out.

"When?" Lidia enunciated, like it was her accent throwing us off.

My sister had a blanched look: immersed in hot water. My mother blurted just then, "This is like Grandma's death, which was terrible, because Aunt Martha was so horny."

Lidia smiled, waiting for an answer.

"Too long," my sister said, putting stamps on outgoing bills.

"Aunt Martha was so *what*, Mom?" I asked, confused, curious.

"Horning in," my mother said, "and she kept me from my last minutes with my mother."

At the funeral I cried because my mother—forced to make a choice, him or us—had picked him. My mother nudged me, asked if I needed

a Kleenex, said, "If you can't pull yourself together, go to the Ladies'."
Did she think I was crying for him? She'd shush anyone crying in public. She'd given high marks to Jackie Kennedy for being poker-faced
during Jack's funeral. Bill Lyman's four daughters were there too. I
sat next to my mother, my sister next to me. The one stepsister who
was reserved but polite sat next to my sister. The rude stepsister—the
apple who'd fallen nearest the tree but still cut her dad off, made an
unretractable vow of not-speaking, not-seeing, a for-as-long-as-we-
both-shall-live quarantine against her father—sat in another pew. If
this were a fairy tale, she'd have been made noble by spending her
childhood with an ogre. But in real life she turned out frantic and
rude. When the organ music started, the kindly stepsister led the angry stepsister to the coffin where she saw her father. The angry stepsister fainted. She didn't tip like a sawed-off tree. Her legs went useless. She sank into the folds of her skirt.

Bill, embalmed, got shipped back to Wisconsin and buried.

My sister and I went home, opposite directions. Our mother
started coming for visits.

Everyone had changed.

I'd turned into a snob on a few subjects, my mother pointed out.
Wine, coffee, men.

My sister's children had grown up. Her husband traveled for work.

My brother liked restoring antique tractors. If I visited, I'd sit in the
kitchen with his wife and kids, and he'd be in the garage, tools clang-
ing, the smell of paint and rustproofer redolent, and the engine would
roar, the garage door open, and he'd head his "cherry" tractor down
the road to the bar. My mother felt welcome there. My brother's wife
liked her. My brother's wife didn't care about the missing years. She
had her own mother.

My brother, sister, and I did care. We were friendly, then remote.
Not friendly.

I wasn't mad. Just impatient. Glad to be reunited. Confused. When
she visited, she'd follow me around, ask me odd questions, for instance, what exactly Monica Lewinsky had done. She had the vague
impression "oral sex" meant talking about it. When I explained, a
wary look passed over her face. She had another question. How did

homosexuals have sex? The same look crossed her face, and I saw she felt unprepared. Familiar turf—TV news, conversations at the grocery store, how-to articles in *Ladies' Home Journal*, which, in her day, covered making pies, or getting Jell-O unstuck from a mold, not "What He Wants in Bed"—seemed like a solid neighborhood turned suddenly risky, the old divisions (us versus bums and whores at the Depot Hotel) fading. When she was married to Bill Lyman she'd been naive on purpose: for protection. But he was dead.

She needed to find her way.

When she first came to see me in Texas, she'd stay for weeks and say: "Did you turn off the light in your room? Who was that on the phone? Do your roofers know to put tarpaper down?" I wasn't used to supervision—though I could have used it once—and she aimed it at the girl I used to be. For my birthday, she gave me a Garfield the Cat nightshirt; my usual style was a black negligee. She slouched, wore a jacket that said "Dew Drop Inn." She talked racist: *spic* and, improbably, a holdover from some "Down Upon The Swanee River" era, *darkie*. She'd picked up Bill's bad grammar. Long ago, she'd told me posture made a woman well-dressed. She'd corrected me if I said "brung," not "brought."

I hoped the new version—sloppy locutions, pointless stories about dog races, the amoral shorthand legible in every comment—would fade, and I'd find my own mother who'd held me when I was a child afraid of the dark. "See what's out there?" she'd say. "Nothing."

She wanted to be that necessary, still.

The summer I was waiting to adopt, she stayed for three weeks. The day I came back from the airport in San Antonio where I'd meant to board a plane to take me to get the baby in Philadelphia, and then the adoption fell through, I was struggling to feel philosophical. So I went to see my neighbor, Clara Mae, to hug Clara Mae, take comfort from her.

Clara Mae put her arms around me and said, "We're two of a kind, we are."

I answered back, our friendship-rite: "Peas in a pod."

I became peripherally aware of my mother in the room, a puzzled look on her face like I see on Marie's face now if she's been left out of a game. Cruel, I hugged Clara Mae harder, as if to say to my mom: did you think I'd gotten by without a mother-substitute?

That same summer, a graduate school friend tracked me down because he was coming to Texas for a wedding and thought I might go as his date. His name was Hessam. The wedding would be half-Zoroastrian (bride's side), half-Muslim (groom's). My mother answered the phone. "Foreigner," she said (Bill's word), her hand cupped over the receiver (her own good manners). I once heard Bill say about anyone who wasn't white: "I don't mind working with some, but that's where contact ends. None of this." He made that wiggling, obscene gesture, thumb and forefinger forming a hole, the index finger from the other hand slipping in. How did I respond? My mother was out of earshot, so I'd said, "You're a pig." Then I worried she'd later on pay the price for my candor.

Anyway, Bill was dead when Hessam called. I chattered on the phone.

I watched my mother watching and chattered louder, happier.

Maybe it was political protest, as in: we don't call them "foreigners" now.

Or it was more.

I hadn't told her I loved her. She'd say: I love you. She'd never stopped.

She'd said it for seventeen years on the phone when Bill wasn't home. Even now, I couldn't say it. I'd answer, obliged: "Me too." But at the end of the conversation with Hessam, I said to him: "I love you." I do love Hessam. Or I did. I haven't seen him for years now. It was a fulsome way of signing off. Showing off. It kept her in the dark, worried.

I've had my own trouble with darkness.

I pursue sleep. I carry a torch for sleep. It doesn't want me.

If I'm in a city, traffic (shriek of sirens, whining brakes) keeps me edgy. Once I moved to the country, in Texas, I'd hear the muffled, crackly noise of animals padding across a dry landscape in a season of drought. I'd think about trouble I didn't have, but could. The word *nightmare* means, literally, a female of indeterminate species, of pitch-darkness, who sits on your chest and torments you. Sleepless-ness is a nightmare with no release. The call from my mother's third husband from a phone outside ICU came at 8:00 p.m.

After my new stepfather called to tell me my mother was in the hospital, Mallory called.

Mallory babysat for me at night, when my regular babysitter wouldn't. Mallory was working her way through school, racking up debt. I had too. Her father was a drunk. Mine too. I had a house, a baby, books I'd published—things she wanted—and I could remem-ber wanting these, how doomed and ideal they once seemed. I'd been her mentor. I was like her big sister, so we said. She was another in the series of faux kin I'd lined up.

I once read a steeped-in-Freud literary critic who thought Jane Austen's best insight concerned vertical as opposed to horizontal relationships: vertical defined as relationships in which influence is unequal and the opportunity for condescension rife. The term *co-dependency* was coined in my lifetime. Its tenet: helpfulness is a racket with a payoff for the helpful one who feels superior, while the helped one stays a loser. This is a useful idea (don't give more than you get) which, taken to its extreme, however, ends compassion: i.e., the Good Samaritan is a closet egomaniac. Consider it. How many peo-ple are exactly where you are in handling a problem, not better off or worse? Family structure is braced by power—experience trumping inexperience (lack of self-protection). Maybe my real sister had been right to rescue and re-rescue my mother, and I'd been wrong.

And I'd expended so much on invented family, temporary, shifting kinfolk.

That night, I told Mallory my mother was in critical condition. Mal-lory cried, thinking how sad if her own mother died. Deep grief, she warned. Deep shit, I thought. *Not now, too busy, too soon.* The phone conversation I'd had with my mother earlier that day—whether to cook the sausage or toss it—had been an attempt at old ritual. The idea behind all rituals, however empty, is that forced use, repetition, creates new feeling, fills them.

Mallory told me she'd arrange a special ticket for me. "You leave when you want, and it'll be on hold, half-price. Airlines call it 'hardship fare.' It's for times like these, family emergencies." I didn't say much because I hadn't yet spent the night awake, worried. I hadn't considered death, just sickness. I had work, my two-year-old daughter.

But we hung up. I didn't sleep at all, no more than an hour or so for the next forty nights, an ordeal I didn't yet know I'd face. I don't burn candles for small causes. I don't mutter through the day: Lord, help this engine turn over, or God save this roast I cooked too long. But I believe in faith for as long as I can stand it, a doubts-set-aside exertion of consciousness that exceeds consciousness. The belief that hope (a vigil) bends steel, parts seas, postpones ruin, is the one comfort that comes with knowledge: knowing the end looms, compulsory. I called the hospital at 3:00 a.m. A nurse told me my mother's condition was serious. I said, "But that's one level better than *critical*, right?" The nurse said, "Um . . . not at all. We're worried about her living through the night."

I moved from my bed to the couch to the carpet—at last onto the hard tile floor.

Lying there, I remembered too many times I'd worried myself sick because some man was late for dinner, late coming home. I'd dedicated myself to men who felt hemmed in by schedules and violated them with spite, with purpose. I'd made myself exhausted, loving men like this, but only one, my college boyfriend, had turned up dead. "What are they looking for with exploratory surgery," I'd asked my new stepfather, "a bad appendix?" He said, "Something like that, something ruptured." In the night, I tried to read meaning into his words. Something *had* ruptured? Or they were looking for *the possibility*? I stopped. I wasn't parsing a text, I told myself. My stepfather wasn't James Joyce. He was a new husband talking on a phone outside the ER to a stepdaughter he hardly knew.

I counted my breaths, pretending their sound was waves lapping against the pier in front of my childhood house with its rose-colored dining room walls and French windows opening onto a lake—the sluice of small waves the happiest sound I know. I also like a box fan in a window, whirring then slowing because the wind waxes then wanes. In those days, people didn't have air-conditioning, not in Wisconsin. My sister and I slept in an attic room, the ceiling pressing near, and my imagination—whetted in that hurly-burly town by the public library and the poetry of Lutheran hymns—believed in slanted ceilings as a lofty edge, heaven's rim. Our pastor had taught us the wind was God breathing. So in the summer my mother put a box fan in the window and it ventilated our highest regions. Thirty years later in Texas, on the cold floor for one night, I pretended all breathing was fed by waves, fans, wind: God's breath. In the morning, I called.

She was alive.

But why waste sleeplessness—strenuous wishing—here?

I found a series of people who'd take Marie to preschool, pick her up, feed her, bathe her, soothe her. I had a strange ticket. The "hardship" in the "fare" Mallory had arranged—I thought later, boarding, unboarding—was the route: a confused scrawl across the West. I left from the nearest airport, Austin, changed planes in St. Louis, then Denver, stopped on the runway in Seattle. I'd get to Portland, rent a car, and drive three hours.

We were parked by the gate in Seattle, waiting for passengers to deplane, new ones to get on. A few of us stayed put, readying for the last leg of the route. The small talk people make on planes begins with the destination, why you're traveling. One woman, dressed spiffy, exuding gumption, said she'd started a self-help business and was on her way to conduct her first seminar. What set her apart was that she covered both the spiritual and fiscal, she said, inner humility and outer glory, Deepak Chopra and Suze Orman combined. She told us she used to be lost and now had found herself, and I realized—standing, but hunkered too, because of the baggage compartment, which did not feel lofty like a slanted, upstairs ceiling—that she was rehearsing. My mother could be dying, I thought, during this dry run of a bad motivational speech. A man going to Portland to test epoxy made for nautical purposes turned to me, "You?" I paused. The news, sickness unto death, was new. Being a daughter was new. "To see my mother," I said.

In the Portland airport, I was so tired I imagined I heard my name called faintly.

No one knew I was coming except my new stepfather, hours away.

At the car rental booth I waited for the clerk to take down my driver's license number, and two women ran in—past Avis, Budget, Advantage, Hertz, back again—shouting: "If someone were renting a car, would you know? Could you find out?" Gape-mouthed, customers looked up. Clerks stared, pens poised. I was at the mind-wandering phase of tiredness, and I'm nosy. Sometimes I tell myself my profession justifies curiosity, that all writers study human tribulations and indiscretion. I thought, as I watched the roaming, brown-haired women in sweatshirts and windbreakers: I wonder why'd they'd ask that? How will it end? We know, of course. But death wasn't in my ken.

"We're looking for a Debra Monroe," they said.

I said, cordial, "That's me. How can I help?"

They paused, air flowing out, deflation. One said, "We're your stepfather's nieces, and he thought it'd be a shame for you to drive so far, so we've arranged to drive you."

I thanked them, saying how nice their family seemed to me at the wedding just a few months earlier—my new stepfather's six children, their spouses, his grandchildren, siblings, their spouses, nieces, nephews, great-nieces, great-nephews, second cousins, the wedding a sea of guests related to him. I remember colossal slabs of pork roasting on big spits. My sister and I stayed near each other. She'd cried about my mother finding a husband just when she'd started standing up straight, buying new clothes, talking like her old self. My sister and I stood under an elm tree, vast branches. As families go, we were small.

During the connubial toast to long life, I said to my sister, "The chances of her marrying a man as bad as Bill Lyman twice in a lifetime are zilch," I said, champagne glasses clinking, "no way a new husband is anything but a step up." My mother had been introduced to him—her good husband—by Aunt Elinor who'd been married fifty years, an omen. He was worldly, educated, cheerful. My mother, like the woman in Chekhov's "The Little Darling," was worldly, educated, and cheerful since meeting him. But I didn't say that to the brown-haired women rolling my suitcase to the car. I said how kind their family was. And big. Incomprehensibly, I thought. Sublime? My brain traipsed through its daily litter. I'd read Longinus on the plane, for a class I'd teach when I got home.

These two step-cousins I'd never met, or couldn't remember meeting, nodded blankly. I remember thinking they lacked a rudimentary talent for chitchat. We were in that white-striped crosswalk, cars idling for us, when one of them said, "Your mother passed."

I made a long sound, must have been No.

You look around when you yell like that. A hundred feet away, a chauffeur with a white stretch limo, waiting for a client, locked his eyes with mine, then reached in the limo, got out a box of Kleenex and ran through traffic. "Keep it," he told me, "the whole thing."

Three hours later I walked into the farmhouse where she'd been married, and my stepfather kissed my forehead and sent me upstairs. It was a low-ceilinged room, dormer walls on both sides. She'd been painting that room pink. It was the shape of a coffin, only roomier, with a peak in the middle like a steeple. Medieval architects who invented steeples thought they helped launch souls. I thought: *not ready*. My mother wasn't launched. She lingered, I felt, sorry she'd missed this part too: my last minutes with my mother.

It was a closed casket funeral because she'd been given Prednizone and swelled up, and no one wanted to see that. But I thought if I didn't see her dead I wouldn't believe she'd gone. The undertaker arranged a private viewing. It didn't work. She looked like someone else. Most of the time I think she's still in Arizona, and she'll be in touch by phone. She doesn't want to see me, but her love doesn't stop—it's abstract, constant.

Most of the time my mother and I pretended she'd never left, but twice she came close to admitting she had. I brought her with me for part of my book tour, to help with Marie. We were exhausted, in and out of cities, though my six-month-old daughter looked ever more amused in each new portable crib the hotel clerks wheeled out. In some cities, friends showed up, and I did the faux-family pageant: they were essential, not my mother. "If you can't stand having spit-up on your best clothes," I snapped at her in a hotel in Phoenix, "why did you pack them?" Dabbing her blazer with a washcloth, she said, "You've never forgiven me I didn't try harder to see you." "Yes," I said, not contrite.

The second time she came with me to a conference in Florida. Marie had just turned two, and my mother would tend her while I taught and attended readings. My mother had been married a few weeks to her good husband and, after the conference, was meeting him at the Miami airport to leave on her honeymoon. I was sitting with my friend, Sofia, and my mother wheeled down the boardwalk with Marie in a stroller. My mother's sleek hair bobbed as she walked, her white capris and black shell the perfect ensemble for a well-dressed woman on a beach. "I can't believe that's your mom," Sofia said.

Sofia comes from a huge Sicilian family in upstate New York—she visits them every year. She has peroxide-blond hair as short as a man's, and multiple piercings, but she took her studs out when she volunteered at her son's high school. She understands loyalty and kindness better than anyone I know. And fashion. "You mom's so cute," Sofia said. I beamed. My daughter was cute too. I'd found myself in this life after years alone. The next morning at five a.m., my mother and I said goodbye. "I'm so happy for you," my mom said, "the baby, your work." I said, "I love your new husband, Mom." She shrugged like we'd baked a great cake together. "Oh, Bill Lyman," she said, "was insecure."

I saw her after she died.

Anyone's dream but your own is dull, I realize. But I wasn't asleep.

On the trip to Oregon, extended nine days to plan a funeral, my insomnia kicked in. I got home and no one understood, least of all Marie. Before I left, she'd slept fitfully.

When I returned, Marie didn't sleep at all. She was afraid I'd leave again. And she had sleep apnea, though I didn't know it yet. I wasn't healthy. I didn't know this either. For forty days, Marie wandered the night away, moving chairs to the wall to stand high enough to flip lights on, or she stood next to me in the dark, her breath raspy. One night, I counted, she got out of bed and turned the lights on fifteen times. I begged, cried, threatened.

I felt insane. But sometimes I felt calm and whispered to her. "Sleep," I'd say, holding her close, "and tomorrow will seem better, brand new." Mornings, I took her to preschool, came home, worked. One day, I walked upstairs to the room my mother used to sleep in and saw the door to a closet, but it was a bigger door now. I walked through it, and my mother wasn't in a closet but a bedroom with slanted ceilings. She sat on the edge of an old-fashioned bed, holding Marie. (Side note: this afterlife is snug and cozy, not infinite.) I said,

"You didn't die." I touched her arm. "I did," she said, "and I'm fine. You, however, will make yourself sick. Go to your doctor and ask for a mild sleeping pill." Then I wasn't in that room, beyond, but on my sofa, a stack of work in my lap.

Maybe I had dropped off.

I never did get sleeping pills. I was too busy. One night in bed, I said: "I don't know if you have control over it, but could you come again tonight?" I did sleep, and then my mother was shopping with me in Target, examining a red blouse on a plastic hanger, but I couldn't get her to turn and look at me. We left, and she walked to the far edge of the parking lot, stood next to a pale-colored car and called out, "I can't keep it up. It's hard."

This one I'm sure is a dream because we were at odds again, bickering. On the anniversary of her death, which falls near the time of tombs rolled open, I dreamed my mother, Marie, and I were going to Easter dinner with a family I know from preschool. Most families willingly attend each other's lives—I used to think this all the time, at 7:00 a.m., for instance, when a teacher would ask for names of relatives because my daughter was making a family tree and didn't think she had relatives. It's hard to describe the attenuated shape of my family, the way it's survived absence, shortfalls. In any case, this couple I'm going to Easter dinner with—call them John and Sally Forthright—tell me about indispensable child-rearing gear. They drive a Suburban with their children in car seats but ask my mother, daughter, and me to ride on benches on a trailer behind—like Okies, but wearing our Sunday best. I'm hardly speaking to my mother, no specific reason. We get to a restaurant. We don't need a big table, I think. Then my mother's gone. I ask Sally, wearing the pearls John bought her for Mother's Day, "Where'd my mom go?" I think: the cloak room? the Ladies'? Sally stares at me. "Into the wall," she says.

What I want back is the sniping, impatient time when Bill Lyman had just died, and I'd lie in my bed long after waking because I could hear my mother up and about and I didn't want to talk. She was visiting only because her husband was dead, I felt. I was her back-up plan. If he were alive, she'd still be gone. Plus, I was used to living alone, the quiet mornings. Finally, I'd get up, pour some coffee, sit on the porch. I liked the sound of birds singing. I liked my house because it reminded me of my childhood house: proximity to water, the old woodwork, the half-story upstairs with low ceilings. She was talking about how she didn't like the way I was doing the porch railing. Had I noticed my rain gutters sagged? I told her I wasn't a morning person, and I would answer her questions later. "You're cranky is what you are," she said, "and being a mother will cure that."

She talked to the carpenters next. They were helping build the add-on for my child, not yet born. I wanted a baby so badly I day-dreamed all the time about her, him, it, a baby as idealized as any looming unknown. Then my mother scolded the carpenters. "I wasn't born yesterday," she yelled from the yard to the rooftop. She looked more irked than she was as she stumped back inside—she'd stubbed her toe on a two-by-four. Greg, the carpenter I liked best, winked at me. I winked back. I went inside, and my mother was talking about crooks, cheaters. I took her to the river because I thought a swim would cheer us up. She was sixtyish, but looked so good in a swim-suit it was hard to realize. She was frail. She needed my help, not hurdles. She was clinging as we walked over slick rocks, and I shook her off. "If you hang on, you'll drag us both down." She said, "But I'm old, and this is harder for me than you." The water was shallow where we stood, but if you looked past the curve, the tree with big branches, you'd see an eddy so deep that currents running endlessly, currents pending, would wash one of us, both of us, away.

Fast-Forward,
A Four Year
Tunnel of Time

My daughter was getting enough love, yes.

But she wasn't getting enough breath.

I found out when she was two years old, and my mother had died, and I was sick but I didn't know yet. I thought it was just grief—I got slapped in the face by it, winded, dumbstruck.

After her funeral, I went back to work. A colleague said, "Sorry to hear about your mother." I said, "I didn't see her for years and years." I wanted to say that death stole her a second time. We had unfinished business. I needed to know she'd regretted the missing years. I wanted to retract moments I'd acted mad she wanted me back only after Bill Lyman died. I wondered aloud how to explain the big blunder that she'd died now—who wants someone else's grief details anyway?—as I tallied up the lost years. We'd talked by phone, I emphasized. She'd visited once. I'd seen her another time at a family reunion her husband let her attend, but we were in groups: cousins, aunts, uncles. Big dinners. Family photos. We couldn't talk alone. My colleague said, "She must have done something really bad." I didn't get it. Then I saw he thought I'd jilted her, not vice versa.

I tried telling someone I knew from around town, Madge. Madge's father had died. I used to drive him to church because both of us wanted to go, and he was blind. I felt fish-out-of water at church, holding Marie. Marie was the only black person in church, one of three black people in the entire town. One of the congregants once walked up to me and said, "You have done a great thing, opening your heart to this child." I'd answered, "I'm the lucky one. I wanted to be a mother." I thought, but didn't say: *I'm proving it can be done without gaps, distractions. I'll be her mother, love like rapture only consistent.* Could I? My mother had been gone a long time. Had unwavering love (a skill) been instilled? All I knew about Madge's father who I'd driven to church and sat next to those Sundays was that he hadn't been blind long and felt embarrassed needing help. So I'd felt connected to him—Martians dropped off on a church pew on the wrong planet.

Madge brought me a sympathy card after my mother died.

"Everyone will say they know how you feel," she said, "but because of my recent loss I do know." A door opened, relief. I tried again. I volunteered information. "My mother and I had been out of contact," I told Madge. "Then we were reunited. Her second husband was . . ." I searched for polite words. "Difficult. Abrasive. Abusive," I said. "He wouldn't let her travel alone, and I couldn't visit her at his house." Madge looked confused. Then she brightened and said, "I saw something like this on *Maury Povich.*"

But I didn't have time to think about a conventional vocabulary for bereavement because, a few weeks later, Marie had surgery so she could breathe at night. And this surgery disrupted her endocrine system and triggered new problems. My mother died, yes. I was sick but didn't know it. Marie, whose breathing had always been labored, had surgery and developed new disorders. I developed my own. Compound emergencies. Certain days or minutes felt interminable, but months blinked past, gone. Years blinked past, gone. I remember taking myself to doctors, taking Marie to doctors, taking myself, taking Marie—and teaching, cooking, grading, cleaning, braiding and unbraiding Marie's hair.

I started sewing. It helped control the disruptive thinking, raking through the past for words I'd said or not said, gestures I'd improve or modify now, my should-haves and could-haves. Sewing made me feel close to my mother. I sewed in the loft, where she used to sleep. Marie and I would drive to San Marcos to select fabrics and patterns for little dresses. "That's a great color for you," I said when Marie picked a print, marigold and purple flowers. "That," I said about a hot pink paisley, "shows off your skin." I complained that kids' clothes sold in stores were boring, pastels, and that she looked beautiful in vivid, dazzling colors. Sewing made me happy, my scissors cutting crisp lines, facings and zippers going in flat, perfect. I kept the iron hot. "Iron-as-you-go is the best tip any seamstress ever gets," my mom said long ago, when she taught me sewing. Marie was two, almost three; she sat next to me to hand me pins. I called her the pin girl.

One day I decided to surprise her with a pair of dresses for both of us, made of matching cloth: a chartreuse watercolor wash. I sewed at night while Marie slept. I made a strappy sundress for Marie, and a 1960s-era sleeveless sheath for me. The morning after I'd finished— the hems, a last bit of pressing—I held up the two dresses on hangers and said: "Marie, look what I made for us to wear." I thought matching dresses would be especially good for plane trips because flight attendants never thought we were together. Marie hesitated. "What about that color?" she asked. "Is it vivid and dazzling?" I said, "Actually, yes. I picked it out because we both look good in this shade." She nodded, approving.

And I tried to make Friday nights always happy. Popsicle night. I'd buy a box of popsicles already cut in half, Bluebell Bullets, and on Fridays we could have three in a row, I stipulated, though sometimes I substituted one of mine for a glass of wine. I'd turn up the music, and Marie and I would dance. Or we watched PBS fundraisers, oldies concerts. We invented a game—whoever saw an old lady in the tele- vised audience dancing crazily and was the first to yell "Rock and Roll Grandma" got points. Once, during a tribute to Johnny Cash, Marie, solemn, turned and said: "Mama, I really like this song." She meant, "Jackson," the duet with June Carter Cash. I bought her the CD, and she memorized the song and sang all four verses at the top of her lungs into a Playskool microphone.

I also taught her easy cooking. One day she stood on a chair—far enough from the burner—and stirred as we made bean and sausage soup. I explained which ingredient went in the pot next, what bay leaves are for and why you take them out later, that thyme is subtle but necessary. She said, "Maybe you could write all this down for when I grow up." Then she reconsidered. "I'd actually like to live in this house with you, but I'd need to redecorate." I laughed and said, "When you grow up, you will so not want to live with your mother. You'll have your own place, and then you'll call me and ask how to make soup."

I used most of the little bequest from my mother's retirement—an old will had split it among her three children and Bill Lyman's four—to start a savings account for Marie. I used the remainder to land-scape. Marie would go outside to check flowers, then race back in. "Mama, we have a new yellow one by the fence," she'd say. Or: "Those bluey-purple ones on the arch are coming on." If I had workers dig-ging or planting, she'd run out and give them gum. I built her a gar-den of her own, a small circle in the center of my rectangular rows of raised vegetable beds, and let I her choose her seeds. She planted carrots, lettuce, and petunias. But she had trouble leaving the plants alone. She'd dig them up, transplant them, and they'd die from over-handling. One day she brought tiny carrots inside. "Those are too small," I said. She frowned. "Barbie doll carrots."

But I also remember that time as constant impulses and worry: worry as lifestyle. My uneasiness turned chronic, my responses me-chanical, the niggling fear I'd caused bad luck an axis I went around like a millstone, wearing blinders, getting my work done, but progress paused. If I try to remember those years in a straight line, memories fall in place fast.

Fast-forward.

At my mother's funeral, I barely understood she'd been removed. Shock made me sick. Then I had grieved, I decided. Done. What could I do to bring her back? She'd been gone most of two decades anyway. I was cooking, sewing, gardening. I was fine.

Our town got Internet service then, dial-up. Even dial-up email is faster than mail, so I wrote letters to Jack Creeden, my friend so long he seemed like family. He wrote back that my emails were lists: chores, different ways my body felt strange. My hands and feet were numb now. My skin felt like bugs crawling. I was too thirsty. My in-attention caused car accidents—one in the parking lot of the office of yet another doctor who said I'd developed hypoglycemia. He said to eat protein. I thought thick, gristly food I swallowed like medicine accounted for knots in my stomach, nagging pain, but pain was the least of my worries because Marie was enrolled in preschool, i.e., in virus incubation.

"Preschool, that racket," my friend, Jana scoffed, as she sat at my dining room table, stacked high with papers I'd graded. "You sign up for it and then your kid catches every bug and is too sick to attend. But you still have to pay for it anyway. But better now than in kindergarten. Their little immune systems have to stock up, either now or later."

"Sounds like a good time," I said. "I can hardly wait."

A few minutes later, Jana said, "You're my third friend ever."

All I knew about her past was that the kids' father had bailed out. "Really?"

She was tapping the table with a pen. She said, "My mother drove off my first friend because my mother thought the two of us combined were macabre, mutual bad influence. I had some compulsive habits—I always pushed myself to the absolute edge of every single one and then stopped. My second friend died when she was twenty-two, melanoma."

"That's terrible," I said. "Sad." Like Jane Eyre, I thought.

She said, "Exactly. So don't die."

I'm superstitious about words, their power. "Don't say that," I said. "I don't want to be negative. But I'm glad we're friends—I couldn't handle *Our Town* without you."

She smiled. "Right back at you. You're great. Except, you know, one thing."

Had I done something inconsiderate? "What? Tell me."

She drew a picture on a scrap of paper. "You said not to say it out loud." She held up the picture: a tombstone lettered R.I.P. I was a little stunned. She started laughing. "Don't say I didn't warn you—my mother had a point. I'm saying get well. I *care*."

And Marie was in preschool and, as Jana had predicted, got every bug going around. When she was three, she was sick for seven weeks. I managed that, my job, a flood, getting to work, the store, the doctor, long routes around washed-out roads. The garbage man stopped picking up trash, and dogs rummaged through it, and I'd go out in the mud while Marie slept and pile up the trash, then wash my hands and give her Pedialyte. We drank bottled water because the county water went bad, and the doctor asked if Marie was perhaps drinking water in the bath because she wasn't getting well. Then she had asthma and wore a mask to inhale a drug that made her heart race. I'd watch her writhe, fight the mask, and I clamped it on her face and thought (profound late at night): *her breath is a bird trapped in this rib cage.* Yet it didn't make sense the next day when she'd look at me with her contented, welcome-back-from-when-I-was-sleeping smile.

When Marie was three, we were in a hotel at a conference—I was sick, but I needed to make money or I couldn't keep us secure and one day pay for braces and college, and, besides, I'd get invited months in advance and think we'd both feel better. One of us never did. Conference days were long, my professional tasks, my scramble to get enough food, to keep Marie happy with her sitter, her routines, her bedtime. When I sat on panel discussions, she'd sit with a colleague. Sometimes I'd think she was stirring too much and when it was my turn to speak about "The Role of Place in Storytelling" or "Autobiography in Fiction," I'd say in the microphone: "Marie. This is Mommy. Please stop tunneling under the chairs and sit down. Thank you." She would. Then I'd give my spiel.

If I was in the audience and someone else was speaking, I'd hold Marie in my lap and give her hand-massages. If I'd stop, she'd tap me to start again, and I'd keep massaging, her hands, her forearms, her shoulders. As I did, I remembered sitting with my mother in church, how she'd kept me quiet by stroking my hands, letting me stroke hers—her rings and polished nails, the veins on the backs of her hands. I'd massage Marie, and she'd sigh, wrap herself around me, and tell me, barely a whisper: "Love you bunches."

But one night in a hotel when she was three, she slept as I read manuscripts, and for the first time in a long time she was asleep while I was awake in the same room, and I heard her gag, and I watched as she rose every minute like a zombie, breathed and lay back down to gag and rise again. We went home, and the pediatrician sent us to an ENT who scheduled surgery for the biggest adenoids he'd ever seen, he said, which fell into her throat like plugs in a pipe. He held her upside down to shake them loose to cut them, her tonsils too. Now she'd grow fast, he said. She'd grow so fast we'd be amazed, he added.

She spent two nights in the hospital during the first weeks of my fall semester, which I missed. I was director of something important because someone important was on leave, and Marie's veins collapsed, and one friend, then another, who said they'd bring food so I wouldn't have to eat hospital food, forgot. The peas were bright green with black scorch marks. The nurse who brought the tray said, "Now is when some family might help." A few days later, a police officer pulled me over for a sloppy lane change. I told him I was on my way to the sitter, then work, and my daughter just had surgery, and he yelled at me for having her out so soon. I told him I couldn't afford more time off work, and his face went soft, disgusted—people who had no business raising children.

A week after the surgery, Marie's skin blistered and peeled, altered reactivity of the pituitary axis, something like that. But it took us a year to figure this out. We saw an allergist, a dermatologist, another dermatologist, an allergist again, none of whom had treated black patients, so her rashes looked unfamiliar. Finally, a doctor from India said to coat her skin every night with Vaseline and wrap it with wet cheesecloth, and it got better.

Next, Marie was four years old already, and one night she said, "Mama, I ate money." Except she said minney. She ate minney. It was raining, a flood watch. I called the pediatrician, and the nurse called me back and said, "If she's not gasping, it's past her airways and unlikely to cause problems, but it's our policy to tell every parent of a child who's swallowed a foreign object to go to ER." I drove her to the ER in light mist, twenty minutes, and the nickel was in her stomach, the doctor explained after the X-ray. But first we'd waited. Hours had transpired in that waiting room where everyone tending a sick person waiting to be checked in probably felt among the ranks about to be thinned. Rain hammered as I drove home, road after road closed. It took me ninety minutes to get home, and I'd left my purse on top of the car and now my credit cards, my ID, gone.

Sometimes, I'd sit on the first step and rest before walking up a flight of stairs. I ate six times a day now. Seven. Eight. Nonstop. I carried a thermal lunch sack everywhere. I lectured with both hands on the podium to stay steady. One day, at home, sitting in a chair, talking to my health insurance company on the phone, asking for a specialist closer to home, I listened as the insurance company representative said I had to use a network doctor, sixty miles away. We were talking about my blood sugar. I told the insurance company representative that it was hard to see any doctor because I worked, and my daughter saw specialists too. "Nearly every week my daughter or I have a doctor's appointment somewhere," I said. I started crying. I couldn't stop. I held the mouthpiece away from my head. Maybe the only sound the insurance woman could hear was my choked-off crying, big breaths. She paused, then asked: "Have you now or ever had suicidal thoughts?" I stopped crying. I said, "I think about a new doctor is all." Marie, standing behind me as I sat in the chair, patted my shoulder. "Poor thing," she said.

Then Clara Mae got sick. I called her relatives in Oklahoma to come help her. They set up home health care, Angels for Elders, but Clara Mae didn't like the food the "angel" made, too spicy, she said, so much cumin, and she wouldn't eat it. I brought her a roast or a meatloaf every Sunday, and I'd cut it into portions to last her a few days. Clara Mae lay in bed, her mouth so dry she could barely talk. As Marie, age four, hurried about the room, moving a newspaper or book, or rustling the bed clothes, Clara Mae would call out to me, confused: "Debra, Debra, save the baby. Save her. She makes a sound like dry leaves rattling." And sometimes Clara Mae would sing in a whisper, an old song about a yew tree: *not once did you speak for the poor or weak who lay in your shade.*

One night the home health care worker called an ambulance. Clara Mae had gotten out of bed to get a glass of wine and a sleeping pill and made a mistake—we said it was a mistake—and took the last seven pills in the bottle. She was in coma now, but coming to. I left Marie with a sitter and drove to the hospital. I told Clara Mae who I was. Her hands were tied to the bed rails. She mumbled. I started singing songs Clara Mae knew: "Harvest Moon," "Over the Rainbow," "Willie, We Have Missed You." Her quavery voice grew steady, and she sang the second and third verses by herself. A nurse came to check on us, looked surprised, then nodded. Then I had to leave. I drove back into the country to get Marie. Her sitter lived at the end of a one-mile, rain-gullied road so hard to maneuver I thought of wagon trails—the steady thump-thump of Conestoga wagons. Sometimes I longed for city sidewalks, for pavement. All the dirt roads, the whacking back weeds, keeping my eye out for snakes and scorpions, I felt like a home-steader, albeit with a Honda Accord and high heels. I pulled into my own bumpy driveway, unbuckled Marie, and thought: Pioneer women pined for letters from back east.

But I had email. I wanted to turn my hard times into a story. Redemption: life was difficult, but I strived and overcame. The reverse: life was good until something went foul and I learned my lesson. I tried to foreshadow my way out, forward. I acted plucky, hopeful—even if hope felt forced. I platitudinized about life, truths I hadn't learned yet, as I emailed Sofia, in Florida. My friends are my family, I thought. Sofia has a fix-it attitude. Her husband, John, once said: "She'll run your life if you let her, and she'll do a good job." She wrote back: "Pour this into your writing. Write a memoir." I wrote back that history, even close-up personal history, doesn't always transmit the expected lessons, a bingo-moment, resolution. "No closure," I said. "It would be an anti-memoir."

Sofia told me to come and stay for a long weekend. I dithered. It seemed like extravagance. I'd never taken a trip that wasn't for work. But then I bought tickets. Sofia installed us in her guest room, cooked tempting, high-protein meals. In the early morning, she'd come get Marie, so I could sleep. One day, as Sofia was explaining to Marie why she couldn't have another cookie before dinner, Marie said: "You're like my other mother." Sofia laughed and said, "That's right. I've got your back. I've got your mother's back." Marie raised her eyebrows, doubtful. "Backs?" she said. Sofia told Marie that if I made a mistake because I could see only so far, Sofia would also be watching.

"Like God?" Marie asked.

Sofia's husband, John, laughed. "We'll have T-shirts made, 'WWSD?' 'What Would Sofia Do?'"

When I went home, Sofia tried to anticipate my blind spots based on what I'd report by phone or email. She switched tacks now. She said I needed to date in a goal-oriented way because I needed to get married. It seemed like a plan to her. A man who was nearby could help me, she thought. She was far away. It bothered her she couldn't help.

I answered that needing help wouldn't make me a date-magnet. Sofia forged on: I needed to date someone educated, she said, so I'd better focus on nearby cities. But she couldn't visualize how far out I lived. She lived in Miami. Forty miles to see a friend is nothing, she said. Forty miles to the edge of the closest city, I said. If I dated someone who didn't live on the right side of town, it might be sixty or seventy miles—on twisty, moonlit roads with leaping deer. Besides, marriage is an institution in which you survive misuse. Hurrying to find a father for your child is a surefire way to find a bad father. I had to factor in babysitting. Did I want to add long drives at night to my schedule? But I'd been solo since Marie was born. I was edgy and turning numb. I understood why people binged on anything, or lost the family fortune gambling. I wanted a risk, a hobby, a lark. I wanted to be distracted into a wild mood. So it wouldn't hurt to go on dates, I decided.

Sofia sent me links to matchmaking websites. "Get First Date Jitters" one ad read. Jitters, I thought. Your self's best version presented: the bait. Snapped up. This is heady entertainment, or so I used to think before I was a mother. But now, I thought—driving into Austin to assess some man—the dressing up and getting acquainted, which should be fun, diverting, seemed labor-intensive. It also hadn't dawned on me this new pool was infinite. I was still thinking in terms of my rural county. ("You won't meet anyone single here," the dean had said.) So I'd settle in fast with someone I'd vetted if he'd meet me at odd times I'd arranged for a sitter. Diffused attachment: jolt, temporary release.

Marie was about to turn five. A few weeks before her birthday, she said: "Mama, I had a dream I unwrapped a present from you, and it was pajama pants, but the pajama pants were big, and there were more presents inside them, more and more I kept having to open." Pajama pants as cornucopia, I thought. I went to Target and bought her pink leopard-print pajama pants, and a half-dozen smaller gifts— T-shirts, toys, stuffed animals—and wrapped the small gifts and stuffed them inside, securing each into its spot in a pajama leg by tying bright ribbons on either side. Then I put the pajama pants in a big box and wrapped it. When Marie unwrapped her present, she got happier and happier, a smile like a sunbeam, and said, "Oh my gosh, Mama. You made my dream true."

Another year went by like that, and I got sicker. A doctor scheduled tests, then exploratory surgery. He wanted to rule out cancer.

"We don't think it's cancer?" I said, as if the doctor and I were allies, partners, sharing this worry. "Probably not," he said, "but it could be." He also said I asked too many questions. "Don't dwell on why you feel bad," he said. "You won't learn a thing." I didn't believe him. Heresy. What's the point of bad times if I don't learn? I didn't say this to him, though. I listened as he told me the new symptoms, pain, bleeding, blood and guts symptoms, couldn't be explained in terms of glucose. I had a new glitch. Marie had just turned six. I had tests, waited for surgery.

One day, on campus, I sat in a thesis defense, and my vision dimmed and the sound in the room turned high-pitched. My breaths went shallow, stunted, small. I can't eat now, I thought. I go to a lot of thesis defenses, but this student has just one, his own, a ceremony. Still, I un-Velcroed my lunch bag carefully, slipped meat into my mouth, chewed slowly, and moments later the room came back into view. I breathed and listened. Another professor was saying to the student, "No, no. Content becomes form, not the reverse—in this case, a plot shaped by the simultaneous compulsion both to avoid and yet revisit the site of trauma." Trying to sound alert, or relevant, I chimed in, "Not linear."

Avoid, revisit, avoid, revisit, I thought.

Not the most straightforward plot, I've since decided, but it's my plot. All ways out were blocked then. I repress the bad memories, and I dwell on them too. I start recollecting, and sometimes I can't stop, poring over the past, expecting it to turn into a cautionary tale: the wrong way never to be detoured onto again. Yet for four years— from the time Marie was two and my mother died, until Marie was six and she stared at me on the couch, feverish, confused—my story just recycles, out-of-sync moments making only the vaguest point: the precepts I'd been taught, Handy Housewife Hints, Motherhood 101, didn't apply. So that day in the thesis defense I just chewed meat and thought about my surgery, too scary, pushed that thought away, thought about my mother (her death preceded by a few hours of flu-like symptoms), and pushed that thought away too.

Then I had surgery and a helpful diagnosis. And complications. And I almost died.

I almost died because of a botched surgery.

I didn't die, I still remind myself. *Avoid. Avoid.*

Fast-forward, but not too far.

Marie, who was only six years old, did have the growth spurt the ENT described: undersized, suddenly oversized. She'd grown five inches in one year. Her endocrine system overreacted, the new specialist said, and there'd be therapies to circumvent this, but not risk-free. This doctor also said Marie had the first symptoms of another illness associated with pituitary disruption, an illness causing blindness, deafness, scoliosis, gross disfiguration, visible tumors. Had I heard of it? A famous movie had been made about it. The doctor himself first saw this disease at the circus. My face felt frozen. I held my breath. I didn't want Marie to hear. But I couldn't stop myself. I moved my face. I spoke: "You mean freak show. You saw neurofibromatosis at the freak show." He pushed his glasses up his nose. "Right. There isn't a test for it, but she has the symptoms." About the symptoms he pointed to, I said, "Maybe you don't know black skin. Maybe the pigment variations are unfamiliar." He said, "Maybe. But I don't think so."

Who's calling who freaks, I thought, my panic pouring out chaotic, lawless, as I drove us away through sloshing rain, my windshield wipers *thwap thwap.* I never saw this bad luck coming or, in its wake, bad decisions I'd make, relying on strangers, callous or kind. I wasn't paranormal. I wasn't even normal. I was on the outskirts of normal. I went through the so-called forward motions. Or we moved forward despite the illusion I kept us alive by worrying, my love shaped like fear all we'd need, I thought. Inhale. Exhale. Inspire. Expire. I kept it coming, air to air, mouth to mouth, my love to her body. Did we have enough? Let me emphasize in this speeded-up version of jumbled time, events occurred in a straight line, but I don't remember a straight line because too much happened. Or I want to forget, let go the infinite regress into foresight I didn't have.

The Time to be
Lovely is Always

The hair-care-as-American-history quandary sprang up immediately. Minutes after I'd signed the adoption papers, I was walking out the hospital door. Using one arm to tote a bag of free samples—a plastic tub, a six-pack of Enfamil—and having taken a crash course in how to bathe, feed, burp, I used my other arm to hold the car seat with its big handle and headed for the parking lot. At last I understood those window stickers: BABY ON BOARD. I felt like bragging. It was late. A stranger, a black woman, brushed past me. "Get some grease," she said, "for her hair. For a little girl, you'll want the pink stuff."

Hours earlier, though most of my conversations with the birth mother had been stilted and sad, I'd tried for a moment to be chatty as ordinary women in an ordinary maternity ward. To be relaxed, cordial, but also to express my longing and admiration for the baby that lay beyond the glass wall in a transparent crib, charmed child, I said, "She has such thick hair." I said so carefully. I'd never been around black babies. What if they all did? I'd been around white babies who are mostly bald as Popeye. It was shocking, this six-pound bundle, smaller than a sack of sugar, with her outsized afro. Her birth mother said, "I mean. My other baby had hair, but I've never seen anything like this."

A few days later I was back in the city at the airport, picking up Shen, my friend from Utah who loves to shop for babies. I was sleep-deprived. I'd taken that spill in the parking lot, dress torn, knees scraped. But the first thing I asked her was: "Do you have satin baby headbands in your suitcase?" When I'd dressed Marie that morning, I thought she looked perfect, but I wanted a bow for her luxuriant hair. Shen nodded. I said, "Do you know where they are and you could get one out now? Or would you have to dig around and look?" Shen smiled, unzipped her bag and pulled out a pink one. We left the airport with Marie in a rosebud dress and pink satin headband. People stared. Two white women with a black baby, one happy to the point of exultation, the other serene as a sage, rolling suitcases overflowing with gifts. People stared because the baby was attractive, I felt.

The three of us went to a beauty supply store next, and I asked for pink stuff. "Grease," I said. The clerk sent me to a little store on the other side of the interstate. It sold colored elastics attached to glittery baubles; red, green, blue, and purple barrettes shaped like bows, dogs, lambs, and daisies; scarves to wear to bed; hairpieces; wigs; packages of fake hair; packages of real hair; packages of pre-braided braids; gel and sheen. I unscrewed the cap on the pink pomade—it smelled like bubble gum. "What's it for?" I asked the Chinese woman who ran the store. She shrugged. I asked how to use it. A regular customer glanced at me, then Marie. She looked pessimistic about the prospect of me doing Marie's hair. She said, "Put it on every day." I asked why. "You just do," she said.

Saturdays, I washed and combed Marie's hair. Grueling work. Other days of the week, I put pink stuff on it, held a section, worked a wide-tooth comb tips to roots. Comb the front. Turn her over. Comb the back. The back matted because she lay on it. Yet the hair on the back of the head is notoriously recalcitrant. It's called "the kitchen." No one knows why. But in the old days, hair was greased and hot-combed bone-straight next to the kitchen stove where the hot-comb got heated. Grease smoked as it protected hair from red-hot metal. Even after emancipation, blacks worked in kitchens, did hair in kitch-ens. Kinky hair was unassimilated, undesirable. The section least likely to conform, the section that wouldn't do its bidding, was a menial place. My daughter's kitchen matted, but I combed it each day, and in a week I'd used enough pink stuff to wax a small car.

If you're white, black hair care is a secret. The reverse is also true. A student one day sat in my office, going over the assignment. She was black, and she looked at a framed picture of my daughter. "*That's* your little girl?" After chatting about how cute my daughter was, the student asked: "Who's doing her hair for you?" My answer was complicated. The student commiserated. "My mother married a white man who has a little girl," she said. "We gave up on her hair. It's like corn silk. We can't do a thing with it."

But white people know even less about black hair.

By the time Marie was a year old, curious strangers had touched her hair so much—"I want to feel it"—she reflexively jerked her head if a hand came near. A white woman in a mall one day said to us, "Please explain to me why black children wear multiple pigtails." A few years later, when Marie's hair was cornrowed, a man in a restaurant said, "I don't get it, the weird stuff black people do to their hair." (He had a bald pate with a foot-long, spindly ponytail.) By the time Marie was eight, if someone reached for her head, she'd say, comic-dramatic, but dead serious, "Hands off the hair, people."

I couldn't find how-to books. In San Marcos where I taught and got my own hair done, I couldn't find stylists who did black hair. People did each other's. Students with the best hairdos went to Houston or Dallas—planned their appointments around visits home. Books I did find were evangelical: the renunciation of chemicals. They were preaching to the choir. Alternatives—other than cutting it short as a boy's—were state-of-the-art, labor-intensive, and stylists who did them were hard to find even in cities like New York.

Another book I found was sociological, describing, first, sculpted, totemic African styles signifying to which clan the wearer belonged, whether the wearer was single, married, widowed, mourning. In America, during slavery, women rolled their hair in string or flattened it with cloth, then unwrapped it—flatter, straighter—on their day off, Sunday. Then straighteners were invented, homemade and commercial. Next, black pride: afros, cornrows. In the eighties, perm companies tried to recapture lost business with the Jheri-curl, touted as more natural than straight hair, but requiring two perms, perm-straightener followed by perm-curls. In a few centuries, African-Americans had learned to conceal "bad" hair, aspire to "good" hair. Hair care turned into a segregated body of inside information, a hush-hush, painstaking record of assimilation, its torture, its toll.

One day we were in a store, and Marie was wearing a pink onesie with a pink-flowered headband, and she smiled—dimples, twinkly eyes—at a black woman who, if I had to guess, used top-shelf relaxer because her hair was long and silky. She touched my daughter's hair, not the way white people do, to experience the unfamiliar, but to see how soft, tractable. "I know someone who'd come to your house and fix that," she said, jotting down a number. I asked, "What kind of baby hairdos are we talking about?" She said, "You could braid it, natural braids, her hair. Or Afro-puffs, or Nubian knots." How long would it take? "Braids or Nubian knots, I suppose two hours." *Hours?* I thought. But books I'd read described some long procedures as an invest-ment—a hairdo that buys weeks of freedom. "How long will it last?" I asked. "The braids, a few days," she said, "unless you add, you know, fake hair. Natural hair mats. No baby could sleep on Nubian knots."

Another day, a woman in Target crept up, whispered, "I could do something with that hair." Another day, I was pumping gas, baby on my hip, and a woman said, "I went to cosmetology school, but people learn how to do black hair at home. I can do her hair." Another day at work, I found a note in my mailbox: "Dr. Monroe, I work in the writing lab and I've seen you with your baby, and I want to say I'm available to comb out her hair."

Could I be mistaken?

When I took Marie on my book tour, people—most of them white, true—told me she was beautiful. I'd slipped her arms into her shaggy, fake-fur fuchsia parka, and a bookstore clerk said, "She's so glam-orous." At her adoption confirmation hearing, to which she wore a cream-colored velour suit with leopard-print collar and cuffs and matching pillbox hat, the judge said, when the officialese was over, "The baby is very pretty."

Wet, her hair measured ten inches. If it was damp, I could fit it in an elastic and make the widest ponytail ever. As her hair dried, shrank, thickened, the elastic slipped off. I'd put it back on. It shot across the room. Then one day as I was watching TV, a documentary about interracial families, I heard a black woman tell a white woman with a biracial daughter: "I know the debate about interracial all that, and I've got no ax to grind with you. But please don't be one of those white women whose black daughter has bad hair."

I'd saved the phone numbers from strangers—I made some calls.

One woman parted my daughter's hair in six sections. It took an hour: straight lines on a tightly coiled head. She combed it, put it in twists, another hour. As she worked, she asked how I came to adopt a black baby. I explained. She smiled. "You'll love her a lot, and she'll turn out fine." When she finished, the twists jutted out all over like short, bumpy commas. "Looks bad," she admitted. "You need to straighten it first. Get a hot-comb you plug in. Grease the hair, or it burns. Careful not to burn her ears or scalp."

The cosmetologist worked faster. But she parted the hair in twenty sections, folded the pigtails over, tucked in the ends. As she worked, she asked: Is this your granddaughter? I said no. Foster child? I said, "She's my daughter." She frowned. I said, "I adopted her." She didn't speak for the rest of the appointment—two hours—except at the end to say, "Nubian knots." I took them out when Marie went to bed that night.

I started tying it up in six pigtails. I used duckbill clips to help make the parts straight. I bought thick, colorful elastics. The first day, washing day, was hard. But tying it up kept the hair easier to comb the rest of the week. This is the logic behind the old method of binding it with string: train it straight. But when "trained hair" gets wet, it "goes back." It took forty minutes to put her hair in pigtails that flared away from her head, fierce and dramatic as plumes on a Seminole Indian. I needed a salon, I decided. I asked a male colleague, black, who asked a friend, who sent me to her stylist in San Antonio. She said, "You don't want to end up someplace where they talk you into a relaxer."

So I drove south for over an hour. I stepped into the main room. A pool table sat in an adjacent room, for men who'd drop off women and wait. "Helps pass the time," the stylist's husband said. I asked the stylist, "Will you cut it?" She said, "Short hair on a girl? Heavens no. I know you're having trouble with that hair, honey. I'll soften it." I'd heard the word "soft" again, again. Keep it soft. I felt bad—I hadn't used enough pink stuff.

She squirted softener in a cup. She asked, "Is this your baby?" I said she was. The stylist frowned. Her husband chimed in. They'd heard it was illegal for white people to adopt black children. I explained that most social workers think a same-race home is the best possible placement, but now it's illegal not to place a child in the best home available at the time, regardless of race. I said, "There wasn't a black home when she was born. She would have gone into foster care. I couldn't have said no. I love her. I can't imagine not being her mother. Her skin, my skin, I just don't care." I'd forgotten where I was. I refocused. "But I need some pointers about hair care," I added, ever-receptive.

The stylist smiled. She put softener on my daughter's hair, and Marie cried, "Mama, Mama, it stings." My jaw dropped. The woman said, "It does now, child, but you'll look a movie star." Witless, I asked, "Is that a relaxer?" The woman said, "The gentlest kind. You can't keep combing that hair." Marie cried hard. The woman rinsed it out, and Marie's hair was straighter than mine, and thin. The stylist said, "Use a blow-dryer, then a curling iron to give her ringlets." Marie wasn't even two yet. I drove home, panicked.

The stylist had said to touch up the roots every other month or the hair would break. I conditioned it, combed carefully. It didn't break except at the temples, also at the nape, her kitchen. But on the rest of her head I had a dilemma: a half-inch, a month later an inch, three months later three inches of kinky hair attached to ten inches of limp hair which fanned out haywire. I put it in twists, lumpy and irregular, that swung past her shoulders.

One day I bought new packs of elastics and barrettes. I wanted her elastics and barrettes all one color, the color of her dress. I spent an hour combing, greasing, twisting. I spent an hour on my own hair and makeup. I carried her to the car, drove to an author event in Austin. I parked the car, turned around. She'd pulled her hairdo out. I shouted, "No. No touching hair after Mama fixes it." I dug around the car for scattered barrettes and elastics, found a comb, replaited ruthlessly. "Ouch ouch," she said. "Bad bad," I said.

When we went to my mother's wedding, we stayed at her husband-to-be's big farmhouse. I combed out Marie's hair. One of my new step-sisters, puzzled, half-joking, said, "Stop torturing that baby." I sat up straight, self-righteous, as in *white people who think they know*, and said, "If this is torture, then little black girls all over America are tortured." My aunt, the former beauty queen, said, "How wonderful you're already so good."

By now I'd enrolled Marie in preschool. It started at 7:45 a.m. I called a woman I knew in Austin, the author of a soul food cookbook. She said, "I suggest braids, the kind with fake hair. You don't have to do a thing to it for two months. Good for you, good for the child. It'll give her hair a rest." From what? I asked. She said, "I do it to give my hair a rest from relaxers, also the stress of combing, styling." She sent me to Dora.

I drove to a salon an hour north. Dora cornrowed fake braids into my daughter's hair to keep it from matting. I was mesmerized by a woman feeding Coca-Cola to a newborn. Dora said, "That woman's been here all day. Her man forgot her." Then Dora said, "My daddy was white, and once a friend who didn't know it said that blacks being with whites made her sick. I said, I, Big Dora, am half-white. So don't be handing me that white-devil talk." I nodded. It was Dora's way of saying: welcome, don't be uneasy. My daughter looked regal for her first days of preschool, but Dora had tried newfangled, silky braids, and soon they slipped loose. I contacted Dora. I paged her. She went to a phone booth and called me back. She said, "Come to my house, so I won't pay rent on my chair."

I drove past winos, hookers. Or just poor people hanging out or lying down, and I wasn't used to their clothes and facial expressions. Dora had fixed up her living room by stapling zebra fabric to the walls. She had four children. The father of the twins gave her the house instead of marrying her, which wasn't what he promised, but she was glad for the house. She frowned. "Sweet Jesus, you left them in." Then I understood I was supposed to have taken out the old braids. "I didn't realize," I said. "I don't know how." She shrugged. "I expect there's no way you could." These came out fast because they were loose, silky, and two of us working. I told Dora I'd pay extra. "That's fair," Dora said.

Then three hours of rebraiding.

Dora's little girl, Desiree, sat on the couch, coloring. "Don't color the trees blue," Dora said, "or people will think you're wrong in the head." Dora talked about her oldest boy. His probation officer had stopped by. She looked at Marie. "Did you sew her dress?" I said I did. Dora used to have a sewing machine, but her sister borrowed it, then pawned it. "I was mad for months." Then she said, "Desiree. Beaver. *Beaver.*" I thought she meant the coloring book, that Desiree had colored a beaver orange or polka-dot. Dora said, "Put your legs together. It looks like a porn store in here." She told me, "This neighborhood so full of useless men—you've got to teach that now." I looked at Marie, oblivious, babbling about whether Dora the stylist knew Dora the Explorer, also waving at Desiree who, age seven, seemed to my daughter like an animated toy, or a celebrity.

When Dora was done that day, she looked at Marie and said: "She looks bad."

"Bad?" I said, worried.

Dora laughed. "Good, honey. Stylish. She looks fly."

Marie had dooky braids—one-inch squares all over the head, and braids the size of your pinkie made of fake scratchy hair that won't slide out. They look pristine for a few weeks, but the real hair gets wet, kinks, and they dishevel. But we were set for two months. Then? In San Marcos one day we were in JCPenney, shopping for towels, and a black woman standing in the door of the hair salon said: "I work here." I asked, "Do you braid?"

She sighed. "I could."

"What about a short afro?"

She shook her head. "That's for grown women who wear makeup and jewelry."

Marie more or less agreed. I'd pointed out a short Afro on TV. "That's boy's hair," she said, despondent. She cried if braiding or unbraiding went on too long, and I'd say short hair would be easier and she'd stop crying. Braiding took two to three hours. Unbraiding took two to three evenings. I used the end of a rat-tail comb to work from the bottom of each braid up, like untangling knots in a necklace—except fifty to sixty necklaces. The idea the hair "rested" was specious. I'd comb out weeks of tangles. Transition days, the days the fake hair was still attached but unbraided and braid-kinks made a uniform pattern, I used a scrunchie to make her look like Cleopatra in an updo. White people would stop me to say they liked this style best—slipshod fake hair tied in a bow.

As the lady at the JCPenney salon braided, she said, "When my children were her age, I quit working." I said, "I'd like to, but I can't afford it." She gave me a clamped-mouth look: her money problems trumped mine. She also didn't like braiding while white clients watched. Some old woman would say: "How interesting, such handiwork." Or: "Are you spending all that time because the little girl is going somewhere special?" I answered that we styled her hair this way every other month. The stylist hissed at me, "Why are you talking to those biddies?" Once, when I said I must be doing something wrong because it took me four hours to unbraid my daughter's hair, and then I still had to wash it and comb it out, her mouth clamped again. "What did you expect? This is our hair."

I went back to my list of phone numbers from strangers.

I remembered the woman in the grocery store with silky hair who'd said her stylist would come to my house. On the phone, the stylist, Therri, said, "You got my number how? That's got to be June Guobadia. That woman would talk to the Pope." Therri arrived on Saturday at dawn. She clued me in. June Guobadia had not used top-shelf relaxer. "She had it long that day? It's a wig, human hair. Chinese." Therri had done hair for almost every black person in San Marcos. I'd say, "You know that woman who works at the deli in the grocery store?" Therri did know her. I said, "I saw her at the park, and her little girl's hair is so smooth. Do they use a relaxer?" A hot-comb, Therri said. I told her about the woman at the JCPenney salon. Therri said, "She doesn't want to work, period. She thinks she runs things, but she runs her mouth." A woman at the library had nice hair, I said. Therri said, "It took me six hours to put her microbraids in."

Every eighth week, Therri sat in my living room. By this time, my mother had died suddenly. Clara Mae, my substitute-mother, had died—not suddenly, a slow, sad process. I'd cried so hard at her funeral, old grief unspooling, I heard people wondering aloud how I knew her. I'd driven with Marie to Galveston Island, to the weeping willow cemetery where Clara Mae had bought her plot, to watch her be buried. A few weeks later, braiding, Therri asked: "Have you accepted the Lord Jesus Christ as your personal savior?"

I believe in God and covert miracles—close enough. "Yes," I said. Therri felt called into people's homes to care for their hair and well-being, she said. She wanted children, but she wanted a husband first. June Guobadia found hers by meeting a Nigerian woman and marrying her brother so he could get a visa. "Look in the mirror," Therri said. "You could get a husband if you wanted." If I put dating at the top of my to-do list, I thought. Also: needle, haystack. Therri said that eligible women outnumbered eligible men. I said, "At our age, they're all married." Therri shrugged. "In prison. On drugs."

I tipped 30 percent. She gave me a doubtful look. I said, "I want to be your best client." She said, "You worry me because you worry about hair all the time. Hair is hair." Easy for her to say. I spent not just Saturday every other month watching Therri braid, but also the Thursday and Friday nights before, unbraiding. I'd unbraid until my Marie's head hurt, and my hands ached. When Therri got ready to go and wrote down our next appointment, I'd stop worrying for two months. She'd hug me, pray for me. She wore perfume, Moondrops by Avon, that rubbed off on me, and all day I felt better, anointed.

She had custody of a one-year-old nephew. The nephew's mother had made bad life choices. Therri brought him along. For awhile, she had temporary custody of a ten-year-old niece. They loved my house—doilies, knickknacks, scattered toys, burgeoning vines and flowers in the yard. Therri said, "You made decisions about your priorities. You get to a fork in the road," she added, "and you've got to choose. I used to be a b-i-t-c-h. I used to beat up other girls." The niece said, "It's important to hang around good people because it's easier to sink down than pull up." I was thinking this was good advice. I was thinking: it doesn't apply to me because I'm lucky, safer. This niece also said, as my daughter hollered "ouch" then, because Therri was braiding her temples, "Poor baby. Therri gets to talking, gets serious about some subject, especially the Lord Jesus, and the braids get tighter, tighter, like she's straightening out the world's problems on your head." Therri said, "You think that's true?" She seemed hurt. The niece said, "True."

The first time Therri came, she cut off the lank, permed hair and cornrowed extensions into my daughter's natural hair. Then she added forty or so minutes onto the procedure by hot-combing my daughter's hair so it would braid in smooth, though it kinked as soon as she got near water. One day Therri said, "If we're going to keep braiding, it would be easier for you taking it out and me putting it in if I'd use relaxer for a few minutes." Not again, I thought. But I'd already made mistakes. What if Therri stopped coming? Therri got on her knees beside my daughter's bathtub and put relaxer in.

One day Therri was packing up. I asked for our appointment in eight weeks. She looked at her calendar. "That's my vacation." I asked: the week after? She said, "I'm doing a wedding, a bride and four bridesmaids." We looked at the week before, but Marie and I would be at a conference. I said, "What will I do?" Therri said, "You can't have just one hairdresser—it's not a good position for any black woman to be in. There's someone working at a salon now, out by the movie theater." In San Marcos, she meant: a fleeting phantom someone. Once an entire salon for black hair opened and closed in two weeks. The JCPenney woman lasted three months. Someone would be doing black hair at Supercuts and, by the time I'd call for an appointment, she'd have quit. I found four salons near the movie theater. I went to them one by one until I found a black woman, Nomie.

She looked good. She looked fly. She said, "I don't believe in relaxing a child's hair." Fickle, disloyal, I threw over Therri in an instant, no decent goodbye, and now I was talking trash. I murmured, "Me neither, but our last stylist didn't braid curly hair." Nomie said, "I'll cut off the relaxed hair, add extensions that are rough and kinky so they blend. Her hair will grow. When it's long, I'll teach you to do free-form twists, no extensions, no braiding." I knew enough to know putting Marie's hair in twists all over her head would take an hour plus, and if I wrapped them in a do-rag at night they'd last a few days, at most. But I like Marie's hair. I hated burying it under fake hair, $5.99 a bag.

Nomie's salon was Miss Francis and Friends. Miss Francis and Friends were white women doing busloads of old ladies from the nursing home. Miss Francis, progressive, had said yes to being the only integrated salon, black and white clients staring at each other. But Nomie's clients would stop by to socialize. One came to show Nomie the car she bought. Another to say she'd fallen back in love with the father of her baby. I watched Miss Francis pick up an empty soda bottle, turn down the radio, rearrange a chair Nomie's friend had disarranged. Miss Francis made new rules. People without appointments couldn't sit. No food, no drink, no radio. But if you spend a span of hours with a person, a span that recurs, recurs, as hair grows, and life spirals forward, you talk, eat, grieve, celebrate. Nomie whispered, "Miss Francis doesn't know that in cities salons stay open twenty-four hours, TV on, fridge stocked. Hair isn't separate from life."

A woman walked in one day, shouting that her kitchen looked nappy, and she had a date on Friday. Nomie walked over, shushed the woman so she wouldn't upset Miss Francis, and made her an appointment. Once the woman left, Nomie said, "Hair is the black woman's anorexia. A white woman who is always 'My butt is so big in this dress' is having the same insane-in-the-brain feeling a black woman gets when she looks at her hair."

The only black stylist in a salon for miles, Nomie was swamped. I'd make an appointment for Saturday at nine, and Nomie would be behind and couldn't get Marie in the chair until eleven. Or we had an after-school appointment—Nomie told us to come back later. We went to the park, to dinner, back to the salon. Marie slept through the braiding, and we got home at midnight. I learned tricks: making an appointment for 7:30 a.m. Saturday. How far behind could Nomie be yet? Columbus Day—most clients were working, but it was a school holiday for us. By now, I carried my thermal lunch sack everywhere. If Miss Francis was in the salon, I ate outside. I slipped Marie little bits of food.

Once, at a late-in-the-day appointment, all the white ladies gone home, Nomie told me to stay inside to eat. She said, "The look on your face says to me that meat is the last thing you want right now." One sign my blood sugar is diving is the thought of food making me sick, but the only cure is to swallow past the queasiness. Then Nomie said she'd sent her daughter to live with her mother. "Girls can get messed up so early," she said. She had a husband—ex-husband, they'd divorced to improve her credit rating—named Kareem. She called him Kreem. "Curdled Kreem, my feelings for him have gone off."

I got to know Nomie when I wasn't used to being sick, and I didn't understand how sick, and I had a useless boyfriend, and then later I didn't. Nomie said, "Start dating again as soon as you feel well." At my daughter's next appointment, eight weeks later, I'd had my surgery, and I spent hours at the salon. I kept leaving messages for the surgeon, but only his nurse called back. Nomie said, "Too polite. Don't apologize to some nurse-flunky you feel bad. Yell at them they did something wrong in that operating room."

My hometown doctor reminded me that surgery taxes the adrenal gland. Crying is an adrenal gland problem. Next, my daughter had the growth spurt the ENT surgeon thought she'd have, though the surgeon had never warned me about side effects, and now some new doctor was laying down a new prognosis, elephant man disease, and I was driving home, rain on the windshield inseparable from my adrenal problem, but I didn't let Marie in back know I was crying with the windshield, the wipers, and Marie's hair looked messy, so I called Nomie, who said, "You okay? You made an appointment for yesterday."

At home, at the salon, time passed by anyway. Come Christmas break, I'd unbraid the fake hair, and Nomie would teach me to style my daughter's real hair. I'd started dating again. I dated a nice man who wasn't interesting—no ideas and feats to arouse and inspire, too many clichés. I dated an interesting man who wasn't nice. Nomie said, "Seems to me you are starting to like the not-nice man. Just get good attention and fancy dinners until someone fine shows up." Then, on a Friday the thirteenth, I met a man who was kind and smart. After a few weeks of dating, I arranged for Marie to stay with a friend, so I could spend a night with him. What did I think? Ideas and feats to arouse and inspire. Would the feeling last? Not in my experience. But you ride it out. Use it up.

Nomie, braiding, frowning, said, "Mark my words, he could be the one." I rolled my eyes and said: "What's your favorite kind of movie?" She said, "Romantic um . . ." I said, "Romantic comedies. Don't mistake this for that." Nomie sighed. Her husband—technically, ex-husband—had swung a hammer at her head. "Life isn't a comedy," she agreed, "but I say you keep going out with this interesting man until you find a reason not to."

At the same time, Marie started first grade with a teacher famous for a rocking chair in her classroom in which she comforted anxious children, but she didn't let Marie near. Marie, ashamed, didn't tell me. The woman who'd been my sitter when Marie was a baby had a grandson in the same classroom. She phoned to tell me her grandson had said the teacher put Marie in the hall every day for asking for hugs, and Marie stood there and cried. I made an appointment with the teacher. I walked in, and she said, "I am not racist."

I said, "I wasn't thinking of race." Unless you are, I thought. She told me Marie was clingy. Yes. Marie had known my mother, who died. She'd watched Clara Mae dying. Since my surgery, Marie kept asking me when I'd die. I tried to tell this to the teacher, who was too officious or angry to listen. I get paralyzed around angry people—my instinct to hold still, play dead, wait it out, too ingrained. And I'd already had trouble with a preschool teacher who'd insisted something was wrong with Marie. "Early childhood nutritional deficit," she'd say, implying Marie had been removed from a negligent birth mother. I'd remind her I'd had Marie since birth, but the preschool teacher always forgot. She'd say "disorganized brain system" or "abnormal cognition" every time we spoke. But right now Marie's first grade teacher said, "She's started out with tough breaks, God knows." She shuddered. "But she has to buck up and remake herself."

I thought: my only hope now is the principal.

I went home. My interesting new boyfriend, Gary, called to ask about my day. When I told him what happened with Marie's teacher, he said, "She's definitely making assumptions based on the fact your daughter is adopted. Or black. I guess a kid could seek hugs in a disruptive way. But I'd think the teacher would tell the parent first, not discipline the child." I thought so too. But sometimes you need someone to tell you what you already know. I mentioned I had an appointment with the principal. Gary said, "Be firm but euphemistic. Don't be the first person to suggest it's racism. Try to let the principal see for himself." This feels like co-parenting, I thought. Also: Get over it. It's not. I told him, "Thank you. I'm not naturally assertive." He laughed. "You? That's funny."

The next day I asked the principal to move Marie to another class, and he said he wouldn't until I met with the teacher again and he'd mediate. The teacher walked in and said, "I taught lots of black children in the most horrible schools in Louisiana, and I never had problems." The principal glanced at me, worried. A few minutes later, the teacher crossed her arms and said, "You, a teacher, should know better than to question me, my intuition." She stalked off. The principal transferred Marie to a new class and thanked me for my patience. I took Marie with me when I left because school pictures were two days away, and I wanted Nomie to redo the braids on just Marie's temples and nape, her kitchen.

Nomie was running behind.

Twenty minutes in the chair turned to hours in the salon, a late night getting home.

I was tired the next day, and I taught until 10:00 p.m., then drove into the country, fifteen miles past my house, to my new sitter who'd take Marie at night, but only at her house, not mine. I picked up Marie, who sleepwalked to the car. In the dark, her hair looked odd. The first day, a hairdo is elegant, but her head feels tender. Then her head feels fine and her hair looks great until, bit by bit, braids get thick, jagged. Edges loosen. Braids on the short hairs, the temples and kitchen, slide out. When I got home and put her in bed, I turned on the light. She'd pulled out the braids in her kitchen. Near the end of a hairdo, she'd sometimes tug on these braids when—because of new growth—they'd dangle, tweak. The hair in the kitchen is short. Braids slip right out. But Nomie had put these in next to the scalp, tight. Marie's kitchen was plucked bald, leftover tufts fluffy as down.

She opened her eyes. Before I knew it, I said, "You pulled out your hair." She thought I meant fake hair. She didn't understand yet she'd pulled out real hair. She was no doubt confused: real and fake hair intertwined for years. "Didn't it hurt?" I asked. She said, "The new braids hurt. I wanted them out." Upset, I flipped off the light. I went to my computer, read an email from Gary: "I hope you had a good class." I'd been dating him eight weeks. He didn't know much about even white women's hair care. But in eight weeks I'd already spent hours at Nomie's. I wrote: "Marie pulled out some of her hair. In the struggle to be the white woman whose black daughter has good hair, I concede."

I went back to Marie's room, turned the light on, lifted her braids, looked at her kitchen. Whose fault was it I'd devolved to a strategy so overwrought? In five years, we'd passed through three centuries of bright ideas about black hair care in America. Strangers had shared secret lore. I'd gone to two cities, the ghetto, the born-again edge, the incompletely-integrated hair care hospice, Miss Francis and Friends,

trying to give my daughter the little girl styles—pigtails, ponytails—
her friends and her black Barbies wore.

In one of my worst parenting moments ever, I found a package of
fake hair left from the days of Therri, got Marie out of bed with the irrational plan I could put some hair back on her head. Or maybe I just
wanted her to look good for school pictures in the morning. I couldn't
accept that I'd spent another year braiding and unbraiding, growing
out hair, and now this. Marie has seen me lose my cool before, for ex-
ample, the day she drew on the bathroom wall with markers. Or that
time she undid her plaits and threw barrettes all over the car. That
night I fumbled with fake hair, fingered wispy clumps of real hair.
Then my helplessness surged. I took scissors I'd been using to cut fake
hair into lengths and chopped the fake hair into bits. It's not what you
wish for in a mother—someone crying and hacking up packaged,
fake hair in the middle of the night. I stopped, apologized.

I put her to bed.

I went to bed myself and prayed: God, make me a better mother.
Help.

In the morning, I drove Marie to school, to school pictures, with
a wide headband covering her bald spot. When I came back I had
a phone message from my old friend Jack Creeden. The message:
"Debra, I dreamed about you last night—at two, because I woke and
looked at the clock—in the dream you said, *Jack, get in touch, I'm
alone and not okay.*"

But I called Nomie first, told her about Marie's hair. Nomie said, "I
did the same thing last fall. I got mad taking out my weave and yanked
my bangs right out." What did you do? I asked. She said, "Same as you
did for Marie. I wore a headband until it grew out."

I hung up because I had a call coming in from Gary. I explained to
him my cryptic email, but I didn't mention my freak-out: scissors, fake
hair. I did say I'd had insomnia and prayed—for help sleeping, I said—
and that in the morning, when I got back from taking Marie to school,
my friend Jack Creeden in Georgia had phoned to say he'd dreamed
I wasn't okay. Gary knew who Jack was because I'd mentioned him,
described him. "Funny," Gary said, "that God turns out to be a semi-
alcoholic poet with a big heart."

A month later I was buying groceries. I looked up and saw Marie talking to a woman in waist-length microbraids, I thought, like regular braids but ever more likely to pull your hair out by the roots. The woman said, "I was complimenting your daughter on her dooky braids and pretty headband." I stared, infatuated. This woman didn't have braids. These were solid, airy, delicate, porous—long ribbons of coiled hair. I sighed. "Your hair. It's beautiful." She said, "Sisterlocks. Not dreadlocks. Tiny squares all over the head. The hair gets twisted with a hook. You leave it alone, let it coil like it wants. It takes a long time to do the first time, but then it's easy. Mine was short at first, but it grew and grew." I remembered books I'd read about natural hair styles. I said, "You must have had it done in New York, or Los Angeles. Or Dallas?" She said, "Two people in Texas are doing this style—one is on the Gulf Coast, the other in Austin, Mr. Day."

Mr. Brand New Day, I sometimes call him.

The same place serving up cant and half-truths might one day serve the truth, I thought. I'd met this woman at the same store where I'd met June Guobadia, who'd sent me to Therri, who sent me to Nomie. As Mr. Day recently did a bi-monthly, one-hour tune-up on Marie's hair, I asked, "How did she find you, that woman who told me about you."

He said, "Who? Oh. Belinda. She heard me on talk radio, a call-in show. She heard me say there is no hairdo besides an Afro if you want it short, or locks if you want it long. You can straighten, extend, weave, braid, but your hairline will creep higher, and your hair will get thin." He started to get mad. "White people look fine. Black people look fine. But black people trying to look white are handicapped from the start. It took Belinda months to decide. You had five years of bad ideas. Other people have heard bad hair ideas since they were born, which their mothers had heard from their mothers, and so on."

When I went to him for the initial consultation, he'd unbraided a few braids and said, "You are to be complimented for not using relaxers." I didn't tell him I'd only just stopped. "But this artificial hair," he said, "stays in because it is sharp. It digs into the hair. This idea hair grows because you have it braided instead of using relaxers is wrong. Some hair grows. The rest rips. And no wonder your little girl pulled out her hair. Would you like something so scratchy rubbing against your scalp?" The first session, he said, when he'd lock the whole head, make coils from quarter-inch sized squares, would take a full Saturday and a half-Sunday. He'd bring a DVD player. He'd lock hair as long as my daughter could stand it. We could leave and come back. "So what will it cost?" I asked.

First session, one-time outlay: he named the price.

I winced. What I'd earn for teaching a week-long class at a conference.

But the maintenance would cost the same as I spent on braids.

I went home. When Gary called me to ask how my day was, I told him about the appointment with Mr. Day. It was a big deal, I said. I felt confused. I needed his advice, I added. He said, "I'm sure I won't be any help with beauty decisions." I said, "It's a lifestyle and economic decision." He listened as I described cost, upkeep. Once the locks were in, every other month I'd take her to Mr. Day and he'd spend maybe an hour twisting new growth—as opposed to the three days of unbraiding, rebraiding. Gary has a son. He's used to the perpetual decisions, your child's future contingent on this or that instant new option. He said, "I think you should try it. You can't keep chasing after that Nomie."

When the long Saturday and half-Sunday were over, Mr. Day laid down his tools. "Done." My daughter charged out the front door of the salon and danced on the sidewalk. Her eyes sparkled. Her hair was short, spiky. The hair on the nape of her head had started to grow back, and Mr. Day had locked the sections that were long enough and trimmed the rest. I looked at her angular cheekbones, the beautiful shape of her head, her elegant neck. Her hair looked good and wouldn't dishevel. It would get better, better. We'd met Mr. Day's twenty-year-old daughter who'd worn locks since she was Marie's age, and her locks were past her shoulders, thick and lush. I asked Marie, "How does it feel?"

Dancing under a tree in sunlight, she said, "Like I don't even have hair."

I shuddered. "All those years of making her head hurt."

Mr. Day said, "You did what you were told. Forgive yourself. Maybe you should have a ceremony—go home and make a bonfire out of pink stuff and braid-spray and acrylic hair." Marie was listening. She told Mr. Day, "Once, in the middle of the night, my mom woke me up and yelled at me and cried and cut up fake hair. She scared me."

Mr. Day looked at me

"I temporarily lost my mind," I said, "that night she pulled out her hair."

He said, "Lots of that going around. I've seen worse."

Now he's done Marie's hair for longer than Therri or Nomie. I knew them well, the special prayer Therri had put in for a husband, her high hopes for her nephew and niece, and I'd listened as Nomie planned to take her kids and escape her husband/ex-husband. And Therri and Nomie knew me too. I had more money, a stable future, but the years of my life that overlapped their lives were hard. I'd never know Mr. Day that way.

I wouldn't spend as much time with him.

The issues that make hair decisions daunting for black women— that the style you choose signifies whether you've opted for an assimilationist ideal or not—weren't mine. My motherhood felt so public. As Nomie said, hair isn't separate from life. As Therri's niece said about Therri's braiding: sometimes you work out the world's problems on someone's head. Marie's hairstyle was one of the first places the odd small talk landed. White people told me, unbidden, if they did or didn't like Marie's hair. Black people felt more bold. Marie's hair was as totemic as hair in books that described the ancient African styles: it was a symbol of a well-run motherhood. I believed the proverb that it takes a village to raise a child, and I misconstrued it too. I thought of my unincorporated village, its environs—if this village was going to help, the village had to see us as well-kept, normal. And I'd been trying to please black and white people simultaneously, an impossibility.

I remembered my first days with Marie, when she was only weeks old, the last days before my semester started, the campus full of students and parents who'd helped them move in, and I was toting Marie in her car seat, waiting for an elevator near a mother and daughter with identical hairdos. Back then, I'd have guessed that a stylist coated their hair with sheen, put tiny braids in, then made braid-ringlets with a curling iron. I now know a stylist hid their real hair in a coil like a braided rug, then attached glossy, pre-curled, fake braids. The mother looked down at Marie, startled. She said, "That tiny baby has such a huge head of hair, at first I thought she was a doll and wondered why anyone would carry a doll in a car seat." At the time I was just proud. I said, "She is tiny. Her hair is great." The mother leaned close, dubious, to assess its greatness.

For most people, black hair is two subjects tangled, cosmetology (how to make a style) and American history (what style means). I'd stumbled into a long argument about old shame: what it means to be black, broken, and fighting for respect. Watching Marie dance on the sidewalk, I thought how finding a way to let her hair be, each lock a perfect helix, meant I had the how-to part handled. Now I had get to work on shame, old and otherwise.

First Date Jitters

To revisit the worst moments, instead of moving toward the blank-slate future, the repression of past pain that's theoretically good for you, let me mention three boyfriends as interchangeable as The Three Tenors. All wore beards. One might be taller or shorter, weigh a few pounds more or less, come from a different country, but they sang one song: self-made, self-obsessed. When I was with one of them, I tended not to notice my self, just his. If I try to understand what I hadn't learned yet, how I was good at my job, at cooking, sewing, building a house, how I was a decent enough mother, how I'd remade myself in every context except the context of sex and love where it's too easy to relive your inherited family muddle, I think about the one, two, three penultimate boyfriends who, like three slaps across the heroine's face in an old movie, woke me from a hysterical dream.

The dream began after my mother died.

Marie needed surgery then, and this specialist or that.

Because Marie and I are a two-person family, we're symbiotic: mutual adoration, mutual need. And Marie was little. She didn't understand my distraction. When I did sleep, I dreamed about my mother. Once, in broad daylight, I saw her on the other side of a window, cleaning it with a white rag. *Surrender*. I told Jana I'd seen my dead mother again, and Jana said, "Stress." Jana was adopted—a happy childhood, she'd emphasize, great parents, conventionally idyllic memories—but after years of wondering, searching, Jana had found her birth mother, who was kind too, but bohemian: a hipster, not a hippie, she'd told Jana. Then Jana's birth mother died, no warning. Stress, I thought. It fractures the world, and we glimpse the big beyond. My mother died in late March. By May, I had bronchitis, strep throat, pink eye. I took antibiotics. I lay on the couch so tired I'd have to will myself to stand, cook, run Marie's bath. I got over the bronchitis, strep throat, pink eye. Then I got rashes, thirst, numbness, passing fits of stupidity and fear.

The first time I fainted, my head clunked down on a coffee mug that left a moon-shaped welt on my forehead. The second time I was in the parking lot at the Baptist preschool. When I came to, the janitor stood over me. I called my hometown doctor who insisted—grasping at straws—we rule out a panic attack. It seemed clear that the failure to sustain consciousness was making me panic, yes. But not the reverse: panic wasn't making me pass out. Even so, he said to breathe in a paper bag for five minutes and call back. Embarrassed, I asked the janitor for a paper bag. Inflate, deflate, inflate . . . five minutes.

I couldn't stand without holding the janitor's arm.

Then he brought me peanut butter crackers. A few minutes later I felt calm, steady. That part stayed consistent. I'd eat. I'd feel fine. An hour and or two later, objects blurred. At the edge of my vision, pin-prick stars blinked then disappeared. I turned dangerous. I ran red lights. Once, a state trooper signaled me to pull over for miles before I looked in the rearview and knew it. I ate all day. I woke and ate in the night. My weight fell, fell. I tried a new doctor who, after five minutes of conversation about symptoms, glanced at my daughter playing with toys in the corner. "Is her father sick?"

"I don't know. She's adopted."

"She's not your biological child?"

I thought I'd just said this. "Yes."

"I'll do an HIV test anyway."

Then a three day wait: negative. Another appointment. "Antidepressants?" he suggested.

A few months later, I tried a doctor at a clinic named The Whole

Woman's Wellness Center. She asked if I'd ever been in an abusive relationship. Surprised, I said, "Um, yes. About ten years ago." She pointed at Marie. "How about now, the baby's father?"

I made an appointment with another doctor, and this time I slipped in a reference to adoption right away. I hate doing this—it means I'm not challenging the implied racial stereotypes. But it does head off digressions. For instance, a police officer once pulled me over for failing to dim my lights, shone his flashlight in my face, then my daughter's, asked if I'd been drinking and, before I answered, said: "Whose kid is that?" I said, "Mine." Silence. "Adopted," I added. He nodded, then asked where I worked and lived. Once we established I was a professor, a homeowner, a taxpayer, he let me go. So I went to this new doctor and said, "The dizziness started about two years after I adopted my daughter."

This sounded illogical, as if I were suggesting cause-and-delayed-effect. I was naked except for my paper gown. I reached for Marie who was trying to lift the lid on the HAZARDOUS BIOLOGICAL WASTE can. My paper gown flew open, and my daughter said, "Oops, I can see your breast." Except she said bweast. This doctor also ordered an HIV test. I said, "But I just had one—it was negative." He said, "Don't take offense. This is standard for mystery ailments." He paused. "Some illness is caused by anxiety. I guess you knew when you wanted to be a single mother it might be hard. It *is* hard."

But he referred me to a renowned endocrinologist who ordered a five-hour glucose test. I fainted during that test. The lab technicians rolled me to ER. Jana picked Marie up at day care, then me at the hospital. I ate fried chicken from a gas station on the way home. At my next appointment, the endocrinologist said he'd tell my insurance company I was diabetic with atypical manifestations. To me, he said, "Your blood sugar drops are so out-of-sync with your lab work, I'm stumped. All I can say is to eat protein six to eight times daily. I doubt this is life-threatening. But it is odd. And I kid you not," he added, "eating this often to stay conscious won't be fun. It'll be a herky-jerky way of life."

So I went to work, to Marie's school, the playground. Also to the grocery store—protein procuring. I was teaching, writing, trying to be a good mother, and I'd think: Pork, beef, eggs, fish, chicken.

Fresh, frozen, thawing, cooked. Jana—a mother of two, overworked, strapped for cash, and worried about Noah's future besides: how he'd fare as an adult once Jana was gone, and then too much responsibility would fall to Zoey—pointed out that people can't live by food alone. As a massage therapist, she said, she had unique insight into the fact people need sex to feel healthy. She had a man friend who proposed to her every third week or so, and she'd set him straight. "If it's too hard for you to be in this relationship that's just physical," she'd say, "okay." She told me: "If you don't have sex, you carry tension in your heels." She reached over and pinched my heel.

I'd been celibate since I was a mother, a choice.

A geographical inevitability too.

A woman I met at Marie's preschool had asked me to her son's birthday party. "Bring your daughter, of course. But you come, for margaritas." She introduced me to her husband's cousin who'd moved here—back to extended family—from L.A., where he'd gone to a music industry vo-tech school. "I had my hair long and permed," he said. "My stage name was Medusa." I said, "Interesting you chose a woman's name." He looked puzzled. "Medusa," I said, "the goddess." He waved his hands in the air and said, "Snakes. My point is snakes." The hostess patted his arm and said, "His IQ is off the chart." He tapped his back pocket. "Card-carrying member of Mensa," he told me. When the cake was cut, the candles blown, the hostess pulled me aside. "So what do you think?"

Maybe educated men in the nearest city, Austin? My friend in Florida, Sofia, had searched the on-line personals for me. She worried I was sick and alone. Also, she's long-married, hasn't dated for years, and wanted to watch me. And she's a die-hard shopper. She got swept away: "I see you dating this paleontologist, and while he's on excavations you write. Then he comes back, and you two go to black-tie fundraisers together."

The email part, eflirting, would be easy. But the first lunch date (you have enough in common to correspond and now ascertain, in thirty seconds usually, if you can be attracted) meant I'd pay a sitter and drive for an hour. And I couldn't get past the lonely-hearts connotation. "Nonsense, this is a social technology that's come of age," Sofia said by phone. We bickered. Sofia: "What if a great man is out there, waiting?" Me: "I'm not marriage material. If you don't figure it out when you're young, chances get slim. Lifelong vows aren't everyone's goal. Men, for instance, have casual affairs." Sofia: "You just say that because you think you can't have love and respect." I said, "I don't *think*. I know." She said, "It won't hurt to start the ball rolling." She asked me to inspect profiles, she at her computer in Florida, me at mine in Texas. She passed on a tip she'd gleaned watching *Sex and the City*. I objected. "This is Sex and the Country," I said.

So, in November that year, I was thinking about slim pickings. I was fretting about Thanksgiving besides. I have fantasies: a groaning table, generations of loved ones. My reality? A woman whose parents died in a car crash told me the way to get through holidays is do good deeds. So I invited people with nowhere to go, the orphaned and friendless. Days before Thanksgiving I bought a monstrous frozen turkey and, because it was thirty-six degrees outside, set it on the screened porch until I could rearrange my refrigerator. I was preoccupied. I forgot the turkey, even the day before Thanksgiving when it was seventy-eight, and I had doors and windows open so I could hear birds and wind chimes as I cooked yams, stuffing, beans, pie. I remembered it Thanksgiving morning: twenty-three pound food-poison colony. The stores were closing, not that they'd have thawed turkey. I rounded up hams, chickens, jammed them in the oven.

The meat roasted unevenly.

I cut off the cooked but tough parts to give to guests. People told polite and garbled lies—chewing rubbery meat—about how good it tasted. I gnawed raw parts myself and realized all at once I had no desire to eat with these people. They had terrible lives. I had a sudden food-chain insight. I was old. I was past tender myself. I'd developed a disease that forced me to eat protein all the time, though I don't like eating protein, which is to say flesh, eating flesh to save my flesh, my own flesh stringy and overdone like meat I'd served to guests, but also—in my mind, my sense of what I hadn't attained yet—also like the meat I was eating: raw, undone. I didn't understand love, not yet.

Too much input from Sofia. That's what I was thinking the next day as the phone rang.

"This is Seth Jones," a voice said. "We met last week."

I'd moderated a panel discussion at an arts event in Austin. The board member who'd called me pointed out I'd better donate time if I expected a spot to promote my own next book when it came out. My own next book was taking years to write; its coming out seemed a far-off dream. Seth grew up here, he'd said on the panel. "I'm an auto-didact," he'd added. A man in the audience had raised his hand and said, "Is that the Biblical word for masturbator?" Everyone laughed; I still don't know if it was a joke. Seth went on to say he'd been raised poor, fatherless. He was a journalist. His current address: Albania, former Soviet Republic. He'd come to the book festival to promote his first novel, a thriller with no comeuppance for the killers. He said the book was realistic because life has no justice. "But," I'd said, mod-erator-like, "you have energy, even a kind of gloating, in the violent scenes. You have what film critics call 'balletic' violence. Yes, pleasure in rape and murder is realistic for sociopaths. But what about your other readers?"

He said, "I wrote a good yarn."

On the phone a week later, Seth said, "I'm going back to Albania in a few days. I'd like to have more good conversation about books. Can you drive in and meet me for lunch?"

Driving to the city and home again would take hours. I said I didn't have time.

He said, "I called a friend in the area, a writer, and he told me you were a single mother. I raised my daughter alone. She's grown now. I have free time. I'll bring you dinner."

Someone would bring me meat? This seemed altruistic.

We sat at my kitchen table and ate ribs.

In the living room, Marie played a game I'd downloaded onto my new cell phone.

Talking about books, Seth offered this: He'd gone to the same high school as a Texas author famous for her racy memoir. They'd been lov-ers. I couldn't think how to answer, so I said I'd gone through a phase when reading tabloids had seemed like a nice antidote to heavy-duty reading I did for work. "And that's a staple," I said, "stories about a rel-atively unknown person having had sex with someone famous, before they turned famous."

He slapped his hand on the table. "I sound like a cad."

I put Marie to bed and suggested we sit in the living room. Seth said, "The couch is too narrow." I was slow on the uptake here. Seth had factored in schedule constraints: no time for "decent interval" conversation. Not that, pre-motherhood, I'd been known for getting well-acquainted. But I hadn't considered having sex with my daughter asleep a few rooms away. Everyone wants to be cherished. I hadn't been. But I understood stop-gap sex: being the site of attraction, the dangling silver and feather bauble the big fish snaps up. Me, the lure, eventually I get swallowed. But first I get the lead-up: Attention. Advantage. Power. I hadn't had sex since before Marie was born. She was four now. I was suffering from what nineteenth century doctors called "female hysteria." They prescribed site-specific massage—midwives did this at spas, the great Victorian vacation destination.

Seth rushed me to bed. I saw this as passion for me, not sexual heat releasing like lightning, random strike. And—an atavistic idea maybe—I feel unfeminine, i.e. the man seems unmasculine, if my desire exceeds his. But I didn't think about that, the sociology of lust, when I locked my bedroom door. Marie woke and knocked on the door.

Seth ran for the closet and crouched, naked—slapstick comedy, in retrospect, since the moral to every story he told was his own courage while skiing the Himalayas or escaping the Russian Mafia. (Was this fiction? Posturing after favorite authors?) Finally, Marie went to sleep, and I put on my glasses to check the expiration date on the condoms. When we said goodbye, Seth kissed my face and shoulders. I felt dramatic as Jane Eyre in the arms of Mr. Rochester, that is, if Jane Eyre had thought this: *get out before my daughter sees me kissing you while wearing this chemise I likely wouldn't have put on until next summer because it's cold now.* He kissed me twenty times, said I was lovely, that we'd had amazing sex, at his age. He said, "I usually don't find it happens like this now. I'll be back in April. When I've felt like this in the past, I've ended up married."

He called when his plane landed in Albania.

He called Christmas Day. He spent New Year's writing me a love letter. I would have dated someone else if someone had materialized. But I scanned the countryside as I made my usual runs: work, grocery store, playground. Lacking corporeal romance, I found the epistolary version enthralling, like keeping a journal that talked back, albeit an opinionated, crotchety journal with a machismo complex and social class anxiety. He liked fighting about what was good writing, genre novels, or obscure books I loved (and wrote).

One night I sat with my laptop on the porch, listening to the first cicada. A snake slithered by. A baby possum, pale, hairless, reared and spit before scampering off. It had been two years since I got the phone call that told me my mother might not live through the night. Seth wrote he was coming to Texas and bringing his Albanian girlfriend. He hadn't told me before because it seemed unlikely her visa would get approved and, if it didn't, he'd wanted to see me. I wrote back that he hadn't lied, but he'd hadn't been kind. Yes, and he regretted the invitation the instant he'd blurted it to Zarza, poor thing, raised under Communist rule, eager to see the U.S., he replied in a last over-wrought prose outbreak.

All those letters. Sex, once.

The last man who'd wooed me in person didn't have teeth. I'd hired him to build a short stretch of fence. He'd said, "You're a fine-looking woman, but you need more makeup." If, reader, you're thinking *all that wasted on a rounder in a foreign country when she could have put her letter-writing to local use*, me too. I wanted a boyfriend to drive to.

Writing the profile came easy—why I'd date me.

I wasn't ready for the wish-you'd-deleted-it-before-reading-it re-plies. Some mentioned penis size, that the letter-writer wasn't single, or de-euphemized the stated profession: if his profile said he was an "engineer," an email might clarify that he in fact fixed plumbing at a Holiday Inn. I eliminated most immediately. Then I ventured forth, lunch.

Sofia had sent me a hip-looking, thermal-lined tote, and before en-tering the restaurant I'd wolf down a preemptive bit of meat. I was dizzy. Nerve-wracking preparation—setting up a time, a sitter. Tweez-ing, combing, powdering, painting. Since getting sick, I'd dropped three dress sizes. My clothes were new. Who was I? I learned to turn off my cell phone too—Sofia might forget we lived in different time zones and call me during lunch. Once she did, and I'd automatically answered my phone, thinking it might be Marie's preschool. Sofia's voice, loud, impatient, fired off questions my date pretended not to hear: "So, did you like him? Who picked up the tab? What did you wear?"

I ate lunch with a man who'd sounded like a rare book dealer but was a fired state employee. An MBA who said I'd look better with flat bangs and reached across the table to flatten them. A physicist, Norwegian, thrilled to meet a woman in the arts, he said, because he needed more right-brain experiences. He sounded well-off because he talked about a house in the city with enough acreage he was beset by the deers, he said, their droppings.

Then Joseph.

His life story was a collage—certain moments vivid, but the connections between them blanks he wouldn't fill. He'd been chief technical officer for the biggest high-tech company in Austin, which crashed when all high-tech companies crashed. Now he was living on savings, working on patents. He had a ten-year-old daughter—waifish, surly, relieved to have me interpreting the mores of *female* and *middle-class*. Once, she had a friend over who cut her knee and, though the friend's parents had insurance, Joseph wanted to sew it with thread because that's how he'd fixed wounds as a kid when his mother would leave him alone weeks on end while she lived with a rock and roll band in Paris.

Facts: He had an accent. He'd also had a car wreck when he was twenty, his jawbone rebuilt from a scrap of hip. His enunciation was both meticulous and slurred.

Slurred facts. At times I thought I misunderstood. I woke him once because I was leaving his house to get Marie at the sitter's, then go home. He said, "I love you." Later, he had a cold, a fever. He said, "I love you." I told him I loved him too. He said, "Too?" He didn't remember he'd said it. When I recounted both times, he shook his head. "The sleeping brain, the fevered brain," he said, "knows more than the daily brain."

One day I made Sunday dinner. Joseph and I and our daughters walked to the river to swim. I was standing in gentle currents when Joseph's daughter, Yvette, started rolling her eyes in a specific direction. She'd done this at dinner because she didn't like cucumbers.

Joseph looked alarmed, dove across the water's surface, swam to Marie—five years old and dog-paddling. She was in a tiny eddy caused by water coursing around a tree. Anyone who didn't know that the river is shallow, or that Marie is naturally athletic and sets up endurance tests for herself, would have thought she was drowning. Joseph wrapped his arm around her chest and swam hard for shore. His feet scraped the bottom. He stood up, holding her. Water came to his knees. "I did not realize." He'd reacted automatically, he said, because he'd learned lifesaving when he joined the navy at age fourteen.

We came back from the river, sat under the oak trees, crickets chirping, and he told me it had been a perfect day. Yvette said, "Do you remember that day I visited you at Shoal Creek Hospital?" Joseph glanced at me. I knew the name from TV and newspapers, a mental health facility. He'd grieved his ex-wife exceedingly, he told me. I had questions. I asked them carefully. "How could you tell you needed to go?" He waited until Yvette and Marie wandered off. He said, "I was required by the court after the police intervened in my suicide. I went on a short course of antidepressants, very efficacious. I came to see what my wife had done was wrong, also that she is human, not ideal."

I called Sofia that night and told her, "Time to cash in."

She said, "Is he suffering from depression still?"

"He said he wasn't." I'd asked him.

Sofia said, "Everyone has bad luck. People change. He deserves happiness too."

This idea—the disadvantaged need my love, too—took me aback. I regressed. Back when my parents were married, barely, my dad said: "Your boyfriends are stray dogs." I'd grown up in a backwater man's town, logging and hunting. My first date, at age fourteen, was riding from country bar to country bar on the back of a borrowed snowmobile driven by a boy old enough, nineteen, to buy me drinks. We'd stop the engine on forest trails—the temperature minus-twenty, perhaps—to smoke pot out of a little stone. I'd inhale and stare at the sky, its ice-like stars, and remember a story about somebody's cousin who'd died of hypothermia. Later, we'd go to a hunting shack and kiss and wrestle, unzipping this or that part of our snowmobile suits for selective access. On the other hand, I went to church. The New Testament seemed true. It wasn't that God or his mouthpiece said so. I believed with every cell that if someone had less you shared yours: your luck, your godsends. Boys I loved had bad lives. By the time I hit mid-adolescence, season of hormones and sorrow, I was the Mother Teresa of Heavy Petting.

Not that I mistook spending the night with Joseph as the dawn of a new day. I didn't bother with hope. Sex, on the other hand, doesn't have to be explained. "You must tell me," Joseph said when we met, "what it is you like to do." I'd said, "You have to feed me. Otherwise I pass out. Dinner is a good start." In my hick town, if I chatted in the Baptist preschool parking lot with mothers in their SUVs, they complained their husbands wanted sex all the time. "He thinks about it all day, every day," one mother said.

I thought: I'm a man then. Or Jeannie C. Riley in "Harper Valley PTA." If it came up in parking lot conversation that my daughter had a sleepover that night and I had a date, I felt like a teenager answering to parents. The mothers asked: what does he do? will he be a good father? All I thought was: who *doesn't* like sex? I just wanted to go home, put on my clothes and makeup to have it all pulled off or smudged later. I wanted more.

But not much time passed before I realized I didn't want to get a sitter every weekend. I used a sitter for work. I wanted to be with Marie on weekends. Joseph had full-time custody too. So Marie and I spent Saturdays with Joseph and Yvette. Marie complained about Joseph's accent. I explained what an accent is—traces of a language you used to speak. I said, "He didn't grow up with English." Marie said, "Can he speak Normalish now?" Yvette, who was embarrassed of her father, his foreignness, laughed: "Normalish."

There aren't rules for this, I thought.

Articles I'd stumbled on in women's magazines in doctors' waiting rooms said to have date-nights when your ex-husband has visitation, and not to introduce your child to your date until marriage seems imminent. But I didn't want marriage. I didn't have an ex-husband with visitation. I wondered aloud about this to Lauren one evening, as we sat on my front porch. She'd been out walking, saw me in the yard and wandered up. As we talked, I heard strains of Mozart, lilting, brilliant, which Marie liked to listen to while she fell asleep. "Don't forget my Mozart," she'd say, tumbling into bed, reaching toward me, a kiss.

Outside, fireflies flashed against the shadows. Lauren, who worked for a county agency that monitored impoverished mothers, waved her hand, dismissive. "You're a successful, smart woman who happens to be single. You're not a nun. You're teaching Marie how it's done. You're showing her what dating is—a way of deciding if someone is right. Someone has to model this behavior for her." What if I don't model it well? I worried. I didn't say so because, at the moment, Lauren's life was hard. Her job was uncertain: more budget cuts, salary reductions. She'd had to sell off a piece of property that had been in the family for years. Her brother had died of liver failure after years of family intervention. "I'd better hurry home and practice my stress relief there," she said, sardonic.

Months passed like that.

Dating with children.

Then a year. And Joseph needed a windfall. He worked longer, later: get-rich schemes.

When we were together, I cooked. I had to feed myself, the children, and Joseph, who was skipping meals. I'd spend hours rationalizing blood sugar drops. I should have had more meat that time, I'd think. That last snack was too small. One night Yvette was at a friend's. I got a sitter for Marie, so Joseph and I could go to a restaurant—special occasion, my treat—and Joseph was late. Crossing the parking lot, I staggered. "You are here and suddenly not here," Joseph said. "If I didn't know it was medical, I'd assume your trouble was," he paused, searching for the precise French/English syllabic overlap, "psychiatric."

That night he found leftover exotic liquor he'd bought when he traveled the world. He got drunk, showed me his military ID with its photo of his little boy face, scared eyes, bruised face. In France, the Army can be your legal guardian if you sign up, self-indenture, attend its school. Scraps of poetry ran through my head: *stunned by a concrete tit at birth.* I understood his emptiness. Joseph rambled on about his mother, his ex-wife, what one, then another, said, did. If this were a story, they'd be redundant. Except life had handed him his mother, and he loved his wife because she was familiar, akin.

I knew we should break up. But Joseph got called for a third interview for a good job, so I postponed. And my body felt weirder. I especially noticed this during sex. Cords like taut rubber bands thrummed. Neither a pleasant nor unpleasant feeling, but new.

And one day I had a blood sugar drop within minutes of eating. Then I started bleeding. Not a hemorrhage. "Dysfunctional," the doctor said. I told him about my unstable blood sugar, also the bleeding, but I didn't describe the webbed, elastic sensation during sex because I didn't want mental health queries and HIV tests I was certain would follow.

I felt confused, my loneliness or helplessness indistinguishable from my meatlessness, craving. The doctor sent me to a gastroenterologist, a gynecologist, a new endocrinologist because the famous one was dead. I saw MRI, CT scan, and ultrasound technicians too—all of them in pale uniforms with serene faces like members of a sect. It takes weeks to make appointments, take the tests, wait for your doctor to call. My tests: inconclusive. Not to revisit the site of trauma. *Revisit*. But it is part of my love story, so-called.

I scheduled exploratory surgery for early January.

Meanwhile, Thanksgiving was the next day. Two years had passed since I'd eaten undercooked meat with near-strangers. I cooked slowly, carefully. I remembered to put the turkey in the refrigerator. I made cornbread-chestnut dressing, watercress soup, sweet potatoes, all ready to reheat. Joseph and his daughter would arrive at six to spend the night.

For Thanksgiving Eve, I'd made tortellini—Joseph's daughter's favorite. My phone rang, Yvette asking me if we could go bowling. I told her that with dinner and the long drive we wouldn't get back until after midnight. She didn't care, Yvette said. She liked to sleep in the day. Thanksgiving was an American holiday anyway. I said I'd made her favorite food, and that I didn't feel well. I hung up. My phone rang again. Joseph, yelling: "Why are you so selfish you can't go bowling? She has been here all day bored."

He'd been scheduled that day to find out if he'd gotten the good job. He'd never yelled before. I said, "You two can go bowling by yourselves." I was mealy-mouthed, light-headed. He said, "You, on top of all else I deal with. I am through." Then, in a meant-to-be gallant voice, he said he'd drive me to my surgery—as my ex-boyfriend, he stipulated.

"I'll think of someone," I said. I hung up.

Marie asked, "Mommy, when are Joseph and Yvette coming?"

I was hungry, ravenous. "We broke up," I said.

My surgery, estimated to last forty-five minutes, lasted five hours. The surgeon lasered away the worst case of endometriosis he'd seen, he said. Or the second worst, he clarified. An eighty-year-old woman had been worse. The starving—eating but growing thinner and more befuddled—was a medical malfunction. Not a failure of attitude. Not psychiatric. Not sublimated sexual need either. I was hypoglycemic, yes. But my body's ability to digest food had been impeded by the endometriosis. Two diseases, unrelated but interacting: co-morbid. I went through all that and came back unchanged. I was still passive, compliant. The surgeon sent me home the same day, a mistake, he later admitted. The rest of his surgeries got backed up because of mine, and he forgot to change my post-op paperwork. He assured me weeks later that, despite pain, bleeding, fever, I was healing but didn't know it yet because I was a single mother who didn't get rest.

I went back to see him twice: two-hour round-trip each time.

He gave me more pain pills.

I called—not too often. I didn't want to bother him. His nurse called back.

Jana told me to switch doctors. "Your own doctor in town. Or someone new in Austin. Or San Antonio. Anyone but that surgeon." When she came to check on me, to cook or fold my laundry, she'd bring her kids with muddy feet and I'd vacuum and mop after they left because I couldn't lie on the couch, hallucinatory, and incorporate a dirty floor.

I was sedated. Bleak days and nights. I drove to campus, parked, walked while holding my briefcase to my chest with both arms because if I carried it the usual way I ached. From deep inside my torpid brain, I summoned years of accumulated knowledge to lecture for an hour and fifteen minutes. The war in Iraq was just beginning, I remember, the meetings with the UN, the failed attempts at diplomacy with France and Germany, because some undergraduate stood and yelled in class, apropos of not much: "Fuck the French." I paused, then steered the discussion back to the novel at hand, *The*

Red Badge of Courage, then drove home to sleep as Marie watched TV. Sickness unto death was amnesia. I tried to forget. *Avoid.* But when I was as sick as sick could be, Marie leaned over and asked me for the first time: "How long do you have left to live?" Hush, quiet, I murmured. "How will Sofia know to come and get me on a plane?" Marie asked.

My dead grandmother leaned over me one night too, celestial tourist. My grandmother's hair was Marcel-waved. White light radiated from her face as she said: "You, the living, it feels better here, like a spa." She was Jewish, the child of parents who'd been chased across Europe before settling in North Dakota, so she didn't mean a place to get pedicures and facials, but the cure. She'd been miserable in life, running away from home over and over, into the snow, hauled back by relatives, neighbors, strangers. She got married young to a good man, but didn't appreciate him. This was the family account. She didn't talk much herself, not in life. In the afterlife, she was chatty. She looked like she'd had a facial, or Botox. "The needs of the body you worry about," she said, "over here, poof, vanished." I woke in the dark, pulled the quilt up and thought: how nice my grandmother I hardly knew came from over there to tell me that death is comfortable. Then I woke up all the way, and I thought: no. I took Marie to school and went to a doctor.

Pain receded. I was still hungry, hypoglycemic, but not as dizzy. I went back to eating six times a day. Food had no relation to pleasure or appetite, I realized. I needed it again, again, even if it wasn't my heart's first choice, meat I had on hand. I ate it to stay upright, not capsize. I stopped feeling ashamed I had to have meat always. I pulled it from my bag, sleight of hand. I hedged bets. I dated two men simultaneously. They didn't know about each other. Marie, age six now, didn't know about them. One bred dogs and pressure-washed houses. We had nothing to talk about besides my house he'd washed, dogs he'd bred, and his mother. He paid her rent because she'd given him everything, he said. She gave him his life. The other had a PhD in psychology and hated his mother who'd been married seven times. Both were named Mike. Jana called them Proletariat and Overanalytic. I tipped both ways. I wanted ignorance and bliss, that old equation.

I also wanted to understand my craving for sex mixed with neglect.

By email, Sofia objected. You and Proletariat have nothing in common, she said.

You and Overanalytic have too much in common.

Jana and I were at town festival once, our kids riding a miniature train, waving each time it rumbled around. Its whistle blared, warning people to clear the tracks. I said to Jana, "Like in *Anna Karenina*, except smaller." Jana answered, ironic: "Perfect for grieving a small, bad love affair. Do I need to keep you from throwing yourself in front of it?"

Seth Jones had taken six months to move from chivalrous to cavalier, to turn toward, then away. Joseph, a year. Overanalytic Mike took three weeks twice. Two mini-affairs: Approach, endearments, withdrawal. Approach, endearments, withdrawal. Whiplash. He knew why he withdrew. He'd done research on "reference behaviors"—the study of how people who've devised useful ways to react in the past apply similar reactions to situations or people in the present, even if the reaction is no longer useful. It didn't bode well, he said, to have two of us with so many unproductive references in one relationship.

I stopped answering his calls and emails.

Proletariat Mike judged dog shows, and the season had arrived. He'd be leaving on a series of trips. The night before he left, Marie spent the night with a friend. He brought me flowers. But he couldn't stop talking about his best dam who'd been accidentally sired by her son, and the litter would be aborted. I asked him to stop talking. We went to bed, his thousand techniques somehow suggestive of "Playboy Advisor," not *The Manual Metaphysics of Love*, if such a book existed. We got up. I took one of the pain pills I'd been taking since my surgery. We looked at the calendar and he pointed out the dates of his brief returns, weekdays all, and I said that because of Marie's schedule I wouldn't be able to see him, not at night, no sex. He said he'd call me. Phone calls wouldn't cut it, I realized. I was wearing a silky chemise— it was hot—and I felt sad and woozy like Patty Duke in *Valley of the Dolls*. He thought I was sad like a girl in a folk song: he would go, and I must bide. But late at night life looks grim, repetitious, and I'd had a new email that day from Overanalytic Mike saying he'd never meet anyone like me again.

Not that I thought Post-Traumatic, Avoidant, Overanalytic Mike was best.

But I went to sleep that night, thinking of him.

I dreamed I was marrying my first boyfriend ever, an Ojibwa Indian with one eye. He covered the empty socket with a black patch. In life, I was his girlfriend when I was fourteen. In the dream, I tell my maid of honor: "I don't want to marry him because I will turn out reasonably successful and fairly smart on most subjects, but not love." It turns out I'm marrying him in the house where I married my second husband, the wife beater. The past and present are scrambled: life not as progress but replication. We walk outside. An SUV pulls up. My mother gets out. As she would have in life if she'd come to my wedding, she pretends to know the groom. She gives me potholders and tea towels. Not what I'll need for this marriage, I think. Shot glasses. Harley Davidson parts maybe. Then I see my grandmother, not the one who loved death, but the other one who married a man she met at a carnival. He gambled and drank all their living days. She steps out of the SUV and vanishes. My mother vanishes. My maid of honor says, "Now everything's set."

I got out of bed.

I emailed Overanalytic Mike: you draw people close to you only to reject them.

I wasn't writing to him exactly. I'd learned this lesson years ago.

So why was I was learning it again now?

Then a real SUV pulled up in the driveway, and Marie came home. She looked so grown-up, I thought. She looked like my mother around the eyes, which is to say, worried. She learned facial expressions from me and, long ago, I'd learned my mother's. Ghosts of my mother, and mothers of my ghosts, had urged me on in my compulsive self-emptying, I realized. I watched Marie as she put a doll into a doll's bed, and she poured down love. When Marie was a baby, I'd poured down love too. I'd wished for her to be happy, confident. And when she grew up and spoke to men, I'd vowed, the men would listen.

She hardly understood I'd been dating, I reassured myself.

I didn't have an epiphany right away. A problem I thought I'd solved—who to trust, how to trust—kept returning, my old problem spinning like a stuck wheel, and, finally, time passed, the wheel rolled around another time, I got traction and understood that my mother taught me enough about love to love my daughter, but what she'd taught me about men hadn't yet been exorcised. Life hands you a lesson and you might not learn it right away, but you get another chance, another. After I felt better, healthy, I knew I was running out of time to demonstrate to my daughter a better way. How to give love for keeps to people who matter. How to know who these people are. How to receive love and not trifle it away. But that day, as I planned my schedule, buying meat, and a trip to the playground too, I just thought how female desire is still a grotesquerie, freakish, and misunderstood. I thought I wanted what a man has, the chance for a physical life without shame. Or maybe I wanted the fusing together to last and didn't know how? If only my failed foresight would yield up instant insight, I thought. I wanted my comeuppance, my end, to end my desire. But no. I wondered what else to do with it.

How to Build a
Better Fence

Delving deeper into this hardest time, my accelerated tutorial in re-
medial love, when Joseph told me by phone the night before Thanksgiving I was on my own, I'd scheduled surgery for January, and weeks
passed as the usual windup to Christmas except for nonstop bleeding, eating, scans, tests. Jana phoned as I passed through a doctor's
waiting room to an exam room and said, "If Joseph calls and wants
you back, promise you'll say no." He wouldn't. He'd once said if his
fortunes fell low enough he'd cast off everyone. He did call two years
later, fortunes restored. By then, he was a symptom of a disease I'd
learned to manage. "What are you thinking?" Jana asked. I paused. "I
need a protein bar."

"What about Christmas?" She'd be going to Beaumont, to family.

"I made a turkey for Thanksgiving. I'm thinking roast beef."

"Your surgery?" Jana wanted to take me. But she worked full-time.
Noah had therapy twice a week, and food allergies. Zoey was gifted—
outlandishly high IQ—but moody. Jana would have to take them out
of school, pay a sitter. She couldn't afford it. Her life was hard. "Because of the anesthesia, Debra," she said, "someone has to drive you."

I'd made a list of people who might.

I'd already ruled out Tess, who'd recently taken a day off teaching to drive me to an endoscopic procedure. The nurses checking us in had assumed we were a couple. I was drugged when we left, not paying attention, and Tess went home with photos of my viscera in her briefcase—the next time I taught, I found the photos in my mailbox in a manila envelope with a kindly Post-it note attached. Tess has helped enough already, I decided.

So I called Ed and Sandy Ware, an older couple from church. They spent their spare time helping this person write a résumé, that person find an apartment—godliness meant loving mercy, helping others. Yet, since I'd dated Joseph, I attended church sporadically. I hadn't been in over a month. When Marie was little, I'd felt housebound by naps and feedings, especially on weekends. So I went to church. To wake, to bathe and dress us, drive us to church, was respite. The weeks after my mother's death, I'd forego the chapel and head for the cry room, a cell-like space with a sofa and dirty toys. A soundproof window faced the pulpit. The sermon crackled through a speaker. Praying is hoping, worrying, being grateful. Marie didn't cry. I did, tears running down my face. And I hated going home afterward, boredom or desolation careening off the edges of furniture.

I looked up Ed and Sandy in the phone book, explained who I was, and asked. Sandy checked her calendar. "We're in town," she said. "I'll talk to Ed, but I'm certain we'd love to take you." I arranged for Marie to spend two nights, school nights, at her sitter's.

I was writing this on the calendar when Ronnie Larkin, the neighbor who lived behind me—his house and outbuildings not far if you're walking, but more than a mile by road—knocked on my back door. He'd climbed through shrub, barbwire. He said he admired the corrugated fence I'd built across the front of my property, seven-foot cedar posts, one after another, rustic, a gnarled, deep-in-the-forest fence, like in a fairy tale picture. I'd planted morning glories and trumpet vines against it. It cost three times more than a fence from Home Depot, but it looked perfect bordering the small clearing in which I'd made a fish pond, planted a swath of grass trimmed by rock gardens and bright flowers. The fence tapered to a graceful end in woods so thick they formed another barrier.

The last time I'd seen Ronnie Larkin he'd been building bonfires with the undocumented workers who lived in his shed. Today, he said he wanted to build a fence across the back of my property to close up a stretch through which we could glimpse each other's houses. We'd split the cost. His workers worked for him free, he said, so I'd get them half-price, six dollars an hour. Half of free is free, of course, yet I wanted the fence—it was still a deal. I said, "But now's not a good time. I'm having surgery in a few weeks." He nodded, eyes swollen behind his glasses. He didn't seem to talk much. Except once he knocked on my door, drunk, to tell me a theory of Christ, Career, and Capitalism. As I stood, dust rag in hand, and listened, he said the Three Cs pointed at a truth, that people missing Christ filled up the void with all-consuming jobs and money lust.

This time he said, "Another way we save money is we thin some cedar from your woods." I told him cedar posts cost seventy-five cents apiece, and the real cost of the fence is labor, wiring posts one-by-one to rebar. "But cedar sucks up water," he said. "Your oaks will grow taller without those weed trees." I nodded and said, "Okay, take a few."

Meanwhile, I'd tell Marie, "I'm sorry I don't feel well," and she wouldn't answer. In the store, as she decided which coloring book to buy for a kid whose name she'd drawn for her kindergarten Christmas party, I said, "Please, hurry. My blood sugar is falling." She snapped, "You should have eaten before you left home." Marie worried that maybe she was in charge. Only by looking back do I see how scared she felt. She was fed, bathed, coiffed, accompanied to and from school, helped with homework, treated for eczema twice daily, but my difficulty staying conscious, my sense of myself entering a chute of trouble without end, kept me dazed. I hadn't shielded her from the conversations about my surgery I'd had with doctors, or Jana. I'd let strange men into my yard, my bedroom. At any rate, I went to her Christmas party, and I watched the short, sturdy kids eating candy and playing musical chairs. We came home, and she was bored.

I opened the closet where I kept my vacuums and pulled out the antique Hoover. I'd had an electrical outlet installed in the closet so the Hoover was always ready for use. It's turquoise-and-salmon colored with all metal parts—especially good on thick rugs. Marie scowled on the couch, as I did a once-over through the living room and bedrooms. Then we went to the playscape in San Marcos. When we got home, every tree, except six live oaks and one elm, was gone, missing. Stumps stuck high in the air as if a storm had passed through, not a crew with chainsaws. My arts-and-crafts fence, which once sunk deftly into lush forest, stopped in thin air, incomplete as a mouthful of perfect teeth, except one side's knocked out. My cottage garden ended abruptly at the edge of a razed field. A car came up the road. Its headlights glared, then tucked behind the truncated fence.

Marie looked astounded. "What happened here?"

Ronnie Larkin said, "How do you like it?"

I said, "It looks empty." I felt sick. Why had this happened now? "I'll have to find someone to build a fence all the way around." How would I fix it? "I'll need to landscape."

He was suddenly embarrassed. "We'll get to work on the fence in back."

They finished the back fence in a week. Ronnie Larkin billed me $400 for cedar we bought, almost all of it, and six dollars an hour for five men, $1200. And five men times seven hours for the day of my deforestation, $210, also lunch that day, five Beltbuster Combos from Dairy Queen, $30.49. As my surgery got nearer and I tried to ignore my intuition—which said to wall up, safeguard, not let a stranger with sharp tools inside my gut, while logic said I had no choice—I worried instead about my land, sealing it up, returning it to private, which meant letting more strangers with sharp tools back inside.

So far, I'd let the wrong people in, I thought. I'd kept the right people—if there were any—out. I had boundary problems. I hadn't expected my life lessons to be this literal.

I tried to find the guy who'd built my first stretch of fence. He'd moved away. I went looking for someone else by walking into places that sold gravel, or rented trenchers and stump grinders, asking: "Do you know someone who builds fences?" A man, Bob, who used heavy equipment to clear land, could get cedar cheap. He'd put together a crew, he told me. "After all, fence-building isn't rocket science," he added. When he came to measure, he looked at the empty, blighted land next to the artful, arranged land, and said he knew a good landscaper. We called the landscaper, Grant. When Grant arrived, I explained I needed to fill the space, then seed it with wild grass. I wanted a stone pathway edged by ground cover, an arbor with honeysuckle, six or seven flowering trees and, in the clump of tall elms, a safe, sturdy treehouse for Marie, like a porch but high in the trees. They wrote bids. I nixed this or that detail, suggested others, settled prices.

Bob was a tall man with a big nose. He came over every day. His crew built the first twenty feet fast. Bob asked me if I'd like to go to town for coffee. I made coffee, carried cups to the yard. He said a roadhouse had opened. Did I want to go on New Year's? I didn't. Why not? I paused. "I'm having surgery after the first," I said. Grant pulled up. He was short. He had dark eyebrows, an entrenched frown. Marie wandered out of the house. When she went back in, Bob said, "So what is it? You don't like white men?"

Grant groaned. "That's the kind of pick-up line you learned in the course of four divorces."

Bob said, "Just because you got married so long ago you can't remember."

Grant looked at me. "I'm half-Indian," he volunteered.

Translation: he was sensitive to slurs too. I nodded.

He said, "In the army, we used to say there's niggers of every color."

I said, "I get your point. But I don't use that word. Ever." Grant blushed. I braced myself against the wind, watched the workers sawing and planting. I'd aimed at spending a third of my savings. But this was costing me more. I turned to Bob. "She's adopted. I'm not racist, if that's what you mean. I don't think black people are in a special category. I know lots of people who are jerks. Race never has a thing to do with it."

Bob stared.

Grant said, "That's what I meant—assholes of every stripe and color."

I went inside, telling myself I'd no doubt been asked the equivalent rude question when I'd hired crews to add on to my house. Preyed upon is how you sometimes feel, hiring men. Still, I thought, it must be lonely for anyone over eighteen and single, living in a small town. These blue-collar guys were looking for the same thing I'd wanted, I told myself, conversation and contact. Love? But Bob was old enough to have manners. Also old enough to think Jim Crow was a good idea. On the other hand, I thought, I could have been less confrontational, more best-possible-interpretation-of-tactlessness, like when I'd built the add-on and I'd tiptoed around every subcontractor's mood swing. But I wasn't Marie's mother then. I had to speak up now. Yet I was sick of being race ambassador, and sick of unwanted attention every time I wanted something repaired or built.

As Marie and I walked the yard one night, picking up scraps left by the laborers, bits of wood, soda cans, I found a cigarette wrapper and thought how Joseph had smoked, and at least I wouldn't have to clean up butts and ashes anymore. I'd made him smoke on the porch, and I'd cleaned his ashtray with a lemon juice-and-baking-soda paste. *A longtime reader from Norfolk, VA tells me this works! Hugs, Heloise.* Marie brushed leaves off her sweater and—just when I'd convinced myself the vagaries of my irregular life had slipped past her, unnoticed—she said: "We wouldn't have wanted a French guy anyway. We had to work so hard to understand him." I was too surprised to answer. She said, "Have you deleted him out of your cell phone?" I hadn't. She said, "Give it to me when we go inside." I continued to stare at her. "I know how," she said. "It's easy." A minute later, she said, "You could get us a dad like that"—she snapped her fingers—"if you would focus." This time I got mad. "It's harder than you think," I said. "He'd have to be a good dad."

Marie said, "But you said Marina's dad was nice."

"He's married to Marina's mother," I pointed out.

Doubt flickered across Marie's face. "Is that bad?"

I said, "You can only be married to one person at a time."

She nodded. "We need sleep," she said, "and tomorrow will seem better, brand new."

We went back inside, and I thought: So I'd screened everyone again.

And still came to wrong conclusions. How was I any smarter than I'd been all those years ago when I'd married the wrong men? I'd scaled back expectations again, I thought. I stuck to that idea. Just days after Joseph had disappeared, my surgery a few weeks away, how could I devise a better plan? Lower hopes: a shorter distance to fall. "Get back out there and date as soon as you feel well," Nomie had advised. Not that she was a love exemplar. When I get healthy again, I thought, I need to date more than one man at a time, so one man won't leave me stranded, so I won't be isolated, pent-up desire, my options finite-seeming, and I'd cling to some implausible love-candidate. And God would speak to me from a burning bush before I'd ever again let Marie meet a man I was dating.

The night before surgery, Marie was at the sitter's. I looked at the shadowy piles of cedar, rock, sand. Headlights blazed out of blackness. I decided not to think about my fence. After the first twenty feet, which is to say after the testy race and sex conversation with Bob, Bob didn't come back to the site. His laborers hadn't built fences before—they drove trucks, shoveled sand. They built the next fifty feet ramshackle. I said so to the one guy who spoke English, and he said he'd shim it up. Next time I looked, he'd jammed a log at a forty-five degree angle between the dirt and fence. "You can't leave that there," I said. Next time I looked, the horizontal rows of rebar to which the cedar posts get wired were looping crazily—huge, cursive Os. Rebar doesn't bend unless you blowtorch it. A new, quick-fix brainstorm, I thought. The fence wobbled when I touched it.

Yet the arbor was finished, I told myself, honeysuckle vines winding around the lattice, waiting for rain and sun. The vinca major lining the stone pathway looked robust. The tree house was half-built. Grant had suggested that for twenty dollars more his carpenter would make a sandbox underneath because I had sand left from the stone floor his crew had laid in the arbor. Grant admired the part of the yard I'd landscaped years before. Who'd designed it? I designed it, I said, though I'd hired a hillbilly with a backhoe to help. He said, "You have a good eye." He told me he'd seeded for wild grass and, come spring, I'd notice he added a surprise. As he said so, the fence-building crew pulled up. I told the one who spoke English to go back to the shop, to tell Bob to call me. It started raining. Work on the fence stopped. But the landscapers wore raincoats, kept on.

One trouble at a time, I thought. I had to get through my surgery in the morning. Ed and Sandy Ware would take me, bring me home. I'd arranged for a high school girl to spend the night when I came home, help if I needed it. My sitter, who had Marie, would take her to school—she was in kindergarten now—for the next two days. By then, I'd be ambulatory.

So home alone the night before my surgery felt like the night before Thanksgiving when I'd made dinner, everything cooked, set to be reheated, only the fifteen-pound turkey to put in the oven, but—late-breaking news, unforeseen upset—no one would be there to eat it except Marie and me. As I'd put leftover food in the refrigerator, washed the last dish, a mouse had scurried down the counter. A good woman keeps a tidy house. A mouse is a trespass, an insult. The next day, I set out poison in places Marie couldn't reach. Yes, the night before my surgery was like Thanksgiving Eve: solitary, silent. I'd planned to spend Thanksgiving with Joseph and his daughter, Yvette. I hadn't cooked a dinner for people I barely knew, the dispossessed and lonesome, because I didn't think I was.

The night before my surgery, I picked up the house, knowing the next time I saw it I'd be too weak. I threw paper Marie had left on the floor into the trash can, and I thought: what's on the floor in the dark by the trash? I blamed my daughter, Miss Mess Up A House. I picked it up and screamed. I was holding a dead mouse. I dropped it, washed my hand. I put my hand in a plastic bag and hauled the mouse corpse to the trash outside.

I came back in, washed my hand again.

Someone rapped on the back door.

Ronnie Larkin said, "Are you all right?" I told him I'd accidentally picked up a dead mouse. "Is that the whole problem?" he said. "You look bad." I said I had surgery in the morning. He looked quizzical. I said, "Female stuff. Plumbing problems." My father's words. My sister and I had learned never to say more than that about things menstrual or reproductive. I've thought since that menstrual huts are a good idea, to hole up with women and let blood be. He rolled his eyes, said, "Sorry to add to your crisis, but I looked at that fence you got going in the front and side, and the first twenty feet look good, smart how he drilled holes to let posts hang from rebar, but it got expensive. Now they're cutting costs and don't know what they're doing. It won't last through a wind."

I said, "It's ugly too. I might need to fire the guy."

Ronnie Larkin stared at me. "You can have my workers, twelve dollars an hour. But understand they can work for you Sundays only. So it would take a long time to build."

I said, "I can't wait too long. Having my yard closed again . . ." I didn't finish.

"Right," he said, and headed into the dark.

Lying in the pre-op cubicle, I listened to the patient on the other side of the curtain. "I know I'm spending the night," she told the nurse, "and I was wondering about my boyfriend who wants to spend the night beside me. He's been so worried since he heard I'm having this hysterectomy." The nurse said, "Tell him to go home and rest up. Tonight we'll take care of you. When you get out of here, you'll need all the help you can get, so he should get his sleep now." A hysterectomy is simple compared to the operation I was about to have. But I didn't know this yet. *Revisit.* I was having a diagnostic laparoscopy. If they found something, they'd cut it out. *Revisit.* I was freezing. A nurse popped her head in my cubicle and said, "You're alone?" I said, "Do you mean in this room?" She frowned. "Who brought you?" I said, "Some people from my church." She said, "Don't you want them with you?" I told her, "I don't know them well."

She must have talked to them because Ed and Sandy Ware popped in. "How are you, darling?" Sandy said. I was cold. Ed went to the locker where I'd stowed my street clothes, got my fake fur coat with satin lining I'd bought for myself on sale, Christmas gift to myself, and laid it over me. I felt like I couldn't swallow. "Thank you," I said. I told them to go to lunch. "Looks like they're backed up. Do you have to be somewhere later?"

"No," they said, smiling. "Don't worry."

But I sent them to lunch. I waited. I thought about my mother's diagnostic surgery. They'd rushed her in. She'd regained consciousness, my stepfather had said, then asked if he'd told her kids: "I hope you didn't make it sound too bad." Then she died.

Were the dead nearby?

Our bodies are like buildings, I thought. The main rooms are the daily self you let people see. The basement is where the plumbing and furnace, the unspeakable business of blood, excrement, desire, the machinery of life, are concealed. Upstairs—attics, crawl spaces— are lofty, private regions where we get insight. That's where I saw my mother after she died, a second-story closet transmogrified into a room. My college boyfriend, who'd lived outside the law, had died, and I'd dreamed I was in an airport, and I saw him on an escalator heading up, up. Guards had him handcuffed. He mouthed, "Stay down here. Earth. They don't know I'm with you." In that pre-op cubicle, wearing a white gown under a white blanket, huddled under fake fur, I prayed: *For all that has been. For all that is to come.* I shut my eyes and asked for—beyond the walls—someone. Clara Mae?

A nurse swished back the curtain and rolled me away.

I had no idea what time it was when I woke.

The surgery went hours past the scheduled forty-five minutes.

I tried to listen as Ed and Sandy drove me home. Ed said I had endometriosis, not malignant. It had damaged many organs. Good news, the doctor got most of it, lasered me in forty places, took out my appendix which he hardly recognized, tried to put the other organs in good positions because they'd twisted. The doctor wished we'd planned a hysterectomy, but we hadn't, so he stripped and cauterized my uterus. Later, at a post-op appointment, he told me I should have spent several nights in the hospital. The nurses checking me out thought I'd had a short laparoscopy, not a long surgery. I sat in the car at a medical supply while Ed bought me gauze pads. We got home. Ed on one side and Sandy on the other helped me walk. Grant the landscaper and Bob the fence guy stared. Bob came back, I thought. I hated his face, curious, aloof—he had me pegged, withered female.

I sent the Wares home. I felt I'd exploited them, asking them to take me to surgery because, like the grasshopper in the fable who never prepared for winter, I'd spent the bit of spare time I'd had with a man who had detachment instead of scruples. I'd turned out to be someone with no one. So I'd asked strangers who, because of their beliefs—I knew when I asked, a calculated asking—wouldn't turn me down. Besides, the high school girl, Breeze, had arrived, the daughter of someone else from church. She'd been unhappy in school, was taking forever to finish her GED. She looked up to me, her mother had said, because I was *unique*, the mother said first, a *free spirit*, she said next.

I called my sitter, who said Marie was anxious, so the sitter was letting Marie sleep in her bed. "We're fine," the sitter said, "just get well." I spoke to Marie. "Hi, Mama," she said, pipsqueak and uplifting. I told her I missed her, that the doctor did a good job. I'd pick her up tomorrow at school. Then Sofia called me. She thinks all problems are solved with research and a plan. I felt drunk from anesthesia. I turned it into comedy, the dead mouse, the crazy neighbor, annoying subcontractors, my uterus which, unlike other uteruses (uteri?) never produced anything nice. When my mother died, I'd sounded so clever that no one, not Shen, not Sofia, no one but Jack, knew I was sad.

Breeze, who'd dyed her hair blue since the last time I saw her, wanted to talk. Had I ever been unhappy? Also, "When did you first understand your destiny?" Homilies strung themselves into logic and rolled off my tongue "At a certain point, you realize that taking responsibility for your existence is a financial and metaphysical gamble, but you won't have a good life until you accept the risk." I was thinking of Simone de Beauvoir. But Simone de Beauvoir had a shitty private life. Corollary conclusion: so did I. I'd underestimated the need for community, shared norms. I'd overestimated individuality, blazing my singular way. Books I'd written, prizes I'd won, good reviews, Best Professor of the Year award, didn't matter. Dan Quayle et al, the Republican National Committee, had been right: the two-parent family is humanity's prerequisite.

Parenting alone is hard, this planned, chancy experiment I'd conducted because I hadn't seen many two-parent arrangements I admired. I'd worried a second parent, a father, a wild card, might make raising a child precipitously harder, causing unexpected trouble. I hadn't meant to be unique, a free spirit facing the world alone, confiding personal facts to strangers or neighbors because the people I know well, except for Jana, lived out of state. I'd been right so far—no man I'd loved would be more help now than Breeze, who seemed not to understand how to slice meatloaf and put it in the microwave. I hobbled to the kitchen. Nothing mattered but Marie, I thought, getting out food, plates, silverware.

The next morning, Breeze left, and the school nurse called me. Marie was sick. I walked carefully to the car, drove to school, walked inside. "Mama!" Marie said. No one else has ever called out to me with such ardor. "I had a little surgery," I told the school nurse, who stared. I eased into a chair and asked Marie, "You feel bad?" She nodded.

"What did you eat for breakfast?" A donut with chocolate frosting. "There's the problem," I said, and took her home, put a blanket on the floor, a bucket. I lay on the couch.

Marie paced. I said, "Lie down, near the bucket." She vomited on her Christmas present, a robotic cat I'd bought because she wanted a real cat but I couldn't stand the thought of being responsible for another mortal being, so I'd bought her a fake cat with size D batteries. It purred or hissed. A bipolar cat, I thought, contented or outraged. Marie vomited on the area rug. Outside, I rinsed it with a garden hose. It hurt to hold the rug.

A week later at the post-op appointment, I said the pain was worse, and the surgeon said, "You never got any down time." I went home. Then I felt worse than worse used to be. I called. His nurse asked if I had a fever. Yes. How high? 101. She'd talk to the doctor. She called back. "If you had an infection, your fever would spike. He thinks you caught a bug from your daughter." I said, "I don't have symptoms. My daughter's not sick." The nurse didn't answer, pause. "I have calls to make," she said.

So I cooked, vacuumed, walked to my car, drove it, parked, walked up long stairs into classrooms to teach. I unbraided Marie's hair, and I took her to Nomie to get it rebraided.

From the salon, I called the doctor again. "You had a big surgery," the nurse said. "It's unrealistic to expect no pain." I drove Marie to school the next day, came home, sat down, broke open again, bled. I asked Jana to pick up Marie from school. I drove an hour to the doctor's office. He didn't do a culture. We didn't need one, he said. He told me to spend a week in bed. I didn't teach for a week, my first sick days in over a decade.

I wanted the doctor to think I was brave. I didn't want to nag him.

I did get out of bed to take care of Marie. But whenever she was at school, I lay on the couch. Once, then twice, a florist's van pulled into my driveway. Each time my heart beat fast, irrational. Someone loved me. I'd set the flowers on the table, rip open the card. *Dr. Monroe, get well, Eng. 3315.* The other, from graduate students: *Feel better.*

I went back to work. Another week passed. And another. In all, four weeks passed as I walked through debris and rubble, past fence-workers who kept coming to tinker with the shoddy fence, and one said, "Pobrecita, you are very sick." Jana came one Sunday and said, "If you don't go to a different doctor than the one who botched this, I'm taking a day off, putting Noah and Zoey in that bad day care center, and driving you to a new doctor." I promised to look into it in the morning, but I felt drugged. That night I dreamed about my grandmother. She was lit up. She told me death is pain's tonic, its antidote.

The next morning I dropped Marie at school, then drove to my hometown doctor. I had on clothes I'd slept in, a T-shirt, sweat pants, my fake fur coat. I'd combed my hair. The receptionist looked startled: "What?" I said, "Remember that surgery? I never got well. I have a quick question." She rushed me into the lavender room, the one with stirrups.

This doctor gets jazzed about emergencies. He'd said to me years ago, "You'd be a great med school project." He did the chandelier test, an exam during which, if a woman shrieks and reaches for the chandelier, she's infected. I shrieked. He ordered a culture. He's a country doctor, so the results wouldn't be back for days. He shot me up with the widest-spectrum antibiotic, gave me pills. I'd come back the next day, the next. "If your blood work doesn't improve," he said, "into the hospital you go." When the culture came back, I was taking the only antibiotic to which the infection would respond. I said, "You saved my life?" He said, "Gosh, well, timing is everything. You had a few days."

I got stronger. I stopped bleeding. I hurt. I couldn't relax. I went back to the hometown doctor's, told the receptionist I just needed a nurse to take blood to see if my white blood cell count was normal. The second time I did this, the doctor passed by and patted my shoulder. The nurse, Mary, a sensible woman, told me he'd called the surgeon and yelled at him. "He said," Mary told me, tightening a rubber strap on my arm, "you dropped the ball on this woman twice. First time, letting her go home the same day." She jabbed my arm with a needle. "Second time, by not doing a culture." My country doctor told me that, true, staph infections are often accompanied by high fever, but not always. He said, "Cookbook medicine. People attracted to medicine are left brain, don't synthesize, and tend not to think outside the usual, discrete categories. They discount instinct."

The surgeon called me. "Hey," he said, phony-jovial. "I hear your doctor found something else." Else? I thought. "Yes," I answered. "You're in good hands now," he said. He hung up. Sofia said by phone, "You could sue him." I was too tired. I was sorting bills, one from this lab, another from that anesthesiologist or facility—making sure I didn't write my check before the insurance company wrote theirs. I was alive. I wanted to blur fears, fade them, etch kindness in stone. Move on. *Avoid.* I was on hold with some billing department, thinking how bad to be old and addled like Clara Mae had been at the end, and then navigate this. Someone knocked on my door. Bob, the fence builder.

I hung up, opened the door. He said, "I underbid it. I'm going to need $5,000."

I said, "I accepted your bid for $2,500 which is legally binding. But I want to be fair. I'll split the difference, so $3,750 total. But you have to redo that bad part. And you said you'd be done by now. So you have to finish up in three weeks." Soon, I'd leave on a professional trip to Georgia I hadn't been able to cancel—I'd be visiting a university to give a reading, teach writing classes. I'd be gone for a week. When I came back, green buds would push out. New shoots. First roses. Spring. I couldn't have my land cleaved open.

He said, "I don't have time for little jobs like this one."

I didn't know who else would build it. Did he even have the know-how? But the first twenty feet looked good. I said, "So let's finish it fast. You and your crew show up tomorrow."

No one did. Not the next day either. But Grant did. On a Friday afternoon, first southern wind blowing, Grant and I watched his two men wrap strips of wire around a twenty-foot remainder of a huge oak that had long ago been split by lightning. I wanted flowering vines to climb it. I'd also bought a wrought-iron archway to serve as an entrance to the new stone path, and we were planting more vines to climb that. Then all we had left was to lay stone borders between the carpet grass in the old, manicured part of my yard and my new, wild side. I said, "This looks great. All I need now is a good fence."

He glanced sideways.

"Have you seen Bob?" I asked.

"We end up on the same jobs," he said. "I've got nothing against him, but both my carpenter and I wonder why he's thinking he can build fences now. He thought it looked easier than it is. I guess you walked in, and he thought you looked easier than you are."

I thought of Miss Manners who always says if someone seems rude switch the tone back, civility. I said, "So he thought I'd be a pushover about quality of work and price?"

"You're kind of unconventional, a freethinker. In the South, some men mistake that."

It wasn't a North/South problem, I thought. It was a horny old man problem. And all this emphasis on me being nonconformist. I'd never set out to be. I'd built my life—a home, a child, a steady job—according to the every-woman's-dream-comes-true template.

But I'd had difficulties with husbands. What was left of my extended family was too far off or blown apart to be a safety net. So I'd made this life by myself, an improvised motherhood, a few traditional features missing. It hadn't been easy. It hadn't been so easy for Marie either. Maybe I did keep good people at bay. I thought some no-love holocaust was coming, I guess, and I wanted my autonomy in good repair. I told Grant, "I landscaped the other part of the yard. I built the other part of the fence. I built half of my house, without a contractor. And never once did I have disputes with my subcontractors." Mostly never, I reminded myself. "No one argued about quality. Or price."

"He's wrangling about the price?" Grant said.

I explained. Bob had doubled the original bid. I'd agreed to split the difference.

Grant said, "Look, I'll measure the part that can be saved and pro-rate it. I'll build the rest for $3,750, minus the twenty feet. I'll have it done in two weeks. Call him, tell him you'll pay for the first twenty feet, and the cedar he's got laying around, and you won't charge him for the labor to tear down the bad fence. But don't say you're hiring me."

I called Bob. "You're firing me?" he said, stunned.

"And now you'll be able to get back to your real work, your big jobs," I said, soothing. In the South some men might mistake that. But I was getting rid of him, I thought.

On Sunday, I was playing Candyland with Marie, and I heard someone knock on the front door. Bob in his zipped-up coveralls.

"Did you want that check for the first twenty feet and the cedar?" I asked. "Let me just get my checkbook." He shook his head. He handed me an itemized bill for $5,999.77. He said, "It's labor and materials I already got in on this job. You don't know the trouble I went to. My crew's been here weeks."

"Yes," I said, "but they don't know how to build a fence unsupervised. And the fence isn't done." I also pointed out we had a "per job" contract, not a "cost and labor" contract.

His face turned purple-red. His eyes bulged like he had blood pressure issues. I hoped Marie would stay where she was, not come into the room and listen. Would he hurt us? Or just scare us? We'd been scared so much lately, I thought. He said, "You pay that entire bill in the next three days or else." He turned to leave. He looked back at me from the stone pathway that curved around my fish pond where the first water lily was blooming. He waved his fist at me. "I'll see you in court, missy. I'm not afraid of court. I go all the time and win. I've been afraid of nothing my whole life, for sure not women."

The next day, in not-worry mode or my best imitation, I drove to San Marcos and hired a lawyer recommended by a friend of a friend—a short, bald man who worked alone, no secretary even. He'd decided to be a lawyer, he said, because his dad once needed a lawyer and couldn't afford it. He said we'd sue first, anticipatory, breach of contract, failure to finish on time, and there was a law against bidding on jobs that require skills you don't have. Like my hometown doctor, he loves risk. His eyes flashed. He said, "I definitely don't want to go to the Justice of the Peace in your end of the county. Those guys are inside each other's pockets. I bet he does win all the time out there. And we can sue for emotional distress—delays, the threatening presence last weekend." Not that, I said. I had medical co-pays. I'd already spent thousands on the yard. "Keep it simple."

A few days later in my front yard, Grant said, "I hear you got a lawsuit going."

I nodded. "He said he'd sue me for six grand for that little bit of sloppy work."

Grant nodded. "My wife's best friend is my carpenter's wife, who is also Bob's lawyer."

Small town, I thought. I said, "So Bob's lawyer works out here."

He nodded. "I was with Bob when he got served. He asked me to go along to the lawyer with the idea we were both working for you and I'd take up for him. She asked if you were a flake, and I said I had no problem with you. She told Bob he didn't have a leg to stand on. But I tell you what, before we tear down the bad part of the fence, let me take pictures. You promise you won't tell him I'm helping with the lawsuit. He'll find out I'm building your fence, but the story we stick with is you asked me to bid on it, and I did."

I paused. "Thank you. I know you don't have to help me."

He said, "Lady, I'm no sap, but I don't take money I'm not owed. Anyone who's paying attention can see you've had had a rough winter. Somebody else saw that as an opening."

An opening, I thought. I was the opposite of impervious.

Bob's lawyer called my lawyer to say if we'd drop the suit Bob would take my original offer. My lawyer sent him back a letter saying: okay but minus legal fees incurred, $500. Bob refused. My lawyer said, "I say we go ahead." I said, "I'd be tied up in court with that creep." The lawyer said, "You can win." I said: "I'll just pay you the $500."

My lawyer twiddled his pen, narrowed his eyes. "I could charge you less, of course."

At the first meeting he'd said he gave special rates to indigent clients. "I'm not poor," I said curtly. Yet I'd had a costly winter. I needed to rebuild my savings. "$400," he said. I was writing him a check when he wondered aloud if being raised poor explained his bad taste in women. He said, "My ex-wife is stripping—says the money's too good." I hadn't yet thought how to answer when he said, "My girlfriend's in love with her ex who walked out when she was pregnant. She has a master's degree—runs Child Protective Services. Why do smart people make bad choices in other parts of their lives?"

I thought how I hadn't seen the warning signs with Bob. Or paid attention to warning signs with Joseph. Or those who came before, smoke and dust. "Beats me," I said.

When I got home, opened my car door, I heard shouting. Grant and Ronnie Larkin stood ten inches apart. I sent Marie inside and stepped carefully across the rocky, bumpy yard. I had on high heels because I'd taught that day. I was taking new drugs for chronic inflammation of scar tissue, lesions from the surgery and infection. I held my stomach as I walked. Grant waved a hammer. "I tell you, moron, we're the heroes, good guys."

Ronnie Larkin turned to me, "I told him he did bad work, and you're sick."

I said, "I appreciate it, but I fired that first guy. This is the new fence builder. See?" I pointed at the now-completed fence, which looked perfect. I looked at the arbor, coral honeysuckle already in bloom, the vinca major showing their first purple flowers. "This is the guy who did my landscaping. I fired the other guy, hired this one to build the fence."

"I was trying to help," Ronnie Larkin said, and stalked off.

Grant's crew packed up, and Marie came out to climb in her new treehouse.

Grant said, "This project turned out well. Do you mind if I show it to prospective clients?"

I said, "I'll recommend you to anyone. You're not cheap, but you stay on schedule, and you do high-quality work." I was writing the last check. New grass glowed in patches, green here, green there, yellow and orange star-shapes mixed in, wildflowers. I said, "I'll bet you have a great yard at home. Does your wife like flowers too?"

He said, "Not really."

Then I complained about my fish pond, how it didn't have enough shade, and with warm weather coming I'd be working on algae control. He said, "I'm not trying to talk you into this because I imagine you're financially tapped out. But you know what I'd put there? Desert willows. Tall with pale, orchid-shaped flowers. They'd set off that pond."

"How much," I said.

"$150 per," he said, "one on each side. $300. I could have them in a few days."

I pictured it. "Yes," I said.

The day he was coming to plant the two last trees, early that day I had a murky, overpopulated, drugged dream, in the dreamingest season of my life. I was at a garden show, walking with ordinary people as I studied wholesale displays of flowers. I stared at purple salvia. "It's a perennial," Grant told me, "and drought-hardy." We looked at succulents. "I had no idea succulents came in these shapes," I said. I saw pink yuccas. "I have those," I said. "Do you like mimosa trees?" He did, he said. "But they struggle. They're not native." It was a sunny day, a fragrant, loamy, greenhouse perfume in the air. We stood next to a flatbed with crates of flowers: yellow, red, blue. He said, "This is my big truck." I stared at it. You do have to make small talk with your subcontractors. I said, "It seems like a good one." He looked at me. "I was wondering if you'd go for a ride?"

In the dream, I was shocked. Angry. "No," I said. I'd thought Grant had helped me because of justice, selflessness. Chivalry. Anything abstract. Not sex. "Not you," I said.

I woke in the dawn. Just an anxiety dream, I told myself. Anxiety about transactions with men who know I don't have a man, and I feel as unprotected as an opening.

I took Marie to school. When I came back, Grant wandered the yard. A worker dug holes by the fish pond. Twenty-foot willows with pink flowers sat in burlap sacks. "They look good," I said. It was his favorite tree, he told me. He pointed at the vinca major. "Did you see this?" I nodded. He said, "Did you notice the honeysuckle is out?" I told him, "And the cottonwoods are about to bloom too. The trumpet vine has clumps of new blossoms." I had my enclosure back, my safety. I felt like I did when I'd added onto my house and had lived all summer with a hole in the wall, and then I could lock up again.

He said, "Do you like motorcycles?"

This threw me off. "Not really."

"I bought a 1947 Indian Chief. And I was wondering if you'd go for a ride?"

I should have had an answer handy. Yet I was too surprised, not that he'd treated me like I was available, ajar, a bull's-eye. But that I'd had an instance of distorted time, a dreamy trance that had landed me in this moment an hour before it turned real. Maybe the dream did prepare me. I said, "No, I'm not interested motorcycles. What about your wife?"

"Nope," he said. "Not even a little. Not interested for years." He drove away.

So I plotted out trees, flowers, stones, a path, a place to sit and think, and what used to be woods became reliable space. As for dreams, since the years I didn't sleep when Marie was a baby, and then my mother's death kept me awake for months, and then I got sick and slept medicated, doped, I haven't had as many that told me so much. When I explained to Jana how the garden show dream had turned real within an hour, she said, "You're clairvoyant." Not reliably. I'd been on an airplane when my mother died and didn't know. Joseph had jilted me—no vision had said to get ready. But once in awhile I'd seen other rooms, a way out of the usual, discrete categories. But even then, when my grandmother came with an invitation to join her in analgesic death, my instinct was to acquiesce.

Say yes.

Not bother anyone with my distrust or apprehension, generalized fear.

I'd gotten used to fear so long ago I didn't pay it any attention.

I'd stonewalled, I thought. Set limits. Only normal people took the hint. Crazy, hard-bitten people, the living and the dead, kept on coming over walls I put up. I'd been confused and let one or two in. I'd been so hell-bent on concealing self-doubts, I never said no in time. But my hometown doctor said I'd feel calm soon, that my body taxed by disease helped generate this hyper-attuned panic. And triggers abounded—a news story about surprise killer diseases, or seeing Ed and Sandy Ware at church, explaining how I felt.

One day, sitting at the only stoplight in town, my heart raced. I sensed danger all around. I needed to save myself and Marie, I thought. I looked in the rearview mirror and saw Bob's big truck idling like a beast and, in its windshield, his flushed, contorted face. He'd recognized me. He'd been afraid of nothing his whole life, for sure not me. I'd been afraid of everyone—Bob was just the latest in a long series. The light turned green. I went forward. Bob went somewhere. I was scared for a while, yes, but I did get better.

Inflamed Scar Tissue

When I was still defenseless, lacking a fence, though I'd been defense-less and unboundaried for years—when I was in fact still dating Jo-seph—a friend from graduate school had called to ask if I'd visit his campus in Georgia for a week that was my spring break, but not his, teach classes, give a reading. The pay was good. "I could have asked So-and-So," Toby said, dropping the name of a writer who'd published dozens of books, "but she has a haughty reputation, and I'm trying to get funds for a regular visiting writer series. You'd be nicer to the stu-dents, and I'll schedule dinner with the dean, because you're good at chatting up old people." He quoted Jacques Lacan: "What does it mat-ter how many lovers you have if none of them gives you the universe?" A lopsided analogy. "What does it matter how much fame she has if she won't get me my reading series?" he said.

Toby loves psychoanalytic theory. At any rate, love and work, the cornerstones of humanness (Freud), let you offer as much or as little as you like. As a teacher, I try to offer a lot because teachers gave me skills that gave me my vocation, my life. Besides, I'd get invitations, go to a campus, and students knew my books better than I did—a flat-tering way to earn money. After I was a mother, I kept going. A student would sit with Marie while I was in the classroom or behind the podium. Then the student handed her back over and we'd have home life as usual, but at a hotel: dinner, eczema treatment, bedtime.

But this gig sounded strange. I'd fly to Atlanta, four hours from his college, and he'd drive eight hours round trip to pick me up because he had to get his daughter from a previous relationship, also his son from a marriage, both children born the same year, same week, like twins but with different mothers. It was their spring break too. My honorarium was generous in theory not fact—no funds for food or lodging, so I'd stay at his house. I could have his bedroom. Marie would bunk with his daughter. "This house is palatial," Toby said. "You can get big houses dirt cheap here." Another incentive, Toby said, was that Jack Creeden and another graduate school friend, Vince, taught in Georgia too, and we'd have an informal reunion. "Think of the times we'll have," Toby said.

But between the time Toby invited me to visit campus and the event itself, I got really sick. Joseph ditched me. My neighbor cut down trees. I called Toby. "I'm having diagnostic surgery in early January," I said, "but I probably should have no trouble coming in March, unless they find something." He panicked. "I told the dean you were coming. I could have asked So-and-So. I asked you as a favor, so students would read your books and you'd earn money." Then his manners took over. "Are they looking for cancer?" My hometown doctor had mentioned cancer, yes. "Not necessarily. I'll probably be okay," I said. Already I dreaded the traveling while working and caring for Marie.

When the trip was just two weeks away, my hometown doctor had diagnosed that post-op infection, I'd finished one course of antibiotics, and I returned to the doctor's office to make sure the infection was gone. Mary, the sensible nurse, frowned. "Back when I assisted," she told me, "doctors I worked for put women on antibiotic drips during surgery." When I went to have her take my blood a second time, she said, "So why do you feel you're not recovering yet?" I hurt, I said. I hurt holding a briefcase, sitting, walking. She said, "You don't trust your body now. Or doctors. But if you had an infection, we'd know. When you get back from this trip, we'll treat you for inflamed scar tissue."

I thanked her. I went home, called Toby. He said, "Great. It wasn't cancer."

We hung up.

I called Jack Creeden.

Two years earlier—having just visited Sofia and realizing I could take trips even if I didn't get paid to go, when I felt at odds and lonely—I'd flown to Georgia to visit Jack. He took Marie and me on outings around town. When he talked to Marie, he'd slip up and call himself Daddy. "Let Daddy fix dinner before you eat that snack, honey." Or: "Sit at the table, honey. Daddy doesn't like crumbs." When Marie slept, he'd pour tumblers of whiskey and say he'd made a deal with the devil, missing his children for the day-in and day-out. "Real life," he said. "I'm their summer dad, a Disney dad. What a mistake."

On the phone now, two weeks before I was scheduled to leave for the visiting writer gig at Toby's, Jack said, "You had surgery? Who took care of you? I didn't know you had surgery. Staph? Why didn't you call? A freaking staph infection. My uncle died of that." I was obsessed with the fence, however, not my surgery and infection, and I told Jack about Bob the fence guy, my neighbor's chainsaws, the landscaper, the lawsuit. *Avoid.* Jack couldn't follow it all. "Sounds like a rough patch," he said. Then I talked about Marie's hair—that I supposed we could go to Toby's even if Marie's hair wasn't freshly braided. *Avoid.* Jack said, "But back to your surgery. Why were you alone? Who nursed you? How do you feel now? Come on to Georgia. I'll take care of you."

I need the money, I thought.

I decided to hire Breeze, the blue-haired girl, to water my plants and feed my fish, fifty dollars. I'd drive to the airport, park, and Marie and I would ride the shuttle, ninety dollars.

In Atlanta, Toby's daughter's plane was already in. "My name is Grace," she said, "and I'm ten." Toby's son wasn't coming after all. "Hamilton is like a long-lost brother," Grace said. "We'd like to be together always, but we're torn apart by fate." Toby winked at me. "She's been reading Russian novels, I guess." We headed out in Toby's van. Toby said to me, "I suppose you have questions about my progeny, how they came to be, the timing. It's a goddamn soap opera. I can't explain now. Little pitchers."

We drove south for four hours. We pulled into his garage. Only a streetlight glowing through windows lit our way as we passed through a big kitchen, a big living room, past an oak-paneled study, to two children's rooms and a mom and pop bedroom suite—a state-of-the-art house, circa 1955. I woke Marie, rubbed her with medicated cream, put her pajamas on, led her to bed. I wanted to take a bath. In dim light, I saw soggy, wadded-up washcloths around the tub's rim, a mushy soap fragment on the tub's edge. I turned on a lamp and looked inside huge cabinets—no cleaning supplies, toilet paper, or towels. The tub needed scrubbing. So I flipped off the light and got into bed, which smelled like gym clothes. Toby tapped at the door and stuck his head in. "Sleep in tomorrow because I'm taking the kids shopping. I'll buy you lots of meat. Anything else?"

"Soap," I said, "you're out."

As soon as I woke, I ate a protein bar. Then I passed through a long hall. Two dogs bounded with me to the kitchen where unwashed dishes sat stacked on counters. The trash can overflowed. Tufts of dog hair floated across the floor. The door opened. "Mama," my daughter said, "he bought Lucky Charms." The girls and dogs went to the back of the house, and Toby yelled, "Old clothes now." He told me, "They'll spend their days at a horse camp for troubled kids. Not that our kids are troubled. It's just reliable daycare."

He'd forgotten to buy soap.

I took a shower, only my feet touching the tub's surface. I used the last soap bit. I was fixing breakfast, three eggs, ham, two apples, when my former classmate from Utah, Vince, stopped by. "I'm on my way to teach," Vince said, "but I wanted to say hi." Vince taught with Toby. Jack Creeden taught at a college three hours north, near Atlanta—he'd come in two days. Toby had returned from taking the girls to horse camp and was taking a shower, without soap. I said to Vince: "I don't remember Toby being a bad housekeeper when he was a student. Last night he said he was tired from cleaning for us."

Vince said, "The sad fact is he probably did clean." He paused. "So you've been sick?"

I'd hardly talked about it—timing, contingency. If I hadn't had that dream, roused myself, wandered to the doctor's, if the receptionist hadn't rushed me in, I'd have died. I'd neglected Marie—no one had filtered the experience for her, given her words and phrases to feel safe. Wanting to feel connected, not alone, I'd even called my dad. I hoped his wife would answer. She's a sweet woman, but years of attentiveness—extreme knitting, furiously monofocused knitting as he drank and fumed—had taken its toll. Or she'd come back from visiting her mother in the nursing home and find him passed out in the snow. She was tired. She didn't like fighting him for phone time. This time, I called in the morning—too soon for him to be drinking— and said I'd had a surgery. I told him I got an infection. My dad said, "You're making this up. A hospital is a sterile place." He changed subjects, telling me how a fellow he'd met at the coffee shop had always looked up to him, and I said, "I've got something boiling over on the stove, Dad. I've got to go."

I told Vince: "The surgeon was in another town. I got a bad infection."

Vince said, "We take these jobs far from cities. I've lowered my standards too."

Standards for doctors? I wondered.

He said, "Bad luck isn't *all* all our fault. The way to see the future . . ."

Someone else pulled up. A woman with flowing hair got out of a car. She checked her makeup in a compact and came inside. Vince said, "This is Carrie, Toby's girlfriend."

"Pleased to meet you," I said.

Vince and Carrie left for work. Toby and I had time before I was supposed to teach Toby's class, so I started washing dishes as Toby talked about women he'd loved, Esmeralda (old girlfriend), Leticia (Grace's mother), Violeta (Hamilton's mother), Carrie (new girlfriend). He said, "I've loved women who are crazy. If our family history is crazy, then we grow up with the burden of our parents' inexplicable choices. At times, I wonder, am I doing research, trying to live a frantic life to get good material? Why do I prefer tragic women? I've decided it's not a crazy life that's attractive. People who grow up that way tell good stories—I just can't fall in love with someone who doesn't cast that spell."

Was this me? I wondered. I liked someone's high-concept back story, acute narrative tension, and I got sucked in? No. I was more comfortable this way. Our pasts matched.

No spending my leisure time with someone who expects me to act normal.

Walking to campus, Toby pointed at a woman in front of us. She was Kenyan, he said, her father an economics professor who lived next door. He flagged her down and said, "I want you to meet Debra, who's inaugurating our new visiting writer series." She shook my hand and said, "I am Mama." That's what I thought she said. Her name is actually Mma. "Mma sometimes babysits," Toby said. "Debra's here this week with her daughter."

"Pleased to meet you," Mma said, and hurried to her class.

As Toby and I stepped into the building, Toby said, "I was going to have Mma babysit for us tonight, for our dinner with the dean. But we'll use Carrie's daughter instead. This daughter lives in Ohio. Carrie left her with relatives to take this job. The daughter is visiting Carrie for the first time. She's handling the transition badly—she just got busted for possession. I figure if she babysits tonight, she won't feel left out over at Carrie's."

My guts hurt—the walking. I thought: if I felt better, maybe I'd be okay with this plan. Or not. I don't like it, I decided. I don't like Carrie. How could she leave a daughter turning into a woman behind? Remove the crucial woman-model from her daughter's life? How bad to be a daughter whose mother doesn't want you—who'd get over that? Having your mother say: I'm done now, go to someone else with your daily this or that. I was projecting, I realized. But I wasn't letting a juvenile delinquent babysit Marie.

Toby said, "We did drugs too, Debra. We just never got caught."

"Not getting caught is key. It means you know when to stop."

Toby laughed. "I still don't."

He meant his infatuation-as-intoxication. I could care less. I want Mma, I thought. I went for broke. I said, "Toby, I'm the most overprotective mother in the world—because of waiting so long to adopt, I guess. I'm nuts." I tried to sound nuts. "I think she'll be abducted. Or fall off a boat. I never go to bed without checking on Marie, checking window latches. I don't let her out of my sight." True. I let hysteria creep into my voice. Bring it on, I thought. "I want Marie to come along to dinner with the dean tonight."

Toby said, "You can't do that. It's not that kind of dinner." He looked at me. "Okay, okay. I'll call Mma, and we'll invite Carrie's daughter too. We'll call it a pizza party."

"I'll pay for everything," I said. We walked into Toby's classroom.

When I finished teaching, I sat in Vince's office.

Vince asked, "If you don't mind talking about it, what was your surgery for?"

I answered carefully. "Female trouble," I said, "which complicated blood sugar problems. I got an infection during surgery. I'm okay now. I don't know why I'm not happy." I thought about a woman from the adoption agency—Nikki, who'd worked with me on an adoption that came up and fell through. Mother of three. She'd died of cancer since. *The essence of immortality is to make an exception of myself.* Wasn't not-dying enough?

Toby started yelling in the next room.

Vince and I stood in the office doorway, listening. Toby had asked the department secretary if accounting had sent my check. She was on the phone. Toby paced. Another woman wandered in. The secretary hung up. Wide-eyed, she said, "Accounting says we'll have the check in two days." Toby's square jaw went more square. His neck muscles flexed. "Those ineffectual ass-hats," he said, slamming a fist. "I'm going over there." I glanced at the secretary. I said, "I'm in no hurry." Toby stormed out. The display was for me—he felt we'd been disrespected. "I'm sorry," I told the secretary, who shook her head. The woman who'd wandered in said to me, "So Brandoesque, I always think." Vince introduced her, a film studies professor. I said, "I've known Toby since graduate school. I assumed time had mellowed him." She said, "Nope."

That night at the restaurant, Toby gave me the honorarium check. "A few turns of the screw." He winked. I was seated next to the dean but thinking about Marie who'd come back from horse camp covered in manure. "I'll have her bathe," Mma had said. I said, "But she has eczema—she needs to have cream applied after her bath." Grace said, "I'll do it." I told Mma, "Make Grace wash her hands after she puts

Marie's cream on. It's prescription." But there wasn't any soap. The tub was filthy. "A shower," I said. This was worse for Marie's skin. "Lots of cream," I told Grace. "Wash your hands with dish soap." Toby was dragging me to the door. I'd barely said hello to Carrie's daughter, a black-and-blue Goth. As Toby, Carrie, and I got in the van, Toby said, "Do us a favor. Relax."

At the restaurant, Toby and Carrie sat across the table, the dean beside me. The dean wasn't much older than we were. I made a note to tell Toby—to rethink his Angry Young Man shtick. But getting Toby his reading series was my assignment. I spoke to the dean.

On the way home, Toby said, "I've never seen the dean so animated. What did you talk to him about?" I said, "North Dakota. He was born and raised there. So was my mother." Toby slapped the steering wheel. "Asking the person who holds the purse strings to talk about his childhood, brilliant." Then he turned up the radio. Someone was interviewing Salma Hayek, who said her father was half-Lebanese. "That explains it," Toby said. "She's so freaking good-looking, hubba." I started laughing—this glimpse of the old Toby falling off a cliff into lust, even if it was a middle-aged rant about a movie star.

Carrie said, "You . . . you have a fetish about foreign women."

"He sure does," I said.

Carrie said, "I feel like I should be more exotic. I'm not."

Of course what he liked best about Carrie was that she was here.

Like Vince. Vince's girlfriend was an undergraduate, half his age. Jack had said Vince used to have a nice, age-appropriate girlfriend in Atlanta, but she got sick of the commute.

"Please," Toby said. "That would be like me getting jealous of, I don't know, Sting."

"Sting?" I said. "Really." We'd pulled up in the driveway.

"I need to get my daughter and go," Carrie said. "I need to go home this instant."

We went inside, and the girls were piled on the sofa watching the Cartoon Network. I paid Mma, thanked her, sent her home. Toby and Carrie were having a staccato, whispered conversation in the kitchen. Finally, Toby pulled me aside and said, "She's upset. I have to go over there. She's insecure about this whole deal, you staying here."

And I'd thought it was Salma Hayek. I said, "Tell her I just had my woman parts lasered. Even if I hadn't, our neuroses don't mesh." Toby grinned. I said, "What about Grace?"

He said, "Will you take care of her tonight?"

I could wash the bedding without hurting his feelings. "Knock yourself out," I said.

Toby, Carrie, and Carrie's daughter left. Marie was asleep on the couch. I stripped the beds, loaded the washing machine. I asked Grace to help me find cleaning supplies, and I cleaned my bathroom, the kids' bathroom. In a closet in the hallway, I found one of those transparent soaps—green, shaped like a Christmas tree. As Grace stood next to me, I asked her, "What did you use for soap tonight when you took your showers?" She said, "Shampoo." Then, glancing at the ceiling, a recitation, she said: "A man and woman are equals. Or should be. He acts helpless about housework and then the woman tries to please him by doing housework for him. That's no way to get a man's attention."

"Your mom must have told you that. But I'm doing this for us, not him."

Grace smiled.

The next night was Grace's birthday. Toby had bought a cake and invited Vince, Mma, Mma's parents, and Grace's horse camp teacher. After Mma and her parents went home, and Marie was dozing in my lap, the horse camp teacher did a shot of tequila. Then she stood with her arm around Grace. She asked me, "Is your little girl a foster child?" I answered, "No, I adopted her at birth. I brought her home from the hospital." She said, "She's so lucky. I started my camp because I didn't get adopted by a good family until I was fifteen. They taught me horses. Horses gave me this easy way to love something, and I want to give that to children who aren't as lucky as I was." Toby said, "You were in foster care?" She said, "Don't ask about those families. I still try to forget."

Vince picked up empties. The horse camp lady went home. The rest of us went to bed. And when the house was dark and quiet, I heard Toby start his van and drive to Carrie's.

When I woke up the next morning, my insides felt like they were falling out while scorched.

Marie tiptoed into my room. I said, "Is Toby here? Ask him if he has a heating pad." I should have packed mine, I thought. If I turned it up high enough, it distracted me from pain. Marie padded down the hallway. A few minutes later, Toby stuck his head in. "Feeling bad?" He drove to a store, bought me a heating pad. As he sat on the bed, plugging it in, he told Marie, "Your mama's going to be okay, sweetheart." He told me: "Take the morning off. Rest up for the reading tonight." Marie stayed home with me.

When Toby came back between his classes, I was making lunch. A peanut butter sandwich for Marie. Meat, carrots, soy milk for me. Even if I'm too sick to eat, my blood sugar drops. It drops faster. I stared at a pile of slick ham. I was afraid—I'd started bleeding again. Too much walking in high heels, maybe? I said, "I need to see a doctor."

Toby looked alarmed. Cancelled reading tonight, he was thinking. Then, embarrassed he'd thought that first, he'd think: so where do I get a doctor? He said, "Why?"

"I'm hurting and bleeding."

"Look I've been married. I watched my son being born. Tell me what exactly is wrong?"

I said, "I'm not sure—my surgery was all over."

"Debra, listen." He reached for my hand. "They've run every test in the book. If you had something, it'd be some obscure, yet-undiscovered disease. I'm sure you're just fine."

I felt dizzy. "I need more food."

He looked alarmed again. "You ate everything I bought?"

I nodded.

He said, "Take my keys. I'll draw a map. Get dressed and go shopping." He left.

Marie said, "Mama?"

I thought: Jack Creeden won't be here until five.

I got my phone, called my doctor's office in Texas and asked for Mary. She picked up. I told her I was bleeding. She said, "You're probably menstruating." I said, "There's a 80 percent chance I shouldn't anymore." The surgeon had told me most women don't get a period again. She said, "So you're in the lucky few percent." I said, "It doesn't feel like a period." Yet the sliding-out feeling did. Only the burning was unusual. She went to get my file. When she came back, I said, "I hurt everywhere." Mary said, "You know staph—it eats flesh. The tissue is an open wound. But your latest lab work came back fine. This period will hurt. Increase your pain meds. Don't stop taking your antibiotics." She was using that hypnotic, rise-fall voice you use on insane people.

"Thank you," I said. I got dressed. Marie and I got in Toby's van, drove to a store.

I was staring at protein bars. Even with my glasses on, I couldn't read the print on the boxes. I held onto the shelf for balance. I ripped open a box, then the wrapper on a protein bar, stuffed the bar in my mouth. You can do this if you leave the price code intact, put the box in your shopping cart. Marie said, "Mama, there are lots of black kids in this store and—guess what?—they all have black moms." Someone behind me started laughing. I turned. A black woman, with two children riding in one of those shopping carts shaped like toy cars. I told Marie, "Most black kids do have black moms, honey. If kids aren't adopted, they tend to be the same color as the mom." Marie said, "Why is that?" I paused. The woman laughed again: "The bird and bees—I'd quit while I was ahead."

I nodded and wheeled my cart away. I bought food and an eight-pack of soap. As I checked out, I could feel my blood sugar sink again. Pulling out of the parking lot, I couldn't imagine standing up long enough to take a shower. Could I stand behind a podium for forty minutes? My vision was blurred. Marie said, "Yay, Georgia has a McDonald's."

I turned into the McDonald's parking lot. I had trouble understanding the menu, and the instructions to order at one window, pay and pick up at another. I was in Toby's old van with dents. I don't go to drive-throughs much. The staff stared, repeated basic facts. "Park over there," the girl in the second window said finally, "and I'll bring you food."

Marie ate a Happy Meal. I ate too, three slabs of burger with four layers of bun. Then—a slow undulation—my peace and understanding returned. This is how a junkie feels after the hit, I thought. Mental note: many burgers with many buns are sometimes the meaning of life. I drove home, euphoric, took more pain meds, hopped into the shower, put makeup on. I washed Marie, greased her skin, put her in a pink sailor dress. I looked out the window at Jack Creeden walking up the driveway toward me, and I ran outside.

We hugged hello. He said, "You're a little pale. But you look great." His hands lingered around my waist. He had that forlorn, carnal look. I said, "Chill out, Jack. I had surgery." Defensive, he said, "I wasn't suggesting anything. I haven't had sex in years. None in fact," he looked around to see if anyone was listening, "since I last saw you." He meant when I'd visited—between my first and second bad boyfriends. We'd waited for Marie to fall asleep. Jack would drink whiskey, and then we'd spend an hour in bed. When we slept together when we were young, we were mutually ungenerous, each measuring the other's overtures. The point of overture-counting is to make sure you're behind: more desired than desiring, more likely to cause pain than receive it. But a few years ago, we were just kind and tender. I said, "That's the problem, Jack. It's not healthy to be so alone. You get attracted to everything." I reconsidered: as if I'd handled it better. My desires had attached unsuitably, like in a Barbara Pym novel: a bookish woman eking out her middle-age in a village. I was bookish, middle-aged, and living in a village.

The horse camp teacher's car pulled up, and Grace got out. The car sped off. Grace said, "You have to promise to help me." She was hiccupping, crying. "Dad is out at horse camp picking me up, but I got tired of waiting and found another ride. He'll be mad."

I said, "I had the van all day. The van's here."

She shook her head. "He's got Carrie's car." She wiped her nose with the back of her hand. "We passed him. We tried to flag him down, but he had this mean stare he gets."

"He won't be mad," I said. But I wasn't sure. All this multi-tasking. A starving houseguest who feared death. A dean who had to be flattered. Carrie's insecurities. Grace who was easy but had routines Toby wasn't used to because she wasn't here all the time. And classes to teach each day. His mood had gone haywire—an overloaded circuit board.

Grace said, "He told me he'd be a better father than his was."

I kneeled. "It's hard to be a good parent. You try. But you make mistakes."

She nodded and went inside.

Jack and I sat in the living room with Marie. Jack was saying he liked *SpongeBob SquarePants*, and Marie was saying she liked *Fairly Odd Parents*. I was listening but thinking how I'd once hurled the quintessential feminist insult at my mother. "You're male-oriented," I'd shouted, "with no sense of who you are apart from what men tell you." Sofia had lately sent me new profiles of eligible men—she wanted me to get over bad experiences by having better experiences. But men looked like time bombs to me now. I didn't want a needy man. Not an aloof man either. Somehow I'd gotten needy and aloof both, two-for-one, in Joseph. I want my mother, I thought. To tell her I understand.

Toby came in, threw Carrie's keys down. "That leaf-eared douche-bag of a horse camp teacher."

Jack said, "Grace caught a ride."

I said, "She saw you on the road and tried to flag you down."

He said, "You know what it feels like when you're picking up your kid, and she's not there. Your heart falls out. The place was a fucking horse wasteland—no humans in sight."

"She's here," I said.

Toby sighed, sat down. "I planned too much this week. I'm not doing a good job." He went to find her. She wasn't in her room. He stood in the yard, calling her name.

Marie, semi-hypnotized, turned from the TV. "Grace is at Mma's."

"How do you know?"

Marie shrugged. She showed me how to duck through a hedge and walk down a path to Mma's door. We rang the bell, and Mma's mother answered. I asked, "Is Grace here?" Mma's mother waved at a curved staircase. "They are up in my daughter's room. Maybe now we tell him to come in from the street and stop yelling." I went up the stairs into Mma's pristine, girlish room. Mma said, "I am telling Grace go home, her dad is calling."

I said, "Grace, he's worried he can't find you."

Mma waved her hand in the air. "So much going on over there always."

That night I stood behind the microphone and, before I spoke to the audience, I looked at Vince, Toby, and Jack—Jack was holding Marie's hand. I thought how, when I met the three of them, I had just one female classmate, Vince's ex-wife, and these boys had seemed like a loud, aggressive cabal. But now they were my friends, taking care of me. Yet I'd had to fly across the country to get their help. Sofia always said: "If you lived in a city, you wouldn't be alone." I'd answer: "I'm a hermit by choice." And these guys were mostly in the same position, I thought, reunited for just this night, all of us teaching in forlorn outposts because our vocation, making stories, isn't practical. Just necessary.

After the reading was over, we went to Toby's. The dean stopped by, thumped Toby on the back, said, "Your advertising did the trick. Even that stand-up comedian we paid top dollar for last year didn't bring out students like this reading." I was standing in a corner of the kitchen, holding Marie by having her sit on the counter as we wrapped our arms around each other. I listened as Vince told me that when he first moved to Georgia, newly divorced, feeling bereft, all he brought with him was one box. "My worldly goods."

I said, "The other day you started to say something about how to see the future."

He looked puzzled.

"You were talking about luck, the future. You didn't finish."

He said, "Oh. It's going to sound too simple. I know you never surfed, but . . . surfing. You don't know what a wave is until you get on it. It might turn out to be tricky, and you ride it as best you can. Two things happen. You get better at riding waves. Also, through no fault or worthiness of your own, once in awhile you get a better wave."

As quotable quotes go, I thought, this is better than Lacan.

Jack came through the door carrying bags of roast chicken and corn on the cob.

Carrie left, because her daughter wanted her. Everyone left. I gave Marie a bath, treated her eczema with medicine and gauze, hauled her to bed. I thought: one and a half more days. Grace was asleep when Toby told me, "I'm overloaded. I have to leave town next week to give a paper I haven't written yet. I was thinking we should just cancel the last class, since you've already impressed the dean. You go back with Jack tomorrow, take Grace, take her to Jack's, take her to the airport—her plane leaves the same day as yours."

I had enough to do by myself. Grace would feel abandoned. "You can't," I said.

Toby said, "Let me rethink this." He told Jack to sleep in the study.

"On that dirty futon?" Jack said. "Forget it. You sleep on it."

Toby said, "You're such an old lady. Listen." They went to another room to whisper.

I was sitting on the bed in my nightgown, taking my antibiotic, my pain pill, my blood sugar regulator. Jack knocked—I looked up. Jack came in, sat on the edge of my bed. He stared at the pill bottles in my lap. He said, "I have a good idea. We can sleep together."

"Are you crazy?"

"I'll hold you. It'll be good for both of us. I'll creep out early so the kids won't see."

"You just don't want to sleep on that dirty futon," I said.

"Maybe." He frowned. "Is that someone's diaphragm on the night-stand?"

"It's a diaphragm case. I honestly never looked inside it."

He said, "It's not Carrie's. They're sleeping together in the van in the garage."

"You mean she left her daughter alone and came back here to have sex in a garage?"

Jack yawned. "It could be some old girlfriend's diaphragm. Esmeralda's."

I shivered. "Talk about your bad housekeeping." I got under the covers.

Jack took off his shoes, got into bed, flipped off the lamp. He curved his arm around me in the dark and said, "I was thinking how your mother has always been the focus of your stories, ever since I've known you. It's like you never had a father." My eyes were closed, and I pretended the sound of Jack's voice was waves lapping. "She was there," I mumbled, "then not there, so I missed her. She came and went a second time, dying. My dad was just not there." Jack said, "Don't you see the parallel? You made the same childhood for Marie, no father, a mother who goes it alone." I groaned. Poets, I thought: everything's symbolic. I said, "I don't obsess about motifs and parallels like you. I'm into causality—first this happens and causes that, and so on."

Or was I? I opened my eyes.

The point of causality is to arrive at a turning point. My theology of stories, I thought.

I said, "Do you mean my mother did more to help me, but I held her to a higher standard than my dad? Is that it?" Then I saw that an outsider studying my life would be hard-pressed not to say: your dad was your first impression of men, a stencil for all future men. No wonder men had seemed like manifest difficulty. All but Jack—and he'd been the exception only in recent years. He used to seem like the enemy. Right now Jack was snoring. Not exactly a ground-breaking insight about family dynamics, I thought. But still.

Jack and I slept curled into each other.

At dawn, he slipped out, the door clicking open, then shut.

In the morning, Toby had yet another plan. He was canceling classes, arranging to spend two days alone with Grace. "I've neglected her," he said. "You can leave with Jack." Toby's previous plan had been that we'd get up at two a.m. to make my flight. "Works for me," I said. I packed. Marie cried. "But I don't get to see the horses again," she said. "I'll miss Grace." But then we were in Jack's SUV, Marie seatbelted in, bags stacked beside her. We drove north on Interstate 75. "One of the most congested highways in all America," Jack said. I didn't pay attention because Jack fusses. He vacuums, then walks on the edges of the carpet to keep it smooth. He takes longer to blow-dry his hair than a woman. On the road, he monologues about bad drivers. I said, "This early?" He scoffed. "We'll hit Atlanta for peak traffic. Rush hour is in fact three hours."

We were ninety miles outside of Atlanta when all four lanes filled up. Progress slowed, stalled, accelerated. Stop, start, stop. I got queasy. "I never get carsick," I said. Jack said, "It's those pills—three horse pills how many times a day?" He shuddered. As soon as he said this, I rolled down the window fast, cool air. "Mama, Mama," Marie called. "Your mama's fine," Jack said, "just a tummy-ache." And he told me his recent news.

His voice rose, fell. I answered. Uh huh. No. Yes. Then someone zipped into our lane, no turn signal. Jack slammed on the brakes. We flew. Our seatbelts whipped us back. "Morons," Jack said. As we regained speed, Jack told me that when he first moved here he was at a party, some arts event. "I met this couple," Jack said. "He was a painter, and she was a writer, and they showed me photos of their kids and asked me if I had kids. I was new to town and having a hard time. I told them my kids were in Utah. Honest to God, I started crying. I couldn't stop. Took me forever to stop. They were so decent."

"Sounds like a nice couple," I murmured.

"We made plans to get together when my kids came to visit, and then"—his voice rose here—"I tried and tried to call them, and I couldn't get through, and I couldn't get through."

"They moved?"

"They were killed, both of them. Dead. This highway. Four kids orphaned."

I supposed those kids had grandparents. And each other. But still. "That's an awful story," I said. I felt sick. My mind went back to the vague days I lay on the couch, sick, sicker. "I feel like throwing up. I can't talk about dying." I started crying. Then Marie started crying. Weeks of suppressed fear discharging. "Of course, sorry," Jack said.

He pulled off at the next exit, bought Dramamine and diet ginger ale. "I haven't taken Dramamine since I was a kid," I said, wiping my eyes. "I'll go to sleep." Marie was in my lap, her head against my chest. Jack said, "I'm in charge today. It's okay if you sleep. Open now." He put Dramamine on my tongue. He cracked the ginger ale. "Swallow. We'll stay here until you're better." He walked around the parking lot, holding Marie. Then he strapped her in, pulled into traffic. He said, "Tonight, I'll cook dinner."

At last we walked into his house, with its basket of beaded fake fruit on the dining room table, the kitchen plaques that say SOUP'S ON and GOD BLESS THIS FOOD. "Lean over your plate, honey," he told Marie. "I don't want to get ants in the house." By the time I finished my bath, he'd started the laundry. "Don't yet," I said. "I need to spot-treat some of that because of horse camp." Marie's clothes had dirt and manure rubbed into the knees and elbows. Jack said, "I saw. It'll come out. I have this great enzyme pre-soak."

That night I slid between clean sheets in the guestroom. Marie lay on the floor in Jack's daughter's pink sleeping bag. "G'night, honey," he told her. To me, he said, "I'll have breakfast waiting when you wake up. I'm headed to the kitchen now to pack you a big high-protein lunch for the plane." He shook out a quilt. It tumbled over me like a cloud.

What you dislike for yourself do not like for me. I can't remember who said this, my brain overstocked from years of reading—important books, and books I'd been hired to review, not to mention bumper stickers and fortune cookies. The opposite must also be true. What you dislike for someone else don't like for yourself. I'd judged people who were parents by rules I hadn't followed. I was a blatantly bad mother on the trip home.

All that time spent with Grace in charge, the Lucky Charms, Mc-Donald's, soda pop—Marie had lost sight of the concept of No. We switched planes in Dallas. We trekked from Terminal A to Terminal D. I told her to hurry, but she'd stare at kiosks, ask for candy, French fries, chips. "I've never in my life seen you cry about pain," I said. "The only thing you cry for is some lost opportunity for a Slurpee or corn dog." My guts hurt. Her lips set into a grim line. She said, "You sound like Toby." I said, "Ask me if I care."

The person reading gate numbers as we'd deplaned had sent us to the wrong terminal. By the time I figured this out, we had to run. "Faster," I told Marie. I was yelling, I realized. I felt like letting rip with a stream of Toby's cussing. People turned their heads to watch, vaguely interested. I stopped trying to use the handle to carry my heavy bag that held my pills, Marie's eczema medicine and gauze strips, my cosmetics, and the big lunch Jack had packed, because I couldn't run fast enough. I held the bag to my chest with one arm, and I used my other to yank Marie, her feet skidding along the floor.

When we got to the gate, our plane was boarding. I set the bag down, unzipped it, sorted through pill bottles—this, no that, that. Pain pills. My hands shook as I pried off the cap. I popped one in my mouth. I was panting from running. A woman stared at Marie, then at me, like I was a welfare mother on drugs. We weren't especially well-groomed that day. Marie looked disgusted too. "Be sure to eat," she said. "Don't get dizzy."

We got to Austin. We got our luggage. We got our shuttle to our car. Now the one-hour drive home. I was pulling out of the airport and

Marie saw a sign on a tall pole. Sonic Drive-In. "Please, can we? Can we have some of that junk food, Mama?" I was idling in line to the booth where you pay for parking. I felt my face twist with pain, anger, or maybe it was the drugs making me cruel, capricious. I yelled at her. "Could you stop talking about junk food for one minute? I promise to buy you junk food as soon as I can. You can eat junk food until you're sick as a dog, if you'll be quiet right now."

I pulled up to the booth, handed the woman my parking stub and debit card. I recomposed. "Hello," I said, calm-seeming. The woman stared with contempt. When she gave me a receipt, she dropped a fistful of candy in my hand. "Give this to that poor little girl in the backseat." She'd seen me yelling. She couldn't have heard me, but she'd seen my face, my daughter's reaction. Even at a distance, through car windows, I'd looked depraved, like one of those mothers who makes you want to call Child Protective Services.

I'd signed on for too much.

But there was no way to say so to a stranger. And it's not a child's fault you've misjudged your abilities. You have to step up. I bought Marie a hamburger, but she was already asleep. As I drove home, I thought about Jack, the abbreviated contact with his kids, his thwarted impulse to nurture. And me, no days off, instincts exhausted, at least now.

When I'd pulled into my driveway in the dark and woke Marie, we stumbled through my torn up, half-completed yard. As we stepped onto the porch and I unlocked the door, I thought how I wanted more for Marie. I couldn't let my emergency, my inattention, this ersatz version of my best self, petrify into habit. I remembered Jack shaking out the quilt over me, Vince asking worried questions, Toby rushing out to buy me a heating pad. No substitute for unsolicited tenderness, I thought. I needed more than solitude and hired hands. I looked at the black sky, crystalline stars, the tall trees, and I reconsidered my life on the outskirts which, when I arrived, felt safe because I was running away, not toward, because the little cabin my house once was had felt like a shelter then, a far-out life that seemed perfect because it was unpeopled. Now it was just unpeopled.

The Uses of Grief

The last time I saw my mother alive was at a writers' conference in Florida, where we'd stayed at a beach house with other writers. One night I sat at a table next to Sofia and, across from us, Marie, age two, sat in my mother's lap. My mother helped Marie slide miniature pretzels onto her fingers like chunky, edible rings. Each night my mother and daughter—Arlene, and Marie Arlene—slept entwined in the same bed. Marie tottered everywhere after my mother. When my mother used the bathroom, Marie banged on the door, sobbing, "Gam, come back to me." My mother would hurry out and say, "Hold onto your horses, dear. I came back to you. I always do." That night Sofia whispered, "You're so lucky you got this second chance with your mom." I nodded. I knew.

I thought back to the first time my mother saw Marie. I'd called my sister to tell her I had my baby and asked her to tell the rest of the family. My mother was staying there, but she wasn't home at the moment. My sister called back. "Mom's packing. She wants to visit." I told my sister Shen was already coming, to tell our mom to come in a few weeks.

Three weeks later, my mother pulled into my driveway in her dead husband's Trans Am, and she stumbled as she got out of the low-slung car. I counted from the day she'd left to the day she'd arrived, and I said, "You must have done ninety the whole way." Stepping onto the porch, she said, "I have a fuzz buster. I even stopped to take some naps." She went inside where Marie lay on the sofa, no bigger than a stuffed animal. My mother, road-weary, stared. "I knew she'd be black," she said, "but not this black."

I said, "Mom, there's a blank in the baby book called 'Grandma's First Words.'"

My mother blushed. Her ideas had always translated awkwardly to speech.

"Another try?" I suggested.

"Her hair," she said.

Daughters need mothers, I thought then. Though you can do without, if forced. But I wanted my daughter's life to be ideal. A grandmother all of a sudden was a must-have.

"She's lovely," my mother said at last, her voice uncertain.

I wrote it in the baby book.

In theory, race didn't bother her. God made all of us, she'd say. But its physical manifestations intrigued her. And she had to tweak her small talk. She wondered if *black* sounded better, or *African-American*, because when she was young it was impolite not to say *Negro*. "This is my adopted granddaughter," she tried saying after she'd shown snapshots to a co-worker who said, "So your daughter married a dark man then." A week later, my mother showed the photos to someone else, and the same co-worker piped up, "That one is Arlene's *adopted* granddaughter." My mother, huffy, phoned me to say she'd told off the old bat like this: "That's my granddaughter, period. She's perfect."

Two years later, in Florida, they sat with their arms around each other.

I said to Sofia, "Check it out. Their facial expressions are alike."

Sofia said, "You should see the three of you. You all have the same look on your face."

"What?" I asked.

Sofia spoke slowly. "You look vulnerable. Alert. Ready for what's next."

A few weeks later, my mother was dead.

Back home, I sat in my living room with Jana, whose birth mother had been killed three years earlier. When Jana found her birth mother, Jana's quirkiness—which her adoptive mother, one-time president of the Beaumont Junior League, had struggled to accommodate—found its corollary, or cause: genes. Jana's birth mother was a painter. Jana went to meet her. Jana's birth mother's house was filled with decaying Victorian dolls, old puppets with leering faces, Day of the Dead figures. She'd hung swaths of antique lace in corners to look like cobwebs. "It was like a set for a Tim Burton movie," Jana said. Her birth mother, alone in the world, had been thrilled to find Jana and two ready-made grandchildren. Two months later, a semi-truck driver mowed her down, road rage.

Another death too complicated to explain to neighbors and acquaintances.

As we sat in my living room, Jana said that, afterward, she'd hated it when people talked about grief. She said, "The five stages of grief. The grief process. Grief processor, I'd think. What am I supposed to be doing? Slicing it? Making puree? My situation was so complicated—I have two great parents. I felt like I had no right to feel sad."

I felt that way too, because I hadn't used time better when my mother was alive. If only I'd tried to rescue her when she'd been with her second husband. Or if I'd called and hadn't waited for her to call me. Or I could have forgiven her sooner for her absence and omissions. I was a grief novice. I hoarded memories of my mother. I made my memories into a fetish. I revisited facts and phases, trying to see them first in one light, then another. I studied my mother's life. In time, I studied my own life, my near-death by inattention. I understood it was life, of course, not a parable. In life, clues arrive in a blitz, mixed with non-clues. Still, I sifted through details, saving this, rejecting that, searching for a moral. But the end of a story that's real, not invented, isn't a plot device, deliverance.

It's not like the end of an old-fashioned novel: everyone married, all ailments cured.

It's conscious choice. The decision to make fewer mistakes. Determination.

Better direction.

I willed my details to add up and point me the way forward.

So far, all I understood about the four-year tunnel of time I'd passed through is that happiness is fragile.

Once, right after my mother died, I was in my car. I told myself: my life has changed now. "Who are you talking to?" Marie asked from the backseat. My future options have changed at least in terms of my mother, I thought, silently now. But I wasn't registering the change quickly. I still had impulses to pick up the phone and call her. Or I'd think—*my mother, what was it she said about lessons, some cost more?*—and then I'd remember: she's dead. And the memory stopped being incidental and turned elegiac, a shrinking currency because if I used it up there wouldn't be new memories to replace it. All the same, I thought, I needed to buy groceries and new shoes for Marie. Then I noticed a billowing black snake of smoke in an otherwise perfect blue sky. I pulled over and turned to see where the smoke might be. "What, Mama?" Marie asked.

It could be my house, I thought, burning. It wasn't a rational thought.

Losing my house would be more than I could stand. Yet if I turned around to make sure my house wasn't on fire, I'd add twenty-five pointless miles onto my drive. I went back anyway. "Where are we going, Mama?" Marie asked. "I forgot my wallet," I said. When we got back to the house and it sat unharmed on its well-kept acre, I pretended to get my wallet, then drove to San Marcos, hoping the frantic double-checking to ascertain we're safe—a compulsion I'd wrestled with anyway—would recede again in time.

Of course it got worse first, because of my trouble with doctors and fences. I didn't believe most people, their expertise or assurances. I didn't trust my body. It seemed like an engine running so rough it should be replaced, not repaired. The status quo seemed fraught with undetected crises. One day I realized Jana could die. In fact, anyone could. But, case in point, Jana had bronchitis. She told me she'd finished her antibiotics. On the phone, she coughed and said, "But I don't feel like they ever quite worked."

I said, "Did the doctor do a culture?"

"Doctors don't routinely for chest colds," she said.

I drove to her house. It's full of children's art work, pieces of used furniture she's painted bright colors. She has dozens of animals—goldfish on the mantle, gerbils and hamsters on a table in the kitchen, two massive cats, and an elastic-limbed puppy. Jana rode in the front seat of my car, our three kids in back, and I drove her to the doctor. I stayed in the waiting room with Noah, Zoey, and Marie until she came out. The doctor changed her drug, Jana said. In a few days, she was getting better. She said, "It was nice, having you take over." Later, she sent me a hand-written note on cream-colored paper (her adoptive mother had stressed etiquette): *Thanks for your kind help when I was sick.*

Close call, I thought.

But the moral of the story couldn't be that I had to double-check everything and everybody. I had to find one problem, I decided. If I'd suffered for a single reason, I could solve all future problems—with doctors, subcontractors, men I'd date—with one solution. And the constant I detected was a too-persistent sense I didn't deserve a home, a family, respect. If someone said *this is all I have, the best I can do,* and it wasn't good, I forgave them; I let them stay on. I felt bad they didn't know better. So I didn't save myself.

One day after the surgery, getting prescriptions for inflamed scar tissue, I said to Mary, the sensible nurse, "I guess I'll be dealing with this for the rest of my life." She said, "Never underestimate the body's capacity to heal. You'll feel fine. Give yourself time."

But before I could, the wheel turned around another time.

Marie was six and had the growth surge the ENT described. This doctor also said she had the first symptoms of neurofibromatosis, which causes blindness, deafness, monster-size tumors, a crooked spine. I drove away from the clinic in heavy rain, windshield wipers slapping, my love for Marie like torment.

It was a wait-for-it-to-manifest disease.

I tried not to picture it. As Lauren said: motherhood is a series of emergencies, and you rise to the challenge, over and over. In the meantime, you stay calm, business as usual.

This emergency isn't here, I told myself.

Only now can I see—this time in hindsight, in my ongoing search for an orderly plot in this disorderly tangle of memory—that I almost always made smart decisions for Marie. When her welfare was in question, I acted swiftly, intelligently. About the sixth time I took her to the pediatrician for a high fever, the pediatrician said, "You should teach a class to new mothers about reacting calmly to childhood illnesses. Some young mothers don't know enough to get scared when they should. Older mothers often know too much and see pathology everywhere." Me? I thought. I seemed calm, but on the inside I was manic. I hadn't made smart decisions for myself—I was habituated to bad breaks, broken in by them—but in time I saw that the decisions I'd make to give myself a better life would make Marie's life better. When I'd stared into her eyes when she was newborn, she was happy, and I vowed she'd stay happy. I hadn't been able to do it for myself.

I'd do it for her.

Heart of my heart, break of sunlight in the darkest time, Marie.

She's sometimes grabby and fast, and she'll climb on you when you're too tired, so you might ask her to calm down, have a seat, give you space. Okay, so she doesn't get it about personal space, the inviolate "bubble." But she's never mean. She's angry or surly rarely—she's happy again in an instant. She doesn't understand grudges, how to hold one. As the delivery room nurse noted, she has beautiful lips. At the time, I'd thought this was neonatal code for likeliness to thrive, like Apgar scores or good reflexes, but it turns out beautiful lips are no indication of health, good nor bad. Beautiful lips mean she's beautiful. To the people who through the years have asked me *what is she?* (ruined by a careless birth mother? HIV-positive?): she's contagious, yes. You catch her smile.

The last year we lived in our little town, her teacher called to say there'd been an "incident." We'd had incidents before—usually on the school bus. After the third incident on the school bus, I said, "Marie, you're going to have to learn to handle mean kids yourself, because I can't be with you always. When that boy calls you that name tomorrow, say: 'You're hurting my feelings and I'm giving you one chance to apologize.' If he doesn't, then we'll talk to the bus driver together. Or you can laugh and call him a name back, to show you don't care." Marie asked, "What name?" I thought about it. I said, "I don't know. Honky white boy?" A few days later, Marie said: "Mama, I called him a tooty white boy like you said and laughed. And you're right, he leaves me alone now."

But the new "incident" Marie's fourth grade teacher called to tell me about was that a little boy had refused to do group work with her because she was black. The teacher told me his parents had been called for a conference. Good luck with that, I thought. Because who teaches a child not to sit with children whose skin is a different color except parents? The teacher said, "I told him you get to pick your friends, but you can't pick who you learn with and work with. School is training for life. In life, you live and work with people who aren't like you." I thanked her for handling it well. She said, "I'm calling because I talked to Marie, and she seems okay. Her self-esteem, my God, you've done such a good job. But I don't see how any child could feel okay. Maybe talk to her?"

That night, I brought it up.

Marie shook her head. "He's mean to everyone. He says mean things to all the kids. So he doesn't have friends, and that's sad. But some people you just have to leave alone."

I agreed. "It's his problem. His parents taught him bad ideas." He was already off her radar screen, I realized. I relaxed a little. I saw she was growing up smart and calm.

Another teacher once said to me: "I don't know how to put it except to say that she's a mensch. She's the class conscience. She has a genius for understanding other people, what they feel—without subtracting an iota from herself, no groveling, not a whit."

And she gets good grades too.

I took her out of school all the time to go to doctors, but she always got good grades. It turns out she has a few learning disabilities, but she gets good grades anyway. An extraordinary brain, tests revealed, but a patchy and labyrinthine way of processing abstract information. She still draws the right conclusions. At the end of the school year, on Awards Day, she always wins prizes for best attitude, cooperation with others, conflict resolution.

I was in the parking lot of Marie's grade school one morning—I'd dropped Marie off and was walking back to my car—when Ronnie Larkin, who lived behind me, slowed down his pickup and waved me over to tell me that Nathan, Lauren's son, sixteen years old now, had crashed his car the night before. He was dead. It was 8:00 a.m. on a cold January morning. I screamed, a reflex. First thought: How do I inoculate myself, keep trouble like this away? Second thought: How will Lauren stand the rest of her life? A third, convoluted thought: Nathan had been removed from his birth family when he was one. He'd had a rough start, a love disorder. It had taken serious work to teach him to attach, to trust, but he'd turned out fine. For what? For Lauren to love him while he was here.

At the funeral a few days later, girls had dressed up. Some wore last year's prom dress—a black strapless, a glittery red halter, a filmy sheath. Goths, geeks, athletes came. They were scared, for him, for themselves: their first acquaintance with death. I saw their anxious faces as I got out of my car, and I stepped through the crowd of undocumented workers who wait each day for work in the church parking lot. When the workers saw us—the crowd, the hearse—they edged away. Because it wasn't my first funeral, I do know what to wear, something plain and warm. A fact: grieving people experience a slight drop in body temperature. When the funeral was over, I stepped back through the undocumented workers who'd huddled, waiting for the funeral to end, the work of surviving to begin again. I heard a girl say, "Are we supposed to go all the way?" I looked up, startled this conversation had begun now. She was wearing an evening dress. With a worried look on her face, she asked a girl in jeans and a T-shirt, "I mean, to the cemetery."

That night, after the funeral, Marie stood naked in the living room. I covered her with salve, wrapped her trouble spots in white gauze. Eczema treatment. "What are ghosts?" she asked. She hadn't been watching *Scooby-Doo*. She knew Nathan was dead. I told her people's bodies go away, but the basic part of who they are lasts. "How?" she asked. "A soul," I answered. Good breeds good, I thought. When people die, we don't lose all they were. What's next? Something. I've seen it. Glimmers. "What's a soul?" Marie asked, ducking, because headlights were shining through the window as if a car had driven straight into the room. Marie ran for her pajamas. I went to the front door, opened it. Lauren stood outside in wet fog. "Take these flowers," she said.

She'd left flower arrangements at the nursing home already. Her parents and in-laws had taken some too. "You knew him," she said. "Here." We hugged. She drove away.

After Lauren left, I looked at the flowers—sunflowers and gay feathers—and I thought they looked too cheerful for a winter funeral. They'd stood sentry over Nathan's closed casket. His car had rolled. Someone I knew had seen the windshield, safety glass shattered in concentric rings. I told Marie that when we cleaned house the next day we'd throw them away. She said, "They're pretty." I said, "This one is wilting." I plucked it out.

I thought about Lauren standing in freezing drizzle, finding a place for unwanted flowers: flowers need purpose too. I thought about her years of effort and patience, teaching Nathan not to say "homo," how to be proud, not cocky. She'd just helped him open a checking account. He'd said, "I don't want to grow up." She'd answered him, she'd told me, "You already did, and you can be bad at it, a loser, or suck it up and get good."

I didn't keep the flowers long. I tried to cast off too-serious ideas about my own purpose. In life, some moments flicker with augury and hope, but you get so many moments, red herrings too: irrelevant information you don't need mixed with essential information you do need. My superstitious fears, gut instincts both credible and useless, that a ripple I caused would turn into a flood, that a failure to act would trigger a plague or pox, I let go. The worst might happen in the rain, the sun, the day or night, I realized. It might be Marie's lungs or endocrine system or freak chance. Or I'd die, leave her an orphan. One of us would die. I hoped it would be me first, when she was old enough, ready.

I'd conceded that much—there's no way to see Death coming and ask it to change its mind—by the time I sat on a patio one afternoon outside an upscale restaurant with gourmet food for parents and a deluxe playscape built of colorful cubes and tubes for the kids.

I'd taken Marie to Austin to a new doctor, forty miles away. Marie had finished her lunch and headed out to play. I watched her moving hand over hand across the monkey bars. Because I treated her skin with Vaseline and cheesecloth, her muscles gleamed. People always said: "She's grown like a weed." I'd smile and say thank you. She grew so fast each test put her this time inside, and the next time outside, the line demarcating normal from abnormal growth. That morning they'd taken her blood, injected her with hormones. They'd take more blood in four hours. When I'd shown this new doctor the first symptoms of the disease, neurofibromatosis, that the other doctor had noticed, the freckling under her arms, this doctor said, "You're not used to black skin." More used to it than most white people, I thought. He said, "There's no test for it. It gets diagnosed by symptoms—how many she has, what size the pigment variations are. Her variations are so minor that, well, unless something changes fast, her diagnosis would be negative."

"She doesn't have it?" I said.

"It's a judgment call. Not in my estimation, no."

I told him what the other doctor had said. He looked polite. No, bored. Was he sure?

"Pretty sure," he said.

And I decided never to think about neurofibromatosis again.

For two years, since we saw that other doctor who first saw neurofibromatosis at a freak show and said that Marie had the symptoms, I'd consciously *not* thought about it, which is to say, on a buried, tacit, smoke-screen level, I never stopped thinking about it. I'd thought the doctor who said she had it was right. Why would he be wrong? I'd researched the disease but found I couldn't research for long without feeling hot, cold, flushed, panicked, organs I never knew I had twisting. Sofia took over and researched for me, then filtered, which is where I got basic facts: when it would manifest and how (slightly? extremely?). Now a new doctor's casual opinion was that she likely didn't have it.

She likely didn't have it.

After he said so, Marie and I went to the restaurant. I still eat every three hours—like an infant. I have to. First, I get clumsy, anxious. I bark orders, look over my shoulder. My vision fails. But not often. I've gotten used to the rhythm, this herky-jerky life. Fear, inattention, bad impulses. Food, better impulses, better decisions. I don't do anything important when I'm hungry. And I was well-fed when the mother of a girl on the playscape wandered up. "Your daughter is so graceful," she said. Also: "You must be a home-schooling mom too." I said I wasn't. She said, "So why are you in Austin today?"

I said we were in town for a series of blood tests.

Her husband was a doctor, she said. "Are you sitting out the time between tests here?"

I said we'd sit out the next few hours at my boyfriend's house—though Gary was at work, his son at school. This was the man Sofia had insisted would be out there if I didn't ratchet down my hopes, the man Nomie had said sounded just right: "the one." I'd told her not to confuse life with romantic comedies. Or, to recall the surfer-dude philosophy, I'd been riding tricky waves—I'd just wrapped up serial dating with the two Mikes, Proletariat and Overanalytic—and I was really good at tricky waves. Then, through no fault or worthiness of my own, a good wave rolled in. After two years, he was still smart and kind. He was a good father to his son. He loved my daughter. He was attentive to his elderly parents. He was tall. He took my breath away in the dark of night. Would I marry him? I'd marry a handsome man who'd see my ambitions as praiseworthy. I'd marry a prince. I'd never been this far, past infatuation and not yet entangled in mutual loathing. When it came to men, I'd had a mild case of attachment disorder, a fancy way of saying cold feet. And just because you have a name for it doesn't mean you get over it. One day, Gary said to me, "You're so ready for this all to go south, you scare the hell out of me. I worry that you'll break up with me, just to be preemptive."

We had a recurring conversation. I'd say I wasn't confident. He'd disagree. I said, "You're wrong. I flinch. I make peace at all costs." He said, "That must be who you used to be." I said, "With you, I don't, because you're not angry. Or selfish." He said, "But you had to be strong to raise your daughter where you did, given the factors that make your life different." He meant that in a small town my This-Is-Not-Your-*Father-Knows-Best* household was conspicuous. He said, "I've seen you be assertive with other people—that teacher who put your daughter in the hall for asking for hugs." He was right, I realized. I had clout now. I'd claimed it. He'd met me just as I'd learned how.

I dated him a long time before I introduced him to Marie.

"Looks like a fancy hotel in here," Marie had said. His house, she meant.

At the restaurant, the doctor's wife I'd been chatting with said goodbye. I stood up to go. Because the restaurant was mostly empty, and the cubes and elaborate tunnels on the playscape opaque, I called for Marie. I wouldn't have called her name if more people had been eating lunch, too much ambient noise and I'd have had to yell and disturb the other diners. If I hadn't felt lazy and contented maybe, I'd have walked down the steps, across the gravel, and found her. I called her name again. She didn't answer. I called a third time, undeniably shrill, anxious, and I hurried down the steps. Marie was nowhere.

Out of a part of the landscape I hadn't registered because I don't have eyes in the back of my head, I heard a quiet, careful woman's voice with sighs built in, "I'll find her. I've had my eye on her all along." I thought: she's obsessed with other people's children, one of those wannabe-mothers who kidnaps. I needed to find Marie and leave immediately. Now. Marie poked her head out of a blue tunnel. I said, "Not good. You scared me when you didn't answer." Marie jumped to the ground, grabbed my hand. To dismiss the woman, lose her forever, I said, chilly, fake-cheerful, "All's well that ends well."

She said, "I lost a child, you see, so I try to help people who've lost theirs."

Impatient, confused, I thought: *lost*? "Where?"

"St. Stephen's." An expensive private school. I looked at her clothes, her glasses, her haircut. Expensive. I must have looked more confused. I thought: lost a child at school? She said, "We didn't find him for a long time. It was hard, the months of not knowing."

The fear I'd held at bay ebbed back. My arm moved involuntarily toward her. I grabbed her hand. She held mine, and we stared into each other's faces. "I'm sorry," I said. She said, "It was very, very hard. Now I try to help parents who can't find their children."

Later, when I went home, Gary called to ask about Marie's blood tests, and I told him about the woman. His reaction mirrored mine. As I recounted her first words, he seemed doubtful. Yet, as specifics accrued, he grew thoughtful. "This sounds familiar." Another lawyer in his office had sent her son to the same school, he said, and he'd ask her. An hour later, he emailed me a link to a website dedicated to a brown-eyed boy who'd attended St. Stephen's and was missing five months when hikers found his body in a ravine, no clues whether he'd stumbled, jumped, been thrown, and to see more missing children just click. The website represented an organization founded by his mother—it was devoted to the rapid exchange of information about lost children. I stared at her face on the website photo and thought about her outward poise and, beyond it, the devastated void.

I recalled how, at the restaurant, as she'd returned to her table, I'd noticed that the people she'd been sitting with had watched our interaction, their faces protective. I gathered up my keys, Marie's toys and books, and I understood. I'd come to the end of a thick passage, the end of a long, circular channel of redundant time to a cleared-out frame of mind, and at last I understood the troth I'd pledged: you want your child to be here, now, so you can see that she's fine, so you can help her, save her, and the excruciating fear that attaches to hope, the fear she might not be fine, is what love costs. Love costs. The woman had waved goodbye, and, an afterthought, blew us a kiss. The people she sat with stared at me, hoping I'd be kind. I blew her a kiss back and headed into the world, the as-of-now, holding Marie's hand, loving her with all my might as long we both will live.

Mother's Day

The year Marie was ten, I stood on my porch holding a tray, wearing my mother's shiny patent leather pumps. I'd brought them home with me eight years earlier when I'd flown up with an overnight bag, and then she died, and I'd raided her closet for clothes to wear to the funeral. Today, the shoes complemented my spring dress cinched at the waist, the ruffled apron over it. I was wearing an engagement ring so big, so new, I still banged and scraped it against the sink's edge or the cupboard door as I did my chores. Gary and I had picked out the ring together. The jeweler had designed it to look old, to look like my grandmother's, the grandmother who'd groused and fretted and run off into the snow without her coat. Later, she'd married a genial husband and took some of the newly-invented psychotropic drugs, and she turned out happy. It was hard remembering that.

Sad years impress deep. Wearing my mother's shoes, I held a tray of parfait glasses filled to the brim with strawberries marinated in wine, vanilla, and rosemary—my old boyfriend Joseph's grandmother's recipe. He'd spent the best years of his childhood at her vineyard where nothing went wasted. Wine too imperfect to sell preserved strawberries ripening too fast. I'd garnished these portions with whipped cream and tiny meringues, except for mine and Jana's son's: plain berries. Noah has food allergies. I'd made cookies for the rest of the kids. I do have parties now, in addition to the infinite cooking for me and Marie, but I don't cook much for Gary because, unlike Joseph, he thinks it's good, salubrious, for me to stop cooking and go to a restaurant. Every holiday, for three years now, Joseph has text-messaged me: "A Joyous Christmas." "Happy Easter." "Fond thoughts for an auspicious New Year." Today, "Warm Mother's Day Wishes. I would be pleased hearing from you." I need to call him, I thought, tell him to stop.

I remembered my mother who, when I was little, ladled out food, love. Festive, gracious. Big servings. Take, eat. Take more. She taught me to be meek and self-sacrificial to inherit the earth. I understood now meek had swindled us. I decided on *humble* instead. So my mother had been humble and content for years, but it was easier remembering her crouched in a bathroom, afraid of her husband, her timid appeasement voice, or how, after he died and I was a stranger, she wanted someone, anyone, a place to attach.

"What perfect delicacy is that?" Jana called from a bench near the fish pond.

"Just dessert," I said, "some berries and cookies."

My other guests—encircled by a well-built fence, every surrounding tree, shrub, and flower blooming fuchsia, saffron, crimson, mauve—sprawled on lawn furniture with that soporific, fed look. I'd given them smoked salmon, then lamb with raspberry-mint sauce, new potatoes, cucumbers in yogurt and dill, roasted eggplant. Jana, looking like a pre-Raphaelite beatnik in her purple sandals, purple spangled dress, and matching shawl, sat watching as the children— her own Noah and Zoey, Marie, and my new friend Tracy's daughter too—jumped through a lawn sprinkler arcing to and fro, water gleaming in lush grass.

I looked at my other guests in the arbor, where honeysuckle bloomed coral. My new friends, Tracy, and her husband, Ron, freelance journalists who lived out here but filed national stories—I'd met them at Meet the Teacher Night when our daughters got assigned to the same class—sat talking to Sofia and her husband, John, who'd arrived from Florida last night, also Will, with whom I'd gone on one date ten years ago, the night before I brought Marie home. He'd recently called to say he was married, that he and his wife had adopted. His wife was inside, feeding the baby in the rocker in Marie's room.

"Mary, Mother of God, and Jesus Christ too," Sofia had said last night, when we'd pulled into the driveway and opened the doors of the car. "I had no idea you lived so far out. I'm amazed you found anyone at all who'd drive this far for a date." The trip from the airport—winding roads, leaping deer, hovering buzzards—had rattled her. For years, she'd been saying by email that living way out meant I didn't live outside as much as inside. Not inside the house—though I did, during one or two cold months or hottest days—but inside myself, my memories. Yet most of the years I'd lived here had been good.

Still, until recently, holidays felt bad. I'd gear up for the big ones. It's a resort town. People retire here. A sonorous hush takes over. Cars fill country lanes, extended families arriving. A few summers ago, Fourth of July, my mood slipped. I thought: Okay, I hate Christmas. I had a bad Thanksgiving or two. But Fourth of July? I took Marie to the town carnival. I was still in the thick of it, worrying as a way of life, just a few months past my surgery, the healing underway, and I wasn't sure about Marie's prognosis yet. I couldn't let Marie know I was scared. I willed the hours to pass. A clown at the festival grabbed my arm. "Listen, lady, how bad could it be? A sunny afternoon, little kids playing games." I jumped. Under the makeup, the clown's face softened. He said, "Bad day? You need a hug?" I'd considered hugging a clown, and shuddered.

Jana stood as her new boyfriend, Kevin, pulled up—he'd had to see his mother before he could join us. Kevin recently told me he'd dreamed Jana was a butterfly, that he'd get near her, and she'd fly away. She thought Kevin was good enough, for now. I understood. You need company, attention. But quick fixes aren't necessarily durable. She had children, Noah especially, for whom she'd tried every therapy devised. A man has to want your love, which is extended divergent ways, has to want a woman who gives her love away like that, and want her kids too. Deciding whether she'd marry him or risk losing him because he needed an answer, she worried more than usual, drank a little more too.

She used to cut herself when she was young. Yesterday afternoon, as we'd cooked while the children played, the conversation turned aimless but succinct. She said she was afraid to live her life alone, but also afraid to risk it on someone who could decide later on she was hard to love. Or she'd be too set in stone, too rigid, to be part of something bigger than herself. "For the first time in maybe twenty years I had the impulse," Jana said. "To what?" I asked. "In April," she said, "I had the urge for a little pre-Easter wielding upon myself." I'd stared, my knife poised over garlic. "Sorry to sound like a Valkyrie," she said. "I admit I felt tempted. But I just ground my teeth instead."

I understood.

When I met Gary and I reveled in the fact he'd had a secure childhood—his parents, oil field workers, had moved a lot, but he was doted on, family scion who stood to inherit love—I felt guilty. If everyone held everyone to that standard, who would love me? He did. I asked him why, and he shook his head. "Your résumé? Your sense of humor? The way you are as a mother? You look good to me? I don't need to understand it."

But for people like Jana and me, love is careful.

We worry about what hasn't happened, or might. Everywhere, books and magazines promise schemes for happiness—proof we lead easy lives now. In centuries when people worried about starving, or in places where people still worry about starving, happiness is beside the point. The Greeks believed happiness is beyond human control— you're happy or hapless, due to mayhap, mishap, happenstance. Fate. Now, of course, we think we're supposed to be incessantly happy, another tyranny. In fact, for the first two years I knew Gary, I wanted airtight guarantees neither of us would die soon, that we'd never fight, never be impatient with each other's children. I wanted out: first dibs. I tried not to say so. He might give up on me if I cataloged all the ways love could turn difficult.

But once in awhile I stall out on old fears.

For instance, my dad recently had surgery and almost died because of a heart attack during it, and he almost died again two days later because of alcohol withdrawal—he'd lied to the surgeon in the pre-op appointment about how much he drank. My contact with him is occasional, visits when I stay at my sister's house, not his, or I meet him and his wife at RV parks. But when my dad was just out of the hospital, Gary flew with Marie and me to Wisconsin—his first visit to meet my family. By the time we arrived, my dad sat in a cranked-up bed in his living room, recasting his worst moments as side-effects of morphine, not DTs. He had two versions of his second near-death, one in which he sounded like a gunslinger: "The doc leaned over me and said 'This one's a fighter.'" Another, like Dickens, Little Nell: "Orderlies from other parts of the hospital knew by my unconscious face I was a good man," my dad said, "and came to pray over me."

A few days later, we went driving, my dad in the passenger seat, gesturing at points of interest. My mother was absent from his ruminations. Not mine. Because of an old will, my mother was buried on the cold shores of Lake Superior next to her mean husband.

I recalled how, when my dad first asked for a divorce, she'd moved out of the family house into an apartment—hoping my dad would beg her to return—but he moved his girlfriend in and changed the locks. My mom's apartment wasn't big enough to keep her compulsion for flawless housekeeping channeled. She came unhinged. She broke into the house, unplugged the deep-freeze so my dad's steaks would thaw. She called the radio station, Noontime Market, and advertised his car for sale. One night she walked into the dining room where my dad was eating dinner with his girlfriend and her parents, and my mother said, "I need my good china." She scraped their food into the sink, put the unwashed dishes in a laundry basket, and drove away. She told me: "Their jaws were swinging. Your dad, that hypochondriac, doesn't have a bad heart. If he did, he'd have died then."

Thirty years later, my dad drove and pointed at the town's highlights. "That's where the strip joint was, with cigarette holes in the curtains so anyone, even kids walking to school, could look in and see strippers. There's that movie theater where that boy killed his mother and father, never convicted, but everyone knew. This house," he said, "is where a guy killed his wife, had a party in the yard until he decided what to do with the body." He turned to me. "Debbie, do you remember the owner of the supper club on Highway 63? The wife finally had it and shot him." My stepmother shushed him. "You'll make the kids think they're in some horror movie, not this nice town." She'd endured years of his tantrums, blackouts, the muddled rants. That morning, as my dad had yelled, she'd said, "Marriage is putting up with things you don't like." My sister had said close to the same thing the day before, wistful. Meanwhile, Gary nodded and smiled.

But when we got back to Texas and Gary heard me telling friends about the trip—in particular, about my father's near-death legend, the mingled versions, a little *Gunsmoke* and *The Old Curiosity Shop* combined—Gary said, "You can't change your father." I'd answered, "I wasn't trying to. If I describe things I don't like, they get more manageable." I realized I'd spent my life doing exactly what my dad does, retelling bad stories to make them better. My dad left out a major fact: he drank poisonous amounts of alcohol for years, and that's why he almost died. Surely I leave out facts too, but I try to be truthful, taking the blame when I can stand it, taking credit if credit feels fair. Gary said, "You talk about it and talk about it—like you're enlisting support, like you don't trust your perspective. At some point, just accept you're not there anymore." He meant Wisconsin.

Or the past, in general.

I have this second chance with my dad now, I sometimes think. But we have more lost years, less time together as a foundation, than I had with my mother. And years of drinking affect a person's ability to talk and listen, to interact. I told Gary I needed to find a way to know my dad better before he died, and Gary said, "This might be a time when the optimistic approach doesn't apply. Just do what you can, and let it go."

I told Gary he was a stoic. "I'm not. I've always been an outsider, and the way I tried to feel normal was to analyze odd things, the things that bother me, package them up into a story, and give them an ending I believe in. But things I hope won't happen," I said, "bad endings, I won't describe. Like the idea behind the name Yahweh— you never say God's name, too scary, jinx factor." Gary looked exasperated. Not that he isn't used to my stream-of-consciousness free association. He said, "My childhood, the moving around, I've always felt like an outsider too. But I handled the toughest parts by being silent."

So, like Jana, I worry. If Gary and I are so different, can we be together without making each other feel wrong? I learned early to judge other people's moods, to fine-tune my mood accordingly, and, doing so, I lost myself, self-rule. I'd been a jester, a diplomat, a spy. I'd placated and cringed. Family values. Finally, I wanted to be in a family of one: me. Then two: Marie and me. Now she was turning into a separate person, not exactly dependent anymore, the pendulum she once was, arms wrapped around me in a clench, my attachment as I went through my day. Lately, she was off somewhere, thinking about her IPod or dance class, her future career which changed weekly: teacher, dancer, social worker, airplane pilot. She thought about friends, crucial alliances, cliques, feuds. When I first wanted to be a mother, it was a selfish wanting, my child. And when she was little, she was in fact mine, a reflection—spiffy, adorable, well-tended.

But already I could see the time coming when she'd contradict and defy me, shun me, need my help while insisting she didn't. Being a mother isn't about the mother but the child, guiding her safely to her own life. I'd be alone again. I didn't think I'd resist, grieve or struggle, letting go, because I've mostly been at peace alone. Yet I've been too alone.

And Gary and I don't disagree much. If we do, we find common ground fast. He said once, "We won't solve this tonight, Debra. Let's keep it on the table, keep talking." We'd just met with the architect who'd draw up plans for the add-on to the house in the city. It was Gary's house to begin with, not mine. And a stranger was designing the house it would be: based on both Gary's ideas and mine, our amalgamated priorities. An engineer would shore up the foundation. It would be a solid, stately, more spacious home. I felt bittersweet, leaving mine. My house was the history of me—the best I could put together with what I had on hand, so by and large a good house. But I understood every mistake I'd made. I didn't want to stay, dwelling on outmoded ways of adapting, surviving.

Having spent so much time in Austin as Gary and I dated, I'd gotten used to city life, the vanishing into the crowd. I'd begun to realize how much—as I'd lived in a small town, standing around the school parking lot, at the meat counter in the grocery store, or waiting to vote at the polling place—I'd dissembled, lied, avoided hot topics and real opinions, pretending to be more ordinary than I felt. I was ready to leave. I thought of my friend, Tess, at her retirement party. She'd had cancer; chemo had been hell. She was moving to England. How did she feel? I'd asked. "Just because you can't see what's next. . ."

She laughed. "You can't see. That's the point. It's bound to be good enough."

Watching Marie now, sleek, tall, pretty, water beading on her skin, her everlasting smile, I thought how, when she was little, I'd worried about every potential or missed chance to help her flourish. And here she was, flourishing. She'd never been anything but fun, besides the expected little toil. As potential adoptions had come up and fallen through, I'd made a secret, selfish list each time, for a healthy child, a smart child, a child whose family history wasn't unspeakable and, if I could be so superficial and vain to add two last wishes, I'd wanted a girl too, a beautiful girl, and then I got Marie. My neighbor, Clara Mae, God rest her soul, had said: "Isn't it funny how you let God know you'd take any child, no matter what sort of problems it had, and God sent this baby, like He was saying I know you've had shitty experiences with every kind of love. Now just enjoy."

Jana's boyfriend, Kevin, called out to me. "Where's Gary?"

I answered, "He had to see his mother too. He's stopping by later."

Last year, on Mother's Day, Marie and I had gone to brunch with Gary and his son in the town where his parents live. Gary's mother, her twin sister, and I wore pink corsages. Waiters and patrons beamed at our table, three generations. It was the first Mother's Day I'd celebrated, been celebrated. With Gary's mother, I'd let my inner housewife show, chatting about cooking, sewing. Her twin sister, on the other hand, once ran a honky-tonk. "Because I liked the music," she'd whispered as we stood in the kitchen. "I more or less had every experience I ever hankered after." I nodded and said, "I married a musician once." She'd groaned and rolled her eyes. "They make terrible husbands."

So, in the end, I got a mother and a spare. In truth, my future in-laws are frail, a little senile, baffled, yet grateful for conversation I offer up they can't quite follow, but they know my intention is kind. They play-act at understanding. I play-act back. I keep smiling and talking because I've been waiting years for a place to spend holidays, the used-to-be lonely days, and I want my daughter to feel family extending. But this year, this Mother's Day, because Sofia and John came to visit, I stayed home and sent my good wishes.

Husband, I'd soon learn to say, which once sounded like a bad word. But most people think it's better, conventional. Saying *husband* instead of *boyfriend*, I'd shed the advertisement I was a single mother who dates, which maybe isn't a strike against you in a city, but in a small town, where church steeples punctuate the skyline, it is. I'd give up my assigned role as conspicuous, brazen. Already I noticed glances I got when I was with my daughter, people wanting to ask *did she come from you, your womb, who's the father?*, were different when I went places with Gary and his son. If people noticed at all, they gave us approving smiles: adoption, so nice. So I stood on the steps of my house, freshly painted for resale, twice as big as when I first crossed its threshold, its grounds so ornate Sofia said last night it looked like a bed and breakfast. I was moving, changing again.

"Debra?" It was Tracy. "Would you like help with that tray?" She was smiling.

I smiled too. I said, "I've been thinking about what it's been like to live here. I'm not a snob about education. But I *was* a strange fit. I had to keep so many of my ideas to myself. Or I told them to strangers in the most stripped-down terms, trying to be understood."

Tracy had moved here from another small town. "The scenery is great. But small towns make for the worst kind of lonely—paring down your real self because it won't go over."

Marriage, I thought. A big house in the city. More vacations. Neighbors I hadn't met yet or might never, because a city's different that way. I'd miss some parts—the birdsong, the rushing river. And there would be bad days ahead. The air's too hot or cold. Someone's in an indecipherable mood. You're worried about this or that. Bad luck comes in clusters, but so does good. Scar tissue never goes away. It stays, like a gnarl, a knot in a tree. Yet it stops hurting always, and you grow around it. I don't want to let life slip past like a bad day, I thought. A good day was here, now, already fading. Marie cruised by, leapt like a ballerina, grabbed cookies. "For the other kids," she said, "for sharing!" Tracy said, "Let me carry those napkins and spoons." So, dressed like Donna Reed, except I was showing more skin, more cleavage— Madonna Reed, then—I stepped off the porch, and I crossed the yard to serve myself and my friends our perfect desserts.

Debra and Marie Monroe, 2009.
Photo by Scott Van Osdol.

Acknowledgments

My thanks to the editors of the following journals, magazines, and newspapers in which excerpts have appeared: *Doubletake*; *American Literary Review*; *Salt Flats Annual*; *Callaloo*; *North Dakota Quarterly*; *River Styx*; *Dallas Morning News*.

I am grateful to SMU Press, which first published this book, and especially to its three-member staff, Keith Gregory, Kathryn Lang, and George Ann Ratchford.

I'd like to honor the memory of Frederick Busch, who sent words of celebration and wise advice when my daughter arrived, and he encouraged me to write this book. Thank you to Madeleine Blais who told me how to begin it (that layover in Atlanta!), and an extra thank you to Kathryn Lang who passionately and painstakingly showed me how to finish it.

I am grateful for the editorial insight of David Haynes, Tracy Daugherty, Cindy Chinelly, and Antonya Nelson. Thank you René LeBlanc, Tracy Staton, Gary Kansteiner, Fraiser Kansteiner, John Dufresne, Shen Christenson, Nan Cuba, Scott Blackwood, Tommi Ferguson, Catfish Petersen, Bob Shacochis, Roger Jones, Ralph Tejeda Wilson, Les Standiford, and Elvin Holt. A long overdue thank you to Robert Ademino, Bruce Taylor, Steve Heller, and Gordon Weaver.

Thank you to Victoria Barrett, Kit Ward, Jane Gelfman, Lisa Bayer.

Book Club
Discussion Questions

What ultimately caused Debra to find her "clout" and helped her to change her life?

How did Debra's mother, and even grandmothers, help and hurt Debra's chances for a successful life? In what ways is Debra like and unlike them? What learned or inherited mothering skills—good and bad—helped make Debra into the mother she became?

How did Debra's father influence her choices in male partners? She says, with regard to self-esteem: "just because you know you don't have enough doesn't mean you get some." It seems clear that she knows all along that she should avoid unstable men but doesn't. Why? In the end, when she makes a better choice for a life partner, why has her judgment improved?

How did Debra come to terms with the "race" issue she and Marie constantly faced in small town Texas? She says she never saw her motherhood as political, "but it has its political moments, and I can't back down." Should she have been more activist? Why or why not?

Strangers comment on the fact that Debra has no extended family. Who plays the role of extended family for Debra? Also, Debra regrets chances not taken to mend her relationship with her own mother and, at the end, worries if she's repeating this mistake with her father. What determines how much contact we have with our family of origin?

Debra seems to see this adoption as her last great chance to enter the ranks of the "normal." Is she naïve about this? Does she ignore the possibility that the way she sets out to make a home and family, and where, will increase her isolation? How does the ending speak to her sense of identity? Has she made peace with this longing for normalcy?

How do Debra's travails with Marie's hair teach her about an unfamiliar culture and, consequently, about herself? Why does Marie's hair care seem so symbolic to Debra?

Debra continually finds herself as the solo female in groups of men: the workers on her house, the workers on her yard and fence, and her graduate school friends. How did her interactions with each group help or hinder her growth toward greater strength and stability?

Debra is both a single mother and a mother in an interracial family. Which circumstance seems most challenging?

How much does the sense of place inform this book? If Debra had bought a house in the college town where she teaches, or one of the neighboring cities, in what ways would the story change?

The book uses a quote from Iris Murdoch as an epigraph: "Emotions really exist at the bottom of the personality or at the top. In the middle they are acted." This quote suggests that we make compromises as we try to be true to ourselves and yet also belong to a community. To be true to ourselves can feel right but isolating. Living in communities can feel cozy, but it requires white lies and self-effacement, too. What does the book say about finding the balance between living alone and living with others? How do we find this balance?

Debra's aunt says at the end of the first chapter, "The meaning of life is children and old people. And death." Has Debra discovered this meaning for herself by the end of the book? Do you agree with the aunt's statement?

Debra writes: "The sprawling mess of life is why we need stories, a fleeting sense of order so we return to life with the unproven but irresistible conviction our mistakes and emergencies matter, so life might make sense too." Do you see your own life as a story that makes sense? How do specific emergencies in the book create a greater meaning and in the end seem to impart a message? What message?